Maureen Lipman

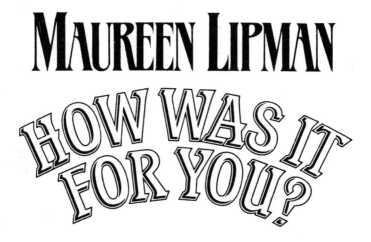
HOW WAS IT FOR YOU?

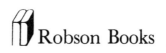
Robson Books

DEDICATION

For Marie Joseph, Gallery First-Nighter and number one fan. To show her what I've been doing all these months.

First published in the United Kingdom in 1985 by
Robson Books Ltd, Bolsover House, 5–6 Clipstone Street,
London W1P 7EB.
Copyright © 1985 Maureen Lipman.

First published November 1985
Reprinted before publication November 1985
Third impression November 1985
Fourth impression December 1985

British Library Cataloguing in Publication Data

Lipman, Maureen
  How was it for you?
  1. Lipman, Maureen   2. Actors—Great Britain
  —Biography
  I. Title
  792'.028'0924   PN2598.L56/

  ISBN 0-86051-347-5

Printed in the United Kingdom by St Edmundsbury Press,
Bury St Edmunds, Suffolk.

Contents

My thanks go to:

LINDA AGRAN: For the hours of loneliness and hysteria involved in writing the book she volunteered me for.

JEREMY ROBSON, my publisher: For making Job look like John McEnroe.

LIZ ROSE, my editor: For pruning.

MY KIDS: For accepting that the mother who used to go out of the front door in the mornings and re-appear with chocolate eggs in the evenings had turned into a hunched-backed recluse with a headache and a felt-tipped hand.

VARIOUS MOTHER'S HELPS: For cleaning round me.

SALLY O'SULLIVAN and BRIGID CALLAGHAN, of *Options*: For giving me two years of Press previews.

SARA RANDALL, my agent: For finding me no interesting work for long enough for me to write this.

MY HOMOEOPATH, MY ANALYST, MY RADIONICS PRACTITIONER, MY OSTEOPATH, MY GYNAECOLOGIST, MY ALEXANDER TEACHER, MY REGULAR DOCTOR, MY ALLERGY SPECIALIST, MY OPTICIAN, MY IRIDOLIGIST, MY REFLEXOLOGIST, MY ACUPUNCTURIST, MY SHIATSU MASSEUR: For my natural good health.

CHRISTINE GOLDSCHMIDT: for typing up and calming down.

JACK ROSENTHAL, my husband: For being a Virgo.

MY MOTHER: For saying 'How was *what* for you?'

M.L.

1

Home. Help!

Au Pairfect

MY HUSBAND JACK and I recently decided that we both need a wife. An old-fashioned, domesticated, dedicated wifely sort of wife — probably gingham-clad and apple-cheeked. She would be required to cook, clean, shop, organize the children, love us all indiscriminately and, most important, bake real cakes which rise and stand upside down on a rack smelling of childhood. She would, of course, leave enough mixture in the bowl for us to lick out whilst she began the pies. Pies with real crusts which overlap the edges and curl up with disdain at the very mention of the words 'Jus-rol'.

Like most wives, her salary would be ludicrously low and her job satisfaction totally dependent on her delight in her creatures' comfort. Unlike most wives, her conjugal duties would be less than minimal — the odd hug when the accountant has delivered a body-blow, or a floury pat on the arm after a hard day at the rehearsal rooms.

At this point reality intrudes. The likelihood of finding Mrs Right is pretty scant. So, in the interim, I've had various Miss Wrongs, a few near Mrs, and the odd obscure object of desire. Au pairs, demi pairs, mother's helps and cleaners have passed through the last nine years of our lives like so many viruses or bonuses.

We started well. Gillian was from the North-East — jolly sensible she was, too. Lived in the boxroom and calmly accepted that the sink was in the living-room, the fridge was in the bathroom and the builders in Majorca. After a year she went off to become a nurse, presumably benefiting enormously from a year's National service with a batch of fruitcakes in North London.

I soon discovered that I was totally miscast in the role of employer. I could be friend, mother confessor, or Rent-A-Dress, but I couldn't be boss. Can't. I still find it impossible to complain

6

about a job undone or wrongly done without apologizing profusely throughout and leaving the room half-way through as though the words sound *nicer* coming from another place. For years 'Will you be in tonight, Maria?' was synonymous with 'It's all right, Jack, we can go out for dinner after all.'

Of course, if they're beautiful you've every right to feel humble. My friend, Louie, tells of a stunning Austrian au pair who came downstairs one night and discreetly asked, 'Would it be all right if I watch BBC2 tonight? One of my films is on.' They were just nicely over the shock of having the toast of Austria doing their morning toast, when she ran off with the husband of their closest friend. Or he ran off with her. Anyway, they both ran. Presumably to the nearest schloss to shloff it all off.

Terumi was our first Oriental au pair. She bowed into Heathrow, after a 22-hour flight from Tokyo, five feet eleven inches tall and so embarrassed by her height that she hid her beautiful face in a Princess Diana-like stoop. She had never slept on a bed and always took her food to her room. She would make a careful salad. Then fry an egg. Then wash up. *Then* place the egg on the salad and carry the warmish clump up to her room.

The children loved her because she said nothing, but said it kneeling at their level. She never went out, except to school, and wore a uniform of jeans and shirts.

When summer came, we took her to Cyprus, where she donned a tiny red bikini and drove the local men insane. The waiters, who seemed unused to pretty, six-foot Japanese girls in bikinis, went wild and began swarming up the side of the hotel at midnight, and following her about the island in an eager, red-coated phalanx. She appeared highly puzzled.

Just before her year was up, she fell in love with a sweet Irish bus driver, and he with her. Her last six weeks were spent at a Kentish Town Irish dance hall, whirling madly to the music of Philomena Begley and the Allstars.

When she left, she cried. And so did I. 'I have been very bad au pair,' she sobbed, in the longest sentence I'd ever heard her say. I joined in her tears, and insisted she was the best six-foot Japanese au pair I'd ever had. She protested vehemently, and, castigating herself all the way to Heathrow, she flew out of our lives.

Providing the right environment for a young girl from a

different country is as much a matter of chance as finding the right person to marry. A friend of mine, finding herself without help at a crucial time of work, hired a sweet Yugoslavian girl from an agency at five o'clock one afternoon. She was plump and amiable in her Laura Ashley smock and seemed keen to please, and glad to have found a home after being inexplicably fired from her previous one. At two-thirty the following morning, one of the children appeared at my friend's bedroom door — 'Mummy, Gerda's making funny noises.' En famille, they stood outside Gerda's room and listened to the low moaning and groaning, issuing from within. My friend went in, to be greeted by a stoical silence punctuated only by groans. 'If-you-don't-tell-me-what-hurts-how-can-I-help-you?' she shouted, her Serbo-Croat being less than perfect. Finally, they called an ambulance. After a brief examination, the ambulance man said, 'Would you mind getting the manual from the driver's seat, and turn to the chapter on Home Deliveries?' 'But I don't know the girl,' spluttered Gerda's employer of nine and a half hours, 'Take her to a hospital!' 'Too late for that, luv, she's three fingers dilated. Hot water — and be quick about it.' The next hour became a 1950s B movie, while she and her husband paced the foot of the stairs waiting for the prescribed yowl. Years later we used the idea for an episode of *Agony* — and everyone said it was far-fetched and couldn't happen...

There comes a time in every au pair employer's life when another three weeks of saying 'Zis is ze washing machine' and 'No, when you pick up the phone it isn't enough to say "Ya, Rosenballs?"' is anathema. At such moments, the urge to buy British is very strong. You then put a carefully-worded advert in *The Lady*. After which, if you're lucky, you get two or even three replies. You then meet the prospective applicants at Paddington, drive them home, show them the animals, and drive them back again.

One such applicant was Sharon from Southampton. She seemed painfully shy, but her erstwhile employer — who arrived with her — assured us of her efficiency, humour and love of children. She arrived a week later, looking cross-eyed with the effort not to cry. She unpacked her case, came downstairs, had dinner, ignored the children — and the dishes — and silently cried. A lot. We comforted her and assured her she'd feel better tomorrow. And, sure enough, the next day she got up about 9.30, came down, ate a hearty breakfast and burst into tears. After two days of this, to cheer her up I asked her what she'd like to do now that she was in London. 'Oi wanna Starsky and 'Utch T-shirt,' she muttered darkly. We got her one, and that night she didn't cry before dinner. *After* dinner she howled like a coyote — while I did the dishes. I asked her what was so terrible about the job, didn't she like us? 'Oh, yes,' she hiccupped. 'It's just Oi miss my owld boss — she used to lark about so.' 'Lark about?' I muttered even darkly-er. 'Well, we'd throw soap suds at each other and larf, and then we'd roll about on the floor together, you know, larkin' about. Oo, we did larf!' Next day, she was larfin' when we took her to Paddington — and we were rollin' around when we waved her goodbye.

Of course, in between the disasters, there are girls without whom you don't believe you can go on living. For two years we had Ruth, who was Swiss with an English sense of humour. After surviving the baptism of fire that my kids invariably impose on newcomers, like screaming tantrums in the Post Office and accusations of cruelty on being denied a £10 box of Terry's of York, Ruth went from au pair to elder daughter. Finally, Jack and I gave her away to her delightful English boyfriend in a marriage ceremony on our lawn. She wore a Victorian dress I'd bought in an auction; and the ceremony was characterized by the delivery of a new carpet for us from John Lewis, causing all the wedding guests to troop into the front room and express their disappointment, after which it was rolled up and returned. The couple continued to live with us for another year, and, in a kibbutz-like way, it was a perfect arrangement.

I'll skip over the one who, for a wedding, 'borrowed' my best silk suit (bought in a moment of madness for the *Parkinson Show*) and came back with it scrunched up in a bag between mud-covered boots and a Braun Ladyshave. It was generously spattered with HP Sauce. All I could think was it must have been some wedding!

For the past couple of years, and at the risk of sounding like an enthusiastic Percy Thrower, we've been having a lovely run of Swedes. Mostly their English is better than mine, and I can't think what they're doing here. But they're loving, intelligent, merry and good-tempered, fond of a good rock concert or two and the odd evening at 'The Bull and Bush' — which suits me fine. The first, the patient and sensible Lisa, we hear is now a balloon-dancer back in Sweden... which leads me to ask, 'Is working for the Rosenthals a high-risk profession?'

I can't help thinking what a dreadful au pair I would have made. At 19, my housework would have been even more risible than it is now, my organization more hopeless, and my only advantage the ability to amuse the kids with vivid impersonations of their parents. Also, my mother would have phoned nightly. And sent fishballs by overseas mail.

When my brother and I were small, a local girl called Sheila lived with us for about twelve years. I console myself in times of crisis with the thought that, if permanence of that nature and mother at home to boot can breed a mass of insecurities like me, then perhaps — with my yearly change of nationalities and natures — I could be doing something right.

Of course, it's always worse when my mother is staying and doing her 'groping around the skirting board looking for and finding evidence of domestic negligence' act. She has a way with a glance (i.e. a five minute stare) or a whisper (i.e. you could hear it in Hastings) which can turn the atmosphere in the house from *Little Women* into *Rocky III*. 'It's nothing to do with me but — she's on the phone AGAIN, don't you mind?' or 'Would you like me to put out Adam's clothes for the morning, as no one seems to have done it...?' I reckon if they survive the grandma, they'll probably survive the kids.

My latest and greatest au pair story, however, began when I placed an advertisement in an Australian paper. This was in the belief that we spoke the same language. I might as well have placed an ad in the *Salonica Gleaner*. Out of sixty replies I picked on the girl who wrote from the 'Arboglen Nursery'. She drove, she worked with kids and seemed very well recommended. She arrived at Heathrow and after she recovered from the journey, came down to meet us all properly.

'Tell me, Sandi,' I chirped during the washing up, 'how many children were in your care at the nursery?' Her face registered pure misunderstanding. 'How do you mean?'

'I mean, how many of the children in the Arboglen Nursery did you actually look after?' Apart from speaking Swedish, I had no other way of phrasing it.

'Oh, no,' the penny dropped. 'Oh, no, you've got it wrong. No. They weren't children. They were pot plants.'

Bring out the Baby Bio, Mother needs some help.

Only Kidding

I'M GOING TO tell you about my children. Before they tell you about me. My children are eccentric. Surreal, sometimes. I expect they get this from their father. I'm very normal. After all, there's nothing eccentric about getting in the bath fully-clothed with a bottle of champagne, as I do every time one of them has a birthday. Perfectly normal. Doesn't everyone?

It all began with Amy. She talked from a ludicrously early age. I was so proud of this one-year-old prodigy who would look out of the window and say, 'What a gloomy day...' At her fifteen month check-up, I tried to show her off to the paediatrician. 'Words?' I bragged to the enquiry, 'Words? Whole sentences!'

The doctor then pointed her spatula at pictures of cats and houses and windows, asking Amy to identify each one, to verify the claims of her over-achieving parent. Amy steadfastly refused to utter a word. Finally, the doctor pointed to a picture of a dog (Snuffy by Dick Bruna, I recall) and said 'Now, do we know what this is?'

'Yes,' said the infant, with some weariness, 'it's a spatula.'

The doctor was rattled. 'No, the picture. What's the picture of, Amy?'

' 'S a dog, of course.'

Once the expected reply came, the doctor prepared to wax lyrical. 'Good girl!' she beamed.

'I've got a dog,' said Amy.

'*Have* you? How lovely.'

'But it can't walk.'

'Oh, dearie me. Has he hurt his legs?'

'No. His batteries are flat.'

Amy lived in an imaginary world called Flagleland. She had an imaginary friend called Doubt, and an invisible help-mate called Fairy Do-Good — a household treasure who apparently

emigrated suddenly to America one day. I still miss her. My son, Adam, had an imaginary world called Boggyland, inhabited by a strange and persistently-naughty playmate called Giggi. Giggi did all the wrong-doing in the house, which Adam got blamed for. We got used to taking him on journeys and leaving a place for him at dinner. One day, he too disappeared. 'Who did this!' I yelled, scraping Boggyland mud off the new twistpile. 'Bloody Giggi, I expect!'
'Don't say blood-with-a-y and no, he didn't. Giggi's dead.'
I stopped in mid-scrape. 'Dead??' He nodded his three-year-old head. 'Aha!' I thought, 'his defence mechanism . . . childhood fears of death, etc.'
'Aaaah, poor Giggi,' I murmured. 'How did he die?'
Not an eyelid did he bat. 'I pulled his skin off.' Alas, poor Giggi. I knew him. Well!
My daughter, who could fell a stampeding herd of bison at twenty-five metres with one glance of her all-seeing, all-knowing almost greenish-brown eyes, suffers no such nonsense from her pipsqueak young brother. An overheard conversation in the car . . .
Five-year-old He: 'I can do anything. I've got special extra-human powers. Me and Tom Dudderidge.'
Seven-year-old She: 'No, you have not, Adam.'
He: 'Anything on earth, I can do. And Tom Dudderidge. 'Cos of our amazing powers.'
She: 'You haven't *any* amazing powers!'
He: 'You don't know about them, that's all. Secret powers, so that I know everything in the world. Go on, ask me. Anything in the whole world.'
Barrister-like, she rapped: 'All right, then. Spell "disillusionment".'
A silence followed, worthy of Charlie Brown at his most flattened. Amy rested her case. A minute later, he thumped her in the leg.
I used to think I'd been very liberal calling a penis a penis and a vagina a vagina. I changed my mind after one explosive bathnight. I was trying to talk to the builder about a new soil-stack, when the noise upstairs threatened the life of the old one.
'Excuse me, Ken. WHAT'S GOING ON UP THERE?'

Amy: 'It's Adam. He keeps trying to put Hans Solo in my vagina.'

I looked helplessly at Ken, groping for the least damaging reply. I failed. 'Well... Well, tell him to stop it. It's dirty.'

It's not just my kids, of course. It's all of them. My friend was driving her eight-year-old daughter from school. Funny how the motion of the car sets them thinking of ways to discombobulate a person.

'Mummy, what's a vulva?'

Mummy nearly hit an articulated lorry.

'Er... I'm not sure exactly, darling. Erm... why do you ask?'

'Well, some of the girls were talking about vulvas and I wondered was it different from a vagina and if so, which bit is it and what's it for?'

My friend bit her lips, swallowed three times, tried to think about her pottery class, gave up and ventured: 'You know, darling, if ever there's anything you want to discuss with me about Mummies and Daddies and how babies are born, you've only to ask and...'

'My God,' her daughter giggled, 'there's not much point in asking *you* if you don't even know what a vulva is.'

While I'm in this area — and I promise to leave it for ever after this last visit — I was recently telling someone the story of Geoff the Gardener, who sliced off the end of his finger in a hedge-cutting machine. The point of the story being the four-hour wait he then endured in the casualty department of a North London hospital. I was so irate in telling the story that I forgot about my son-and-heir sitting wide-eared in the back seat of the car. (From the sound of these stories, you must think I moonlight as a chauffeuse. I do.) Suddenly, the piping falsetto: 'Mod?' — they call us Mod and Dod for purely eccentric reasons — 'Mod? When you see Geoff, tell him not to worry. Tell him I had the top of my willy cut off when I was a baby, and *I'm* all right.'

I refrained from pointing out that you don't dig weeds with your willy, because I thought it might lead to an immediate demonstration of how you could if you really tried.

At seven to nine years old, they both hated the opposite sex. The mention of boys brought an immediate 'Yuk!' from Amy; and Adam recently announced he plans to marry two boys.

'Darling, boys don't marry boys.'

'They do in San Francisco. Tom Dudderidge says.'

I know it's an old cliché, but they really do say all the things you only dare think. How many times have I agreed to jobs or a personal appearance, simply because the person on the other end of the phone sounded so *nice*. Not so my daughter. All her little life she has fought shy of acting, dancing classes, children's workshops, except in the safety of home where she often behaves like a cross between Lilian Bayliss and Peggy Mount. Once (again in the car!) when I was reluctantly driving her home from a delightful Anna Scher Drama class which she'd steadfastly refused to join, she heard my anger through the silence and the snap of gear changes.

'It's all right for you, Mod,' she said. 'You like things like that, you're good at them. I'm shy, that's all.'

'You just don't give it a chance, Amy. You'd have loved it if you'd stayed. You could have played parts like Mummy.'

'But, Mod! When will you understand? I don't want to be an actress. I want to be a *pet shop!*'

Game, set and match. And, possibly, new balls.

Imagine my amazement when, a year or so later, a TV producer friend rang to ask if Amy would be interested in the part of an autistic child in an episode of *Nanny*. 'Bernard,' I said, apologetically, 'she doesn't like acting. I'll ask her if you like, but she says she's shy.'

'Well, ask her,' he said, 'and if she is interested I'll pop round and explain the script to her.'

I ran upstairs to see her sitting reading, in the dark, in the top bunk. As she guiltily put away the book, I told her with studious nonchalance what Bernard had said... 'Anyway, it's a main part and he's hanging on if you'd like to talk to him about it.'

A long, solemn-eyed pause, and then: 'Tell him I only do musicals.'

I ran, spluttering, downstairs and relayed the cryptic remark to Bernard, and of course, as in all good Hollywood stories, he found her refusal intriguing. They met the next day. With great gentleness and precision, he told her the story and outlined the character, ending with 'So, do you think you'd like to do it?'

Again the perfectly timed pause. 'I think I'd like to see the script, please.'

I fell in the fireplace. In time, came the director from Shepherd's Bush in a taxi, and our unrecognizably-assured child asked Jack and me if we'd mind waiting in the other room, so that she could talk to him in private. He presumably passed his audition, because she did the part, behaved like a real pro, and never mentioned it again.

Oh, blood-with-a-y-hell— What wouldn't I give for that attitude! Goodbye to opening-night nausea, that cardboard feeling in the solar plexus. Hello to cool, composed enjoyment of the job, and total disinterest in its effect.

Both children were, of course, in their time, persistently in disguise. Amy, at the age of two-and-a-half, watched one episode of Edward VII, and homed in on Annette Crosbie's Queen Victoria as the model for a perfect lifestyle. The next year-and-a-half became a parental nightmare. The metamorphosis was total. She found a long black lace blouse and a tea towel, crowned them all with a lace doily, and proceeded to rule us with a rod of iron. Breakfast became an ornate ritual, since she could only be induced to take food when coaxed by her father, in a heavy German accent. Many were the mornings I came downstairs to find the blackclad figure of my daughter, spoon imperiously poised over the plate, surveying the figure of her father on his knees, saying, 'Vill Your Majesty haf ze scrembled eccs or ze Gricicles?'

My part, being that of the deaf Princess Alexandra, was simpler. I just had to wish her 'Gut mornink, Your Majesty', and 'Vat did you say' in a vaguely sing-song accent which owed more to Pontypridd than Copenhagen. I couldn't wait for the phase to end. When it did, I wished it hadn't. Its place was promptly taken by an obsession with *Tales from Shakespeare*, a book compiled with great love and attention by Sir Bernard Miles. Soon, she knew more of the plays than I did, which is not saying a great deal. One night, in the bedroom, she asked Jack to make up a song about Hamlet. After a panic-stricken interval, and with naïve foolhardiness, he came up with:

> 'Now Hamlet killed
> Polonius,
> 'Cause he thought he was
> Claudius,

And Ophelia died
Of a broken heart.'
She sniffed. 'Not a word about Laertes, I notice.'

As she began to grow out of these delusions of grandeur, Adam began to grow into them. True, he started each day dressing up like a miniature version of his Dad, but for a full seven months he dressed exactly like Superman. This included a trip to Florida for which I actually packed a spare *cape*! Within the next few months he changed rapidly. Physically changed, that is. His clothes, I mean. He would watch, say, *Buck Rogers* for five minutes on TV, then race out of the room, returning virtually an hour later in Amy's white tights, a leotard and a crash helmet. By that time the Muppets would be on, and back upstairs he raced, crying with frustration at not having the right shade of green jumpsuit to attain Kermitness. This would go on all day until he collapsed in a heap of tangled personas and his wardrobe door fell off. We hardly saw him, although we heard him a lot in those days. Zelig-like, he transformed himself so much, it was as though he was in training to be a showgirl at the Crazy Horse Saloon in Paris. When he watched *The Evacuees*, Jack's play about two small runaways in the last war, he forced us out into the street in search of a red school-cap, and demanded for his birthday a tin of corned beef and a gasmask.

Last week Adam left home. After a slight contretemps at the table involving a pancake, he left the room, banged about a bit, and returned half an hour later with a face like February. 'I'm not talking to you,' said the face, 'but before I don't, I want a long wooden stick and a red-and-white spotted cloth.'

I realized this was in earnest and, deadpan, supplied the order, substituting a blue-and-white curtain sample for the real McCoy. I tied it to the pole, and off he went to pack. Not much later he returned. 'Mod, I can't make the things stay in the cloth.' He was still not talking to me ten-to-the-dozen and had clearly forgotten his reasons for leaving. The problem was obvious. When Dick Whittington left home, he wrapped the cloth around a piece of bread and cheese and a clean tabard. When Adam left, he attempted to do the same with twenty-four Star Wars men, a Manchester United football and Donald Duck.

Religion plays a large part in their eccentric behaviour. 'Is everybody Jewish?' was Amy's first real sentence. Even the cat came under her curious scrutiny. 'Is Pushkin Jewish?' she asked. 'Or is she Catholic?' Once they refused to come down to lunch because their Star Wars game had just reached Luke Skywalker's barmitzvah! Another time Adam crept panic-stricken into bed with us. 'Dod,' he said,' it's only seven years to my barmitzvah, and I don't know a word of it.' The obsession came to a head at last year's school Open Night when I read in his essay: 'And so the monster chassed the hunter threw the trees over the hill down to the river over the brig threw the shule and nocked the rabbi over.'

And then there's the naming of parts. In my own defence may I state that the accused children possess the following accout-rements? Amy's tooth brace is called 'Brian', its connected rubber band, 'Vanessa', and the box they sit in, 'Henry'. Her bottom, on the other hand, is called Harry. Should vengeance be taken on her in the form of a smack, she screams out on Harry's behalf, 'It's not fair! Harry didn't do it — it was me!'

Like I said, 'eccentric.' Like their father's side. After all, I am a solemn, erudite woman of letters who only occasionally pops up on *Blankety-Blank*, waving maniacally from a box with Paul Daniels on my head. I did, however, sell out recently, it can now be told — they both appeared on *Whose Baby?* Well, you'd have done the same for a couple of BMXs, wouldn't you? Considering you can practically buy a new oven-with-variable-grill element for the price of a BMX, not to mention the accessories.

Anyway, they looked divine and hardly showed us up at all. Matthew Kelly, who guessed them immediately (not surprisingly, since Amy and I look like the definitive version of 'Send in the Clones'), said 'Is your Mummy pretty?' All I can say is that the pause which followed would have shocked Harold Pinter. Finally, Amy waved a dismissive hand and said, 'Well, *we* think so.' The 'kvelling' Mother (look it up in *The Joys of Yiddish*) in the corner of the screen collapsed with an excess of devotion. Later in the programme, Beryl Reid said, 'I think your Daddy's rather famous too, isn't he?' Delighted to reply to a question to which he definitely knew the right answer, Adam piped, 'No. Not very.' 'It's a compliment, darling,' I reassured his troubled father. 'How can you be famous for sitting in a room all day lighting fags and typing?'

Now they are eleven and nine acting has hit hard. They were lucky enough to be in the television series *Robin of Sherwood*. Playing two small Jews in the Forest of Sherwood. Not all that taxing really, since it was filmed there and they are. Since then they've been embarrassing me constantly by writing letters to the Casting Director announcing their availability. 'My brother and I and our friend, Simon Apple, have formed a theatrical group called "The Rosy Apples", and we are considering offers of work in TV or the stage. Please write if you have any.' Adam's not too keen on all this, but the threat of reprisals keeps him hanging on in there.

A play is being rehearsed — or rather has been in production for nine months, rather like they were, in the cellar. It is called *The Management Will Decide That*. It's the 'That' that kills me. It's written by Amy Rosenthal and stars Adam in the challenging role of Lilli, the hotel temptress. Potential backers, please send vast amounts of cash in plain brown envelopes.

Nowadays we can only communicate with our son in sporting metaphors. 'Adam, will you sit down at the table and finish your *innings*! Then straight upstairs into the Pavilion, wash your face, clean your teeth and that's the end of the *over*!' To see him at all is to see him duck, swerve, dive or bowl. To speak to him means averting your eyes from the ceaseless off-drives his clenched hands make, with or without a bat in them.

Bleary-eyed from a night spent learning Wisden or Matt Busby's Life Story, he staggers down at 7.30, throws himself on his ducking, long-suffering father and says: 'If a batsman hits a boundary, but someone in the crowd throws it back and it hits the umpire and bounces back on to the wicket, is he out, and did it ever happen to Don Bradman?' This represents 'Good morning, Pater.' He wants to play football for England and cricket for Australia. This latter is as a result of watching *Bodyline* and poses certain naturalization problems for the family unit. It also poses the problem of 'faction', where documentaries imitate life as interpreted by the film-maker, but based on real people. As far as Adam is concerned, the programme was the 'truth', and Douglas Jardine is forever relegated to Despot and Tyrant-land, along with the entire England team.

As for his adored sister, she retains her power over him only by playing his game. 'Strachan! Strachan!' she screams, having taken a fancy to the diminutive United player, and nightly catechisms now include questions like 'Who's your third favourite Man United player since 1968?' They both watched a video of the Munich Disaster and cried hopelessly.

As I said earlier, I blame their father. Who was it, after all, who attended a *Coronation Street* story conference in a red fez and *floor-length* rosette the Monday after England won the World Cup? Who was it who chose, for his first-ever sculpture, to make a model of a certain Mr B. Charlton, a model of such complex structure that he had to hire a 'Bobby-Sitter' to wet the clay whenever he was away for the weekend with this, your patient authoress? And who is it who's eccentric enough to fill his wife's champagne glass on her birthday, whilst she's sitting in a bubble bath, fully-clothed, with her incongruously naked children?

Of course, I accept responsibility for Adam's award-winning gift for jumping in where angels wouldn't be seen dead. Which brings me naturally enough to Barbra Streisand. Jack had been working with her on the script of *Yentl* for what seemed (to him, anyway) like years. It was a project which was more than a film to her, it was a memorial to her late father, and, as such, very intense, very personal and very difficult to intrude on, even as a co-writer.

For the co-writer's wife, who was dying for a bit of personal detail and/or gossip, it was totally frustrating. Even when he stayed at her house in Malibu, he had virtually nothing to report. Steven Spielberg never called round, there was no tantalizing glimpse of Bo Derek, nor any whiff of scandal from Warren Beatty. All there was, was Scene 47, Page 47, or at one point, it seemed, *Draft* 47.

When they worked here in London, my frustration intensified. 'What was she wearing?' 'Did she mention Ryan O'Neal or anyone?' 'No,' Jack would sigh, examining a new crop of grey hairs. 'We spent most of today in fierce dispute over whether or not they used the word "cookie" in late nineteenth-century Poland. According to the director, they used it all the time...'

One day, however, he came home smiling. No, it's not what you think. Barbra had played him her new record. It was

'Memories' from *Cats*, and he said for the first time he'd actually felt 'the presence'. Being in such close proximity to *that* voice, played on superb sound equipment, with the Real Thing sitting on the opposite sofa was a *thrill*. It was pure showbiz, but it made the hairs on the back of his neck do a little dance.

I don't mind admitting I was jealous. And envious, to boot. The following day I had a matinee of *Chapter Two* at the Lyric, Hammersmith, and I left the house with the kids to pick up a baby-sitting friend of mine, with the intention of dropping them all back at the house. The plans of mice, men and Maureen gang oft a-cock-up... I'd locked myself out. The only course of action was to get Jack's key. (I know what you're thinking; there's no such thing as an accident — you're just like my mother!)

All four of us drove down to the hotel where he and Barbra were busy working. Once in the foyer I phoned through to the suite. A minion took the call: 'Yeah?'

'Er... can I speak to Jack, please?'

'Yeah. Who is that?'

'I'm... it's his wife.' (I was beginning to sound like Joyce Grenfell.)

'Hello, luv,' queried his familiar voice, 'everything all right?'

'Er... yes... but I'm locked out and I've got Karen and the kids, can you bring the key down, sorry to disturb you.'

'Okay, luv, I'll be right — oh, wait a minute — Barbra says would you like to come up. She'd like to meet you.'

'Jack,' I hissed, 'Just bring the key down. I'm not ready. I've not go my face on. I've got the kids, so don't ask. I'm not up to it. Just bring the key down.'

He brought the key down.

We were just leaving, when the hall-porter's phone rang. He turned to me.

'Mrs Rosenthal?'

'Yes?'

'It's for you.'

'Hello?'

'Hi, it's Barbra.'

'Oh. Helleow.' (As English as a muffin again.) 'How are you?'

'Foyn. You sure you don't wanna come up?'

'Ahhm... It's really very nice of you to ahsk, but... ahhm...

I hev to do a matinee, end Ay've got the kids... ahhm...
children... end...'

'I'll play you my record.'

'I'm on my way.'

We went up in the lift, me rubbing ketchup off Adam's head,
combing Amy's face, applying the only lipstick I had, which was
green — it turns pink after a while, but only after a while — and
primping my babysitter. The kids were very excited. 'We're
going to meet Barbra Streisand, we're going to meet Barbra
Streisand...' They'd heard so much about this person over
the last two years — she was bigger than Babar in our
house.

She opened the door of the suite, and (for the benefit of the
star-struck) she was wearing a wrap-around black dress of no
particular style or cut, no make-up, hair haphazardly pinned
up, and she looked very pretty. Her features are all in
proportion, so you don't have this nose walking towards you as
photographs suggest. Her skin is lovely and she looked... well,
very pretty.

She was also lovely with the children. 'Hi, Amy, hi, Adam,
you wanna cookie?' (Old Polish word for biscuit.) 'You wanna
strawberry?' We sat down and, after a while, she played us her
record.

Now 'Memories' is a good song and Streisand is a great singer
and, I kid you not, the goosepimples were body-popping all over
my skull. I felt like crying. Thank God, I didn't. Saved that for
later, didn't I? Out of the silence came the high-pitched sound of
my Number One Son, then aged six, clear as a bell and twice as
metallic: 'Well, it's very nice — but it's a bit loud!'

We all laughed. A bit loudly.

'Oh, you think so, Adam?' said Barbra, with mock-solemnity.

'Yes, it's terrifyingly loud, your voice, isn't it?'

'Uh-uh.' I had the feeling the mock was deserting the
solemnity. 'You figure maybe when I get it released, I should
take the sound-level down a little...?'

Pleased to be consulted in this major decision, he replied
promptly: 'Yes, because your voice really hurts your ears,
doesn't it?'

More laughter all round the cries of 'Oh, Adam... ha! ha!...
he's so cute... ha! ha!... all right, darling!' ('*Shuttup!*')

She turned the strange blue eyes on to me. 'And what do you think?'

'I think it's wonderful,' I enthused, 'wonderful.' But she continued to look at me, and I had the most appalling brainstorm. It suddenly occurred to me that what she wanted was Honesty, not Flattery. I suppose somewhere in my head I had this idea that Superstars don't want to be surrounded by yesmen all the time. It is my bounden duty to tell you that they *do*. And preferably ones who, after saying 'Yes', add 'And, my, don't you look beautiful today!'

The eyes, however, were still on me, and I heard my mouth open... 'There's just one thing...'

'Uh-uh?'

'The middle section.' Jack's eyes began to imitate my mouth. 'When the orchestra cuts out and it's just your voice... er... is it... um... is it a bit... er... is it a tiny bit... um... low — not *low*! — but low*ish* for the rest of the... not that I know *anything* about music 'cos I don't... but is it just a teeny bit... well, when I say low, I mean... is it, would you say, or are you happy with... you probably think it's fine and... I mean, what do I know?... It's terrific, wonderful, not at all *low*... I don't even know why I...' And on I blathered, sinking inexorably from a falter to a babble and finally petering out into a small high-pitched squeak and a silence you could cut with a cheese-straw.

'Mmmm,' she said eventually. 'You think *so*... mmm... well, who knows... mmm.'

'GOSH-IS-THAT-THE-TIME!!' yelled the culprit, leaping to my feet. 'We must go... Kids, say thank you to Miss Streisand' (dreadful middle-class creep that I'd become) 'for the tea.'

'Thank you for having us,' intoned my angels, as their mother sprinted for the nearest exit. THAT VOICE, however, slightly lower than before (or did I imagine it?) stopped me...

'So what's the play you're doing today?'

I racked my brain. 'Er... *Chapter Two*. Neil Simon.'

'Oh, that's the one about Marsha Mason and him, right?'

I agreed that it was.

'Gee, I don't know how you can work in the theatre. I really hate it.'

'Oh, really. No, I love it. Well, I like it. Mostly.'

'You play it American?'

'Yes. We do.'

Then I thought she said: 'Can you do some for me?'

So I laughed. 'Sorry, I thought you said can I do some for you... Oh, you *did*... Oh, yes. Er. Certainly.'

I couldn't remember a single line of the play I was to perform in less than forty-five minutes. I remembered a lot of it took place on the phone, so I said: 'Hello, this is Jenny Malone. Is that you, George?' Except I said it in broad Humberside, laced with a little Manchester Ship Canal. It was very impressive.

Once outside the door of the suite, I lay on the carpet making low, well, lowish groaning noises with the children above me, saying: 'Get up, Mod. What's wrong, Mod?'

That afternoon in the show, I walked into George's (Gary Waldhorn's) flat, and slammed the door so hard that the dining-room table fell in small pieces to the ground. I knew just how it felt.

Later, Jack told me that she'd wandered around for a bit after I'd left, saying: 'I *told* Andrew the middle section was too low... I wanted to do it over... it's too late to call him... fix another session... etc.' But I, in my dressing-room at the Lyric, had no idea of this — or anything. I was wondering whether, in asking me to do the American accent, she might have been auditioning me for the part of her stand in for *Yentl*. I must have been the only Jewish actress in England who didn't see her for a rôle. (Memo: Must stop sleeping with the writer and insulting the director and star. It's just not how you get *on*.)

The funny thing is that what, to me, was first a great embarrassment, then later a great after-dinner story, probably didn't *exist* to the subject of the story. It's what we do with the Famous. We forget how to be ourselves, make silly noises and turn them into self-deprecating stories which the public loves to hear because someone famous figures in them. Unauthorized biographies are full of such hearsay. No wonder the stars lose their rags. Only recently someone asked me to tell the 'Streisand Story' and, when I got to the end, said: 'That's not how it ended.'

'How did it end, then?' said she who still bore the scars.

'She re-recorded the whole number,' said he who hadn't been there.

She didn't, of course, but I guess it makes a better story.

It would be interesting to hear it from Barbra's point of view, if indeed she remembered it at all ... 'Saturday: Met Jack's wife and kids. The kids were real cute. Sunday...'

P.S. The night of the *Yentl* première, I was onstage in *See How They Run*, so Jack took my mother (who managed to feature prominently in the Royal line-up) and I joined them afterwards in the restaurant for the 'do'. Barbra looked astonishing in white silk with matching turban. I took my place at a table and saw by the place-card that on my left was a Mr Sheldon Streisand. My heart sank. I hadn't even seen the film, what could I possibly talk about? He was a dour, moustached, bespectacled version of his sister only in real estate and was accompanied by his girlfriend, a fellow New Yorker. After a few abortive attempts at assessing a film I only knew about from the 'tsorrus' it had given the writer, I opted for the personal touch — 'How did you meet one another?'

'Well, as a matter of fact, our horses share adjoining fields.'

Now, you know what a horsey type I am — I've never seen one in real life except under a policeman — but was I stumped? Was I heck. It so happened that I was sharing adjoining dressing-rooms with Liza Goddard, who, she won't mind me telling you, is to all intents and purposes a human filly. When not acting or managing her family, she lives, eats, sleeps *horse*. So after three months in adjoining dressing-rooms there wasn't much she didn't know about the chaos of Lipman-land and there was even less I didn't know about creatures which whinny and sport hooves.

I programmed the computer, and pressed the key.

'Ah, you both ride? Do you favour a German saddle? I find them quite superior, myself.'

Sheldon lit up.

'Well, it's funny you should say that. This very morning I was looking at some German saddles here in Jermyn Street, with a view to shipping one over. You find it satisfactory?'

I then described the joy of riding Olive, Liza's horse, now that my German saddle had arrived, went on to discuss the problems of seedy-toe disease, and, by the end of the meal, we were all virtually eating sugar out of one another's hand.

So, you lose with the sister, you win with the brother. Wonder if he sings?

As a perfect end to the evening, Princess Alexandra, my favourite Royal, was the guest of honour. As she rose to leave at midnight, the room rose with her. She passed through the crowd saying 'Good-night' and 'good-bye' to people. When she got to me, however, she said, 'How did you enjoy the film?' For once in my loquacious life I was utterly speechless.

Zuckerman: A Life

A TORTOISE IS, I suppose, a Jewish pet. It knows its place. Outside on the lawn. It doesn't bark. It doesn't tear the Dralon. And it never raises the question of kosher dogfood. It's also not unlucky, like birds, unluckily enough. To this day I can't even buy a tea-towel with a bird on it. For fear. Of what? I hear you, not unreasonably, ask. Well, historically, mythically and somewhat obviously the bird is a symbol of flight; and a symbol of flight is the last thing you want to look at when you've just unpacked your bags after the last pogrom and said, 'Never again!'

Be that as it may, and it may be or not, depending on how much you believe my Auntie Bella, the entreaties of my brother and myself thirty years ago for a fluffy friend to take on walks to the car and back, fell on house-proud ears. Finally, after one particularly-protracted 'last of the summer whines', we were allowed a four-legged friend: a tortoise. Ecstatic with joy, we gazed at its four legs, waited three days for its head to appear, saw the marked similarity between the expression on its face and that on its leg, and lost all interest.

How little we knew. And how empty of reptile lore, therefore, have been the next thirty years. Accompany me, if you will, to the Muswell Hill pet-shop, on the occasion of my daughter's sixth birthday and a lip-biting dilemma. Stand with me, before a shelf of tortoises, all slightly variable in size, all identical in expression. Or lack of it. See the hope on my face, as I pray that the right reptile for the Family Rosenthal will show, by some small but meaningful gesture, that my choice is inevitable. Nothing much — just a minor shell adjustment, an imperceptible 'Hi, there, Mother!', even a lewd wink. Nothing. I shut my eyes and chose Zuckerman. For it was he.

I took him home in a Winalot box, with a nice Webb's lettuce and no idea what to do with him. I showed him the garden, newly terraced, and put him in a sunny spot with the nice

27

Webb's. Headless, he retained all the appeal of a piece of crazy paving, and showed no interest whatsoever in his dinner. 'He's probably getting his bearings,' said Jack. 'I'll take the outside leaves off the lettuce for him. He'll soon settle.' Thus began the first hint of the relationship that was to form between my husband and a thirty-nine year old Greek female of dubious background and highly eccentric character. But more of that later.

The kids showed nominally more interest in their tortoise than my brother and I had in ours. They offered some birthday cake to what turned out to be his tail, and that was more or less that. (They named him Zuckerman after a naughty schoolboy in Jack's play, *The Evacuees* — all snotty-nosed, trailing shoe-laces and wily wit. The kids would watch the play over and over, on the video, on wet afternoons.) By and large, he was mostly ignored. And the feeling was mutual.

The turning-point came when Zucky began to sprint. It was an astonishing sight. We were sitting at the living-room table, when a flash went past the window. Was it a bird? (Unlucky for some.) Was it a plane? No, it was old Supershell, actually legging it across the lawn towards the wire fence separating us from next door, if not at the rate of knots then certainly not at a bad rate. You could've knocked me down with a week-old Webb's.

Was this rare streak of tortoise athleticism a flash in the pan? Or was it time for a fast call to Mr McWhirter? Or perhaps the *Sun* newspaper — 'Phew! What a Tortoise!' Breath bated, we waited. Place him back at the other end of the lawn and — whoosh! — all four legs akimbo, head and tail erect, he went for that gold like a prehensile Seb Coe.

But what exactly was the nature of the gold? What luscious scent could make a taciturn tortoise turn his back on today's Cos and hare off towards next door's fence? (Yes, in this story, Zuckerman plays both the Tortoise *and* the Hare.) The following day we found out. Enter the man next door. Jim. Short of temper and red of face. (I'm sorry this sounds like a Worzel Gummidge story, played out in North London, but it is, and was.) In his hand, one tortoise, legs waving sheepishly — if that's not too tautological (sorry, couldn't resist) for you.

'It was at my lettuces!' by way of explanation.

'My goodness, Jim,' I grovelled, 'I *am* sorry. I can't understand it. It must have dug a hole under the fence. I'll check it and nail it down. The fence I mean.'

'Garrumph!' Yes, he actually said it. And left.

We checked the fence. It was secure. Two days later it happened again. Jim's face was even redder. 'I'll have to put it over t'back fence if it does it again.'

Over t'back fence. The death-knell for small, slow creatures of ill-heated brain. Into the British Rail Experimental Paint Yard section of Ally Pally Park. Surely Zucky wouldn't end his days tethered to a stake through a shell painted Buffet Car beige? We checked the fence again. The next day we watched in shifts. During one of mine, I glanced through the window and did a triple-take worthy of Zero Mostel. Zuckerman was not on the lawn. Zuckerman was not in the flower-bed. I rushed upstairs to spy on next door's lettuce. Zuckermanless. And then I saw him. It was a sight that filled me with awe. Zuckerman was halfway up the garden fence. He had climbed roughly two feet up the wire netting, and now hung on with three legs while exploring with the fourth for the next crampon or whatever the word is if you're a tortoise. Tampon, I suppose. Yes, Zucky was now going for the Decathlon. By the autumn, the family was treating him with a new respect: he was growing as eccentric as the rest of us. Occasionally he would fall off the fence and lie in an undignified position on his shell, revealing what a ratty little reptile he'd be without it. His legs and toes would wave wildly until someone came to turn him the right way up again, at which point he would attempt to look as though it had never happened — and certainly not to him — and saunter over, casually, away from the fence. Almost whistling.

Then came the winter of our discontent. As the book says, in the winter tortoises stop walking, stop eating and finally — just stop. It soon became clear, however, that although Zuckerman may be Olympic standard in night-time pole-vaulting he was somewhat ignorant of one of the three instincts with which the Lord endowed his species. Hibernation. He tried. His idea of a *good* try was to bury his head and front paws, then knock off work for a week, and sit there like a rejected meat pie. In vain, we tried boxes filled with straw, warm cellars, garden sheds, etc. At one point Jack had him in his study where he worked, cementing the strong bond between them. One would type and the other would potter. One would occasionally shit but the other didn't seem to mind. Greater love...

Finally, and well into December — like an overtired and recalcitrant child — he fell into a deep and presumably dreamless (but who knows?) sleep, and was put in the garden shed for the duration. For the next couple of months it was as if he'd never been. And had it not been that with that first rustle of a warmish spring came the first rustle of a friendly gardener popping round to do the 'few bits and pieces that can be done', which obviously included a trip to the shed, we might never have known that Zuckerman was out of his straw. Jack raced to the bedside. The patient, who was alive (but as Dorothy Parker said after Calvin Coolidge's death, 'How could they tell?'), wouldn't eat, move, or bring his head out. Was it 'Hang up your climbing boots' time for Zucky?

Jack said no. He took Zucky to the vet, filled in all the forms — 'Zuckerman Rosenthal' (ethnic enough, do you think?), Age — nine months since bought, Past Medical History — none, Complaint — inability on owners' part to know whether animal is dead or not.

'Oh yes,' said Mr Hill, 'common enough.' Jack and Ruth (our then au pair girl, whom he'd brought along to hold the patient whilst he explained the situation — presumably expecting Zucky to throw a tantrum) listened, rapt, while the expert gave him (Zucky) his first life-saving injection. He explained that people shipped these poor creatures over from the Continent, in their hundreds, thrown into the hold like a batch of live lasagna. Then other people bought them, with no knowledge of how to keep them (I needed Tortoise Guilt to add to Working Mother and Loving Daughter Guilt).

It seemed that Zucky had woken up too soon due to a combination of not having eaten enough to feed him during the full hibernation, and the warmish spring. His brain was now too frozen for him to know that he was alive. Jack's glasses, I expect, gleamed with attentiveness.

'He'll have to be made to eat,' said Mr Hill briskly, as though it was the easiest task in the world. 'Lucky you spotted him. Lots don't, and then, come the summer, they look for their pets, and what do they find? Liquid tortoise.'

When I arrived home, it was to find Jack, Ruth and the kids and the corpse (?) of Zuckerman, standing contemplating the pantry. Jack had a small syringe in one hand and two cotton buds in the other, and was engaged in the mind-boggling decision of whether to give the patient warmed-up chicken soup or tomato soup. For obvious reasons, that night Zucky ate Jewish.

But first, Jack gently swabbed his crusted eyes, placed him in a bath of lukewarm water — elbow in water, just like the old days — up to his haunches...fetters...plimsoll line... whatever, then he forced his jammed-up mouth open with tweezers, revealing a sight which made Jaba in *Return of the Jedi* look attractive. Finally — the warmed-up chicken soup (minus matzo balls) was syringed in. If Zuckerman felt any surprise at a regime which would cost £150 at a good health farm, he certainly didn't show it. The main problem was keeping his head out once they'd got it out, which required a merciless grip where his ears would have been had he had any.

Sweating with triumph at the amount accomplished so far, Jack gazed up through soup-misted glasses and said, 'I've got to get him some herring. It's full of iron. 'My nose twitched, and it wasn't just the mention of herrings. What was occurring was more than paternal duty. It was undoubtedly love.

Each day, Zuckerman's smorgasbord grew more varied, until at last the day came when, confronted by iceberg lettuce and wild strawberries, he gave in; opened one eye, raised his upper jaw and clamped it firmly on the lettuce. He didn't eat it, you understand. But it was a start. The old, evolutionary instincts came surging back, and within a few weeks it was midnight feasts for the two of them in the study...Jack eating his herring chopped, and Zucky raw. Neil Simon could write a play about it. Jack Rosenthal could write a play about it. Who needs me?

Anyway, a life had been saved and a bond strengthened, and the spring and summer passed in a now-familiar manner, tortoise-wise. Zucky, once more, climbed, ran and stole next-door's lettuce. The boy was a hooligan. Disturbed certainly. The signs were that Jim would shortly take out a contract for his life. British Experimental Tortoise. Each night, Jack battened down the fences and put his little friend to sleep on the patio. And came the autumn. This time Zucky obliged us by hibernating at the right time in the right way. You know, like he was a tortoise. Then the dumb cluck went and woke up in February.

This time Mr Hill sent Jack to a Reptile Expert. His receptionist was sympathetic. 'Oh poor thing,' she crooned, 'I've had just the same thing with my python.' The Expert himself was alarmed by Zucky's appearance. In the course of his examination, he weighed him, took his temperature and revealed, almost en passant that Zuckerman was Greek, probably about thirty-nine years old, and not surprisingly when you think about it — a female!

Without allowing a second for this extraordinary revelation to sink in, he added 'And she's dying.' Madame Zuckerman had one week to live. During that time she had to be bathed as before and kept under a 300-watt infra-red lamp, placed exactly eighteen inches above her head. If she lost more bodyweight then presumably — liquid tortoise! And she couldn't eat until her body temperature reached a certain heat.

As I left for work, Jack was tearing off in the direction of the North Circular, heading for every hairdresser's suppliers in North London, or if need be the world. Six hours later, he returned triumphant. He'd managed to borrow one until Friday. He measured eighteen inches above Zucky's shell and with trembling hands and many a glance at the clock, he began the tortuous (sorry!) business of fixing the heavy lamp by means of double-sided tape, piles of books and much amateur Heath-Robinsonry into its exact position. Ten minutes later it blew, and so did Jack. This time he headed for the West End.

In due course, another infra-red lamp was installed in the study and yet another was returned to the wholesalers off the North Circular at a cost of— but what cost love? It stood on a piece of hardboard, which was liberally strewn with out-of-season Iceberg lettuce (from Harrods, yet, special delivery), two or three herrings and the odd apricot, another great favourite of tortoise according to a lady on a tortoise phone-in on LBC. (You understand my meaning when I say tortoise phone-in. Of course I mean tortoise-*owners* phone in; although sometimes I'm convinced these programmes would be a hell of a lot more articulate if it were the tortoises who phoned.) Impassive and headless as ever, Zuckerman sat, and no doubt somewhere in those semi-frozen brains he awaited the next set of inexplicable indignities.

Meanwhile Jack's behaviour grew more and more suspicious. As the hours and then the days passed, he would often come out of his study, looking green and complaining of dizziness. 'Could it be the infra-red herring cocktail giving you radiation sickness?' I suggested. 'Why not move her to the cellar?'

'No, she should be where I can keep my eye on her,' he said stoutly.

Every day the ritual continued . . . the twice-daily bath in a deep tray, the deep all-over tanning. The syringing had stopped, thank goodness, as I was down to my last can of Bean and Barley, and the apricots lay rotting on the hardboard. As did Zuckerman. See what I mean about a Jewish pet? You work, you slave, fingers to the bone, you bathe, you syringe, you work in a dangerously hot room — and what thanks do you get? Nothing. Not a thank you, not a gesture, not a nice box of Black Magic. Nothing. And the times he'd told her to keep warm!

Do you know, I even caught him playing thirty-nine-year-old band tunes to that tortoise on his violin one day. Actually thumbing through *Favourites From the War Years*, looking for a jolly, rejuvenating, hopefully Greek ditty, no doubt. The nearest he came was 'Kiss Me Goodnight, Sergeant Major' — I tell you I was shocked. I thought of writing to Anna Raeburn, but I feared she'd say she was going through the same thing herself.

Matters came to a head, as matters and pimples always do, on the Friday when Jack was *still* working on *Yentl* with Barbra Streisand. With only one day left of Zuckerman's life expectancy, he was called in urgently to discuss Draft Eleven (sic[k]) with herself and the Heads of United Artists (which sit on the wafer-thin, silk-shirted bodies of the heads of United Artists). I wasn't working that day, so I was asked to Zuckerman-sit. With some reluctance, but already thinking no doubt of dining out, one day, on this Magnificent Obsession, I agreed. He left the phone number of the hotel, where they were 'taking meeting', and clear instructions to check on Zucky's condition every half hour.

The kids were at school. I began listlessly to do some

housework. Perhaps if I had a list I'd be a better housewife. However...

Suddenly distracted by the need to chat to my friend, Lizzy, I sat down by the phone in Jack's study. The smell was rich and the vegetation on the floor somewhat noxious. The Melina Mercouri of the tortoise world (equally without her marbles) sat giving her Sidney Greenstreet impersonation. I placed her under the lamp and put a fresh apricot (again out of season, of course) by her nose. And rang Lizzy. We'd been chatting for some time, a long time when I come to think about it, about Life and Art and the price of rawlplugs, when my attention was caught and the words dried up in my throat. Zuckerman's head was out.

'Zuckerman's head's out, Lizzy!'... presumably she thought this was a coded message. I put the phone down, crept towards the floodlit animal, pushed an apricot near her nose, and picked up the phone again. 'It's the tortoise,' I began to whisper, 'she's— arrrgh!!' Even as I spoke, her snake-like head came forward another inch revealing much-gnarled neck. Then, as if by divine command, her head twisted on its axis, her jaws parted and she sank her teeth into half an apricot. I began to cry.

Typical, wasn't it? The bloody animal wakes up for me, whilst Jack, who'd nursed her back from near-liquidization, gets a faceful of Megastar. I put the phone down on a confused Lizzy and phoned the Berkeley Hotel. I'd give Jack a real coded message this time.

'Miss Streisand's suite,' I tried to sound authoritative. 'Who are you calling?' came back the regulation bark. 'Mr Jack Rosenthal... it's his wife... it's important...' I petered out. Relieved, I heard Jack's voice, 'Yes, love?'

'OK,' I whispered, 'show no reaction. I'm sorry to disturb you... it's just that Zuckerman's eaten half an apricot and I thought you'd—'

Show no reaction! The man was beside himself... 'She ate a half?? Will she eat the other half? Look... Oh, God, that's wonderful! Oh, thank God! Look, try her on the herring! Oh, love, that's fantastic... Oh, well done! Listen, I'll be home in an hour — just keep her...' He faded out a bit and his voice took on a slightly more formal note. I knew what had happened.

In his ecstasy, he'd glanced up at a sea of Californian faces, gold pens airborne, glossed lips open, gazing at their deeply deranged screenwriter with a mixture of pity and despair. 'Everything okay, Jack?' Finally the Megastar spoke. 'Oh, yes, thanks,' he wiped his brow and grinned. And for one minute made the fatal error of imbuing Hollywood film executives with a sense of humour. 'It was the tortoise . . . er, Zuckerman . . . she was dying . . . today was her deadline . . . and that was Maureen telling me she's just had a bit of . . . er . . . apricot . . . and . . .' The room was rife with lack of interest.

'A tortoise?' said the head of bottom-lining and scripts. 'You mean like a turtle or something?'

'Well, er yes,' said Jack, willing and able to launch into his favourite topic. 'You see, she was too cold to know she was alive and I've been bathing her and . . .' The silence was cavernous. The ground failed to open for him, but the mouth of the head of scripts did. 'Great, OK, fine, well now . . . page 43, Draft Eleven, you know when Yentl says to Avigdor . . .' So ended United Artists' part in Zuckerman's life, another example, as Jack so rightly put it, of Hollywood getting its priorities wrong.

Meanwhile, back in Muswell Hill, we were a merry throng. Zucky regained her strength, and, after a long convalescence, much helped by songs from *Zorba the Greek* and the *Best of Nana Mouskouri*, played by her loving benefactor, she grew strong enough to venture outside for increasingly longer spells, and ultimately to play her old part of the Lettuce-Kleptomaniac again.

Impossible though it may sound, the story isn't over yet. One day, well into the summer, when we'd stopped watching her and stopped apologizing for her lack of social graces and due regard for property, she disappeared.

In vain we questioned Jim as to whether he'd been practising discus throwing with a four-legged discus. His answer was no, but his face read 'But give me half a chance . . .' En famille, we scoured Ally Pally Park, all six of us, including au pair and cat, shouting 'Zuckerman!' at the tops of our voices. We somehow hoped our cries would penetrate the sides of her head where her ears might've been. Tearfully we told the Park Keeper of our loss. He promised to keep his eyes open. We thanked him and headed back for home — Jack lingering behind the rest of us hopefully whistling 'Take the Water or the Wine'. Believe it or not, on our second search we found her. Plodding her way across the park in search of sex with a perfect stranger, Ally Pally Park being her idea of a singles bar, I presume. It was hard to tell whether she was pleased to see us or not. She gave a low hiss when we picked her up which seemed to me remarkably low in gratitude.

Back on the lawn she seemed to be back in her anorexic phase and turned up her nose, indeed turned up her whole head at whatever we offered. The summer was ending and we reckoned it was probably hibernation time again.

Two days later she was gone. You know, when a kid leaves home enough times you finally gotta get the message. We searched again but with no luck. We informed the Park Keepers to start looking for her again, having first informed them to stop, and this time they fixed us with a baleful look not entirely unlike one of Zuckerman's, who could be full of bale like you wouldn't believe!

The days turned into weeks and we finally had to admit that Zucky was probably headed for the Greek mainland now. Sadly we resigned ourselves to her loss — some of us with greater difficulty than others. Her final joke at our expense came, as usual, whilst Jack was out. It came in the form of a Park Keeper — he stood on the step, brown-suited with a carrier bag. Which moved.

'Who's a lucky lady, then?' I wasn't sure whether he meant me or the contents of the bag, but was too happy to care. I flung my arms around his neck, got out the fatted lettuce from the fridge and with many a pat, stroke and admonishment, I put her back once again in her verdant prison.

I couldn't wait for her 'father', the fiddle-playing maniac last remembered giving her the kiss of life, to come home. I actually kept running to the front-room window whenever I heard a car. The kids were all excited, too, and kept checking on her progress on the lawn. She seemed pretty well fixed in one position — maybe her Houdini days were over.

'Hello, love.' The front door banged. It was he.

'All together now [to the tune of "Hello Dolly"] — Hello Zucky, well hello, Zucky, it's so nice to have you back where you belong. You're looking swell, Zucky, I can tell, Zucky...' etc.

He was stunned with disbelief and delight. We dragged him on to the lawn and looked at the expression on his face. He took off his glasses, bent down to greet his little taramasalata. He stood up again and blinked.

'It's not Zuckerman,' he said.

'What's not Zuckerman?' The thought had never crossed my mind.

'That. It's someone else. Different markings. Not Zucky. It's just a tortoise.'

It's difficult to describe our feelings really. How can you start again at the same point of love and exasperation and dependency and history for Godsake, with a totally new tortoise? With different markings? We tried. But two days later when she disappeared off the face of the lawn, I can't say we were anything but relieved. Presumably Zucky's understudy was a forty-year-old Turkish tortoise looking for exactly what Zuck was looking for, regardless of race, colour and markings. Presumably he was mad as hell when, just having got within sniffing distance of the tortoise equivalent of casual sex, he was picked up, placed in a Sainsbury's bag, and thrust into the smothering world of North London Jewish Family Life. Presumably before the winter set in they found each other — please God. Let's just hope, for all our sakes, that the sodding earth moved! Particularly the earth around the British Rail Experimental Paint Yard.

We're just a one-animal family now. Same old cat — Pushkin Rosenthal. Her eccentricities are confined to Grievous Bodily Harm to Wilton carpets and chintz-covered furniture. The kids want a gerbil but they've no chance. No chance at all. I know who'd end up cleaning out its cage, mincing its morsels and supplying it with old scripts to tear. And he's not doing it. Honestly, wouldn't you give anything to get under the duvet in October and wake up in May to a warm bath, a mouthful of chicken soup — and to a face full of love ready to tend your slightest whim?

We now have a large yellow tortoise made of stone, every bit as responsive as her predecessor. We bought it in a Cuffley garden centre out of sentiment and a deep desire to avoid buying patio paving stones. Some weeks later, sitting in the garden, Sara, my agent, mused, 'That tortoise hasn't moved an inch in

three hours.' Adam sprang to Zuckerman II's defence —
'Neither have *you*,' he countered.

Now that's my sort of pet, silent, anorexic and able to project
a doting mother through a plastic garden chair.

Amy now wants a duck. You'll be surprised to hear that I said
'No.' The following day, I kid you not, at a recording session in
Bushey, someone (Helen Nichols, to be precise) offered me one. I
looked upon it as an omen. And said 'No' again. Recently, a
gentleman in the wholesale publishing world told me that ducks
make the loveliest pets. He had fourteen. Indian Runners,
they're called. 'They don't need much water,' he said in reply to
my doubts about bringing home a pond from the garden centre.
'They only go in when it rains. And they'll eat anything. If you
haven't got any corn, they love a bit of lettuce or mashed-up veg.
Ours poke their heads through the cat flap at feeding time.'

I could feel myself falling in love, so I spoke to myself severely
about piles of duck-poo and constant quacking. Then, just as I
was beating my better nature into a fluffy pulp, he said it. The
sentence which is surely going to change my life for the duckier.
Are you sitting comfortably? Then I'll begin:

'In the summer,' he smiled, 'when it's a lovely day and all the
windows are open, I love to sit in the lounge and watch the
cricket. One day, I heard a quack which sounded quite near —
but I didn't pay much attention till a flash of white caught the
corner of my eye. I looked down and there were three of my
ducks, Big Daffy, Daphne and Doris, sitting in a line, glued to
the telly, following Botham with either side of their heads. They
watched solidly till my wife came home and I had to shoo them
out of the lounge. Now they invariably come in for *Sportsview* to
check if there's any cricket. If not, they don't bother.'

And you thought 'out for a duck' was an allegory, didn't you?
Must dash, the garden centre closes at 6 p.m. and this house is
short of another eccentric or two. The family argument at the
moment is whether to call them Aqua and Via Duck or Duck
Whittington and Duck Turpin. Watch this space.

Kitchen Made

THERE WAS A time I used to go to bed with Richard Burton and Elizabeth Taylor. I'll tell you about it sometime. It was pretty tame, really. It was about thirteen marriages ago — theirs not mine. I'd be in my chaste bed in Hull, imagining what erotic things they would be getting up to somewhere on the Nile. Their photograph — she of the elongated eye and chubby chops, he as battered and pock-marked as my school homework — was stuck to my ceiling.

'It's just a phase she's going through,' my mother apologized to our daily — well, twice weekly. She was right, as ever. In the fullness of time, and in rapid succession, I went to bed with Cliff Richard (there's optimism), Dr Kildare, all the Beatles (and John Lennon more than was good for me), Neil Simon (who said sex can't be funny?) and Noël Coward. Strange bedfellows indeed. Then, after years of going to bed with *Cosmopolitan* in an effort to acquire what everyone else appeared to have such a lot of, I got married, began to beget, and started going to bed regularly with Dr Spock. Which is tricky in hard-back.

You take my point, though, don't you? What could be more erotic, more utterly absorbing than whether they've got German measles or an allergy to strained prunes?

'Where is all this leading?' I hear you yawn. It's leading, my friends and fellow adulterers, to my last beau. I moved house. And, strictly *entre nous*, I began to go to bed with Neff. No, not a Swedish lumberjack with steely-blue eyes and a lopsided grin accentuating the thin duelling scar on his right cheek. But an oven. To be precise, a white, enamel, circotherm, easy-to-clean under worktop, illuminated oven, with thermostatic controls and variable grill element, Model 1078 HCSG-7. Be still, my beating heart.

And that was not all. Not all, at all.

There was the integrated fridge-freezer, overall dimensions

whd 560 × 1120 × 1200, with three temperature zones, Model L225 5li. And that wasn't all, either.

There was the hob. With removable pan supports. And cooker hood with ventotherm. And dishwasher with diagnostic sockets. And fourteen place settings. (Memo: still haven't bought a bigger table.)

You've got it. I became a brochure freak. The bedroom was now knee-high in them. So was the Victorian bathroom with claw-feet bath and mahogany lavatory seat. (Can you hear me, Posy Simmonds?) They dropped out of my bag, my car and my conversation. They nestled uneasily with the piles of *Ideal Home*, *Homes and Gardens*, *Garden and Gnome*, *Ideal Garden*, *Home Beautiful* and *Architectural Digest*. Incidentally, did you know that a twelvemonth's supply of *Interiors* magazine will pay for one and a half sessions with a good psychiatrist?

Dear Doctor, I used to love train journeys, settling down with a sweaty, film-wrapped sandwich which wouldn't unwrap, to several hours of *Plays and Players*, *Time*, *Newsweek* and *Private Eye*. Then, one day it became workety-work-workety-work, rustling frantically through *Which?* to read a survey on whether enamel sinks chipped less than porcelain. Nineteen-eighty-three, and I ask you: it's which of them chipped *less*, not which was totally Lipman-proof like I'd wanted it to be! I even scoured the back pages of magazines, the one with adverts for portable conservatories and wrought-iron circular staircases, and lines like: 'So you thought you couldn't afford a pool? Ha!'

And *taps*! A whole new world emerged. I could've gone on *Mastermind*, specializing in 'The Tap — Then and Now'. *Then* being when I used to wear bright red tap shoes and blithely lumber through shuffle-tap-step-tap-tap-step-step... shuffle-tap-step-tap-step-step etc. The *Now* became with or without soap dispenser, integral shower-head, elbow-action and — wait for it — swan-necked versatility. It's like an old-time Variety Bill, isn't it? 'And now, at enormous expense, all the way from West Germany — she's Franke... she's Compacte... she fills the stage with suds, she's your very own swan-necked Miss Versa — I once tried tap dancing but I kept falling in the sink — Tillaty!'

I'll tell you something. I resented it. Deeply. It wasn't me. Great Bores of Our Time used to refer to *other* people. Older people. Less gay. Heterosexually gay, I mean. Although even sex became a question of Which Bedhead? Which Duvet-Cover? And, by the time you'd got all the lace cushions off the antique bedspread, who had the strength?

I became a human sample. Minute pieces of fabric were crammed into my handbag and pinned to every surface, giving a curiously likeable patchwork effect to every room in the house. How could I have made one decision, when it all depended on twenty others still to be made? I'd been clutching a picture of Monet's restored house in Normandy in my hot little hand, on and off since the previous November. Perfectly pleasant people in Selfridges' Basement turned into Darth Vader (before he got paternal) when confronted with my grubby little picture. They repeated their information re melamine versus pure English oak, denied the very existence of a yellow-painted wooden kitchen with cobalt-blue tiles — and by the sound of it, can you blame them? Only Mr Smallbone, left to his own Devizes, could see that I was merely short of Monet.

A few weeks later I stood in Elon Tiles (go in, I dare you, you'll faint) in a trance-like state, mentally tiling the whole house, inside and out, with rustic, hand-glazed, sun-baked Mexican clay. A man standing next to me, who'd travelled all the way from Warwickshire with his sample in his hand, said wistfully, 'Moving house is like standing under a hot shower in an Yves St Laurent suit, tearing up £20 pound notes.'

I'll tell you something else. I didn't care a Bosch for the new me. On a pouring wet day, the last place on earth I wanted to be was on a double yellow line in Hanover Square, screaming at a traffic warden that if I didn't find the Amtico Flooring Showroom by one-fifteen, the whole bloody kitchen would sink through the concrete. The old me would have pushed it. Zanussi the difference? The old me used to hob-nob with the great and near great — then suddenly, hobs, knobs and grates meant something completely different. And infinitely more depressing. The old me thought *Carousel* was a hummable show. The new me knew it to be an obligatory plastic-coated basket which swings malevolently from a corner unit, hitting you in the knee with thirty-one tins of baked beans and a packet of fibre-filler.

If I dropped in to see a friend, or went out to dinner, I headed straight for the kitchen. And before they had time to ask if I was working or resting or what I thought of *Amadeus*, I was under their sink, groping to see what model their waste-disposal (I know the verb shouldn't come at the end, but I wasn't myself, okay) was.

Not to mention, and I wish I hadn't, carpets. Plain or geometric? Man-made or pure wool? Arguments for and against. Mine came equipped with ready-made stains. Hard to believe, but true. It's not that the Carpet Shop — like the Blind Shop (if you see what I mean) — weren't willing to replace their beautiful but tarnished goods. It was the seven-week delay, the twenty-three phone calls, the pithy and brilliantly perceptive arguments I conducted with myself in the car before I said, 'I'm awfully sorry to trouble you, and I know it's all my fault but . . .'

I mean, how would they like it if I was billed to appear on television at 7.30 on Monday 28th March in *Coronation Street*, and turned up four hours later in *Die Fledermaus* instead? Don't answer that.

And why does every window need a curtain? And why does every curtain need a curtain-maker? And why did every curtain-maker tell me their life story instead of making curtains? And why couldn't I tell them what I wanted without changing my mind fourteen times per swatch? It was so humiliating. How could I be so certain of my position against Cruise missiles, unemployment, and Mrs Thatcher — surely the most undiagnostic socket of them all — and yet be reduced to sleeplessness by pinch pleating?

Oh, I know some people thrive on it. *Other* people. Like those women who suit pregnancy. You know, the ones who waddle happily to school in an advanced state of inflation, pushing a double-buggy bursting with Emmas and Matthews, all the while chatting *interestedly* to their elder progeny. You can tell by looking at them that there's a pot-roast in the slow-cooker, that she's on her way to Class 2B to make a crocodile's head out of four egg boxes, and that they will soon deliver their fifth child in one hour twenty minutes to the sound of Vivaldi. Under water. I, on the other hand, looked like a furtive ostrich for nine months, and ended up trying to take the gynaecologist to the International Court of Human Rights. Other people have a flair for it, you see.

Take antiques. I wish I had a Synchromax waste-disposal for

every time I've admired someone's mahogany commode/ dresser/chiffonier only to be told, 'Yes, isn't it lovely? I picked it up in a junk shop in Stow-on-the-Wold for 75 pence. Frank stripped it and waxed it and now it's worth £880, apparently.' Somehow, for me, it works in the opposite way. I 'picked up' a chaise longue in the Fulham Road for more money than I'd earned all month, paid extra for delivery, and then was told by a friendly antique-shop lady, 'If you're going to buy, darling, don't buy crap.' I defended my taste right until it was stripped down to twelve sacks of rolled-up copies of *Tit-Bits* and a well-munched pine floorboard. They could actually see the new me coming.

It came to a head one balmy summer's night when my husband and I, dressed to kill, went out for dinner à deux. After two pina coladas and a salade niçoise, we gazed long and deep into each other's eyes. Then, by mutual consent, and without a word passing between us, we drove off into the night to press our noses against the pitch black windows of every closed kitchen showroom in North London, in search of the perfect Trash Compactor. For all the world like Burton and Taylor on the Nile.

After this nadir, the old me staged a come back. She started gently with a shifty glance in the designer department of Harvey Nichols and gradually weaned herself into a restaurant without a fabric department. She didn't crawl on the floor to inspect the wickerwork under the upholstery, nor did she embarrass the maitre d' by asking him if he had a self-defrost button on his freezer. Slowly, gradually, with faith in her heart and her bank manager by her side, she re-entered the safe, sure, positive well-tried world of show business.

Nowadays, of course, the dream kitchen which caused the nightmares has been installed for several years and paid for in several instalments. It's been used, abused, grained and stained, and both potatoes and paintwork have been heavily chipped in it; but still its bright yellow paint, bright blue tiles and blue and white gingham curtains thrill me whenever I see them, which is most of the time I'm in the house. Next year, when I'm sick of living in North London's answer to the Swedish Embassy, I'll paint it black, or trompe l'oeil it to look like a lounge.

In the meantime, I've not bought a single copy of *House and*

Gardens, Gardens and Home, or *Home and Breakdown* for almost two years. And suffered not a withdrawal pang.

The news for all of you people about to step into brochure dementia is as follows.

Don't buy a two-bowl sink unless one of the bowls is big enough to wash up in. (You'd have thought that might have occurred to me when measuring up, but no. I just thought it looked pretty.) There is even a 'sauce viande' in my pretty porcelain sink with no existing attachments as claimed by the French manufacturers. I've never found out what it's for, but it holds the soap, I'll give it that.

Do have a draining board, even with a dishwasher. Correction, especially with a dishwasher. That way you'll avoid the teetering pile of roasting pans, frying pans and large, plastic salad drainers which daily form a Tate Gallery-like erection on my soggy tile grouting.

Don't buy an under-worktop oven with integral grill. Not if you like grilled food, that is. For that I'd favour an oven with separate grill section like the ones they've brought out since two years ago, when they'd never heard of such a thing. Ovens which claim to grill mean much crouching of man and wife with furrowed faces till both sets of glasses steam up and tempers and oven gloves fray. It sounded easy at the demonstration. '*Just insert the variable element. Remove and invert drip tray. Adjust switches and slot stainless steel guard in partially opened door.*' 'Aah, I see.' I nodded brightly, not bothering to write it down. The following morning I bought a toaster (which is even lousier than the variable element) and we've had baked, fried or roasted ever since.

Also, *don't* buy an automatically igniting gas hob. They automatically don't ignite for several days if you've had the temerity to wash them. Furthermore, have great respect for your microwave should you buy one. It's bound to be temperamental. I only bought it because a free food processor came with it which, friends told me, they couldn't live without. I should have known better. I sliced circular gouges out of its plastic mixing bowl the first time I attempted coleslaw. Now it sits there since my mother, on her last visit, covered it in a large plastic bag for tidiness, looking huge and forlorn, wondering if it will ever be forgiven. It won't.

Still, the microwave is worth having, if slightly temperamental. Sometimes it takes longer to cook things than the regular oven. Sometimes it sucks the 'micro-film' into the casserole, making the vegetables resemble pre-packed plastic toys. Mostly, however, it gets you out of tight corners when strange rugby teams descend on your house saying your brother said they'd be sure of a good dinner at Number 30. God bless Marks and Spencer.

Finally, when entertaining in your dream kitchen in July, don't make the entire meal from the 'Entertaining' section of a magazine. Not, that is, if the magazine was the November issue. I had nine distended guests on the hottest evening of the year, unable to rise from the table after consuming a pea soup, rack of lamb and fruit pie dinner. Once hauled from the kitchen chairs, they had to be laid in groaning lines in the living-room till it was time to boule them home.

Recently, I snatched a week in Majorca at a friend's villa. On the plane — as the moment came when it stops taxiing and everyone leaps up, grabs their hand-luggage and then stands sheepishly for ten minutes until they decide to free you — a lady across the aisle waved to me. I waved back and looked hurriedly away, unsure whether she really knew me, or whether it was the telly, and I was about to be told I was thinner/plainer/tireder/ shorter than she thought, and she'd never liked me anyway. Inevitably we met up as the two queues mingled by the door. 'Remember me? I'm the lady you came to for your "Monet" kitchen. How did it all go?' 'Have you got an hour or two?' I yelled as I descended the steps into the cold (of course) Majorcan air.

Believe it or not, the day before leaving we were basking by the harbour feeling the noonday sun on our faces for almost the only time of our stay, sipping white wine and watching the fish eating bread rolls, when a smartly-dressed lady from the next table rose to leave. 'Excuse my butting in on your lunch,' she said, 'but may I ask you a personal question?' With fish-baited breath I awaited the inevitable 'How do you learn your lines?' But oh, the power of the ego to deceive. 'How was your Smallbone kitchen in the end? I'm having one installed next month back home, and I'm desperate for details.' She got them.

Let's face it, if the glamour of show biz ever begins to pall, there has to be a job for me in the Finchley Kitchen Centre, with an armful of brochures and a face full of the wisdom only bitter experience can bring.

In My Natural Habit 'at

IT IS A habit of mine to observe the habits of my fellow
eccentrics. (Yesterday I saw a man at the Archway Road
crossing, wearing a yellow hat, a khaki jumpsuit, brown boots
and a tortoiseshell cat on his shoulder. He looked like a poster for
a panto. I wondered if the cat always went for a walk, well, a sit,
with him; and, if so, how the habit started. Were the matching
outfits an afterthought or was the cat perhaps velcro'd to his
shoulder pads?)

I myself have no habits worth mentioning, unless you count
falling over my own ankles a lot (but only when walking —
never when sitting, lying or crossing the Archway Road). Oh,
and I don't like whistling. It makes my teeth itch. A visit from
the window cleaner can virtually turn my mouth inside out. Oh,
and when I was a child, I couldn't stand anyone touching me —
unless I touched them back. This was irritating at the age of
nine, but positively lethal by the time I reached sixteen, and
could be said to answer for a lot.

My husband has a lot of habits. Indeed, one of the bonds
between us during our early courtship was his ability to catch
me just before I fell over, and his apparent appreciation of my
touching him back every time he touched me. One of his
strangest is his 'cigarette routine'. Years ago, he was working
with a writer who was paralysed and worked in a wheelchair.
During a long, dour session over a comedy half-hour which
wouldn't have made a tortoiseshell cat laugh, Jack reached for
his customary cigarette. 'Don't do it! Don't do it!' shrieked his
co-writer. 'I was just going to light a fag,' murmured Jack,
somewhat taken aback. 'I know you bloody were!' said Harry.
'Do you have any idea what *happens* every time *you* light a
cigarette? Every single time?' 'Yes, I lessen my life by twenty-
five minutes, now do you mind if I—' 'No, you soft sod, what
you actually do — what I have to *watch* you do, thirty times a
day, six days a week!'

47

Jack blinked in puzzlement.

'You take a cigarette from the packet, then you tap it on the packet, filter side down. Twice. Then you tap your chin. Twice. Then you take a match, tap it on the box, twice, and light the cigarette.' By this time, Jack's jaw had tapped the ground. Twice. 'Then,' continued Harry (his calm was deadly), 'you take the cigarette out of your mouth, tap your nose twice and your chin twice and carry on as though all you'd done was light a cigarette.'

This story has two morals. One, which has nothing at all to do with the subject, is that a guy in a wheelchair can't walk away from other people's lunacy. The other is my dear old man's total ignorance of his own ornate ritual, the like of which could create a new school of advanced anthropology. Actually, he went to a hypnotherapist last week to give up the habit altogether — the smoking, not the tapping. Once there, he was played a tape, the gist of which seemed to be that if you never pick up a cigarette again — you won't smoke. Logic, innit? Habits are every bit as addictive as addictives, but it's the first time I've seen him in fourteen years when he hasn't been on fire. We shall see.

Our secretary, Christine, popped by the other day having terrible trouble with the car she's been driving for the last six years. It refused to reverse. It would do everything else it had done before — like start, stall and attack old ladies at pelican crossings. But it just wouldn't retreat. She said it was out of spite because she'd driven her father's car for three days while her own car was being serviced. She had to drive miles out of her way, in ever-increasing circles and bounce it out of parking spaces by hand. Finally she went storming back to the garage and was faced with the irrefutable evidence that her car would indeed reverse. But only if put into reverse gear. As opposed to the position used for reversing her *father's car*. It seems incredible that six *years* of habit could be broken in just three days. A marvellous argument for brainwashing or even carwashing. Christine took it well. Her face just reversed from red to white and back to red again and she was forced to back down.

Her little girl has a lovely habit. She licks her fingers in a precise curving movement, little finger first, over and over again. When asked why she's doing it, she says, 'I'm just keeping

The Boris Fridkin Troupe. Three of whom, I discovered at the tender age of 39, were my great-aunts and uncle.

Having a *wonderful* time at Butlins.

Waiting for perm to come out and teeth to go in.

Age 14, going on 45, emoting as president of the youth club.

Stiff petticoats, a waspie and a night on the town in Hull, with mother, brother Geoffrey and my father.

School play: *The Lady's Not For Burning*. Newland High School, Hull, with non-naturalistic scenery and — no doubt — performances.

Age: 21. As I liked to see myself.

Age: 22. As others saw me in the film *Up the Junction*, 1968.

Feet off the ground, having met future husband in Manchester.

Feet on the runningboard — during filming of husband's play *The Evacuees*.

my fingers ready.' For *what*? A lifetime with the Post Office? A page-turner for the LSO? A short-order cook for cannibals?

Adam recently completed what we lovingly called his 'Burgess and Maclean Habit'. The one where he continually glanced over his shoulders (or up in the air) or out of the corner of his eye as though trying to see who was following him. In vain we asked him what he was afraid of. Monsters? Kidnappers? Keith Joseph? Where had we gone wrong with our child? His eyes flickered in his sleep and he began to resemble one of Ken Livingstone's salamanders. Then, one day, he stopped doing it, and we stopped asking why, so he told us. Apparently, he'd been told by some passing mystic — probably his grandfather — that God was everywhere, so he was trying to catch a glimpse of Him before He dematerialized; an attempt to outwit the Almighty at his own game, I suppose. It's as well to give up on that one as early as possible.

Amy's forte as a baby was 'gurning'. You've seen those octo-genarian toothless wonders who win a yard of Real Ale by wrapping their gums round the back of their left ear while squinting up their own nostril. Well, Amy, who, in retrospect must have been teething at the time, was a brilliant face-puller. She could twist her tiny features into two terrible expressions. One like a well-weathered gargoyle. The other like Marlon Brando in *On The Waterfront*. Passers-by, when I wheeled her out for a walk, would peer over the coverlet and coo 'Aaah, what a lovely ... er ... *pram!*' She could also pretend to be non-verbal, thereby encouraging folk to 'Goo-goo', 'Ga-ga', 'Who's a booty? Who's a dinky-winky?' etc. She'd let them finish, then turn to me and say, '*She's* stupid, isn't she?' It never failed.

My mother counts. Well, all mothers count, of course, for a great deal, but mine counts under her breath. Stairs, as she goes up them. Socks, as she rolls them. Fish balls, as she packs them in Tupperware containers. Sometimes she takes on a resemblance to those old Greek ladies counting their rosaries. Mostly I think she's muttering under her breath how sharper than a serpent's tooth it is to have a thankless child, but no, it's just another knaidlach having its number taken before it hits the boiling salted water. She also hums in the middle of sentences, comme çi:

Her. Do you think I should go back to the Dental Hospital

with this crown? The hills fill my heart hmmm, hm, hm...

Me: Well, yes, if it's still hurting. Is it still hurting?

Her: Well, no, not really — My heart wants to hmmm, hmmm, hm, hmm. Well, it did this morning — hmmmm, mmm, hmm — once more.

Me: Well, go back there and tell them.

Her. (*adamantly*) Nooo! It's perfectly all right! Hmm, hm, hm, hm, like a lamb when it, hm, hm. Except when I eat. But I'm not going *back*. Hmm, mm, would you?'

My mother's habits have always been legendary amongst my immediate friends. Since I was interviewed by Bel Mooney on Channel 4's *Mothers By Daughters*, they've reached a larger audience. I was terribly worried about how she would view the programme, since when I accepted the job I had honestly thought it was all going to be all sweetness and light and a few gentle anecdotes. It turned out to be a rather harrowing analysis of the mother-daughter relationship, with said daughter in a pretty tearful state.

I persuaded Mum and Dad to come down before the programme was broadcast so I could show them the video. I couldn't watch. I paced up and down outside like a pre-natal parent. Afterwards I went in. The subject was wreathed in smiles.

'*That* was the *best* television programme I've ever *seen*!' she said in her special over-emphatic delivery. '*Fancy* them being able to make a *whole* programme all about *me*! And so *long*! Wasn't it *marvell*ous!' Etc., etc., etc. It was only a few hours later over the dishes that she turned to me and said: 'One thing I didn't understand. What were you crying for?'

Is it true you only see what you want to see? I felt light-headed and exonerated. The question which had precipitated my downpour was 'Do you love her?' The answer of course was 'yes'. Who could fail to love someone with such hilarious aberrations? Once, we lived in a flat where the gates were flanked by two concrete balls. Inevitably she would tell the cab driver: 'It's the one with the two round white things on the gate.' If we entered a garage she would wind down the car window and ask 'Do you happen to have such a thing as a mechanic on the job?' She would then look round in wonderment when we all snorted. After the SWET Awards, when I had missed out on the Best Actress Award for *Messiah*, she phoned me and said:

'I watched the "do", on television. Did you enjoy the evening?'

'Well, it was OK. You know . . . a bit disappointing.'

'Why? Wasn't the food any good?'

She also has an unerring need to clean behind my fitted furniture, use vats of Vim on my cookware, re-arrange all my clothes in my wardrobe and dictate to me the words I should use when phoning a complaint: 'Just phone them. *I* would. Say "*Hello*, are you *there*? *My* name is Mrs Rosenthal and I'm phoning to *complain* about the *flood* on the floor of my *utility* room. My husband and I have been *unable* to go to *Marbella* and I have had to *wait* in . . ." Then, if he says . . .' and so on and so on, until I hand over the phone and suggest she does it for me. A suggestion greeted by a loud 'NO O-O-O-O! I wouldn't know what to *say*!'

My father has one major habit, and that is his forgetfulness. It's a familial complaint. Once, my brother and I, after weeks of long-distance intrigue and laborious Geneva/Hull/London arrangements, bought him a car. It was to be delivered, with a huge ribbon round it, on the morning of his birthday. At about noon I rang through and sang two choruses of Happy Birthday To You, before he replied 'Thank you, sweetheart, that's very nice of you, very nice indeed. How are you?'

'Fine. Have you had a nice day so far?'

'Very, very nice indeed, love. How's Jack?'

'Oh, he's OK, thanks . . . Get any nice . . . er . . . cards?'

'Oh, yes, thank you very much. How are the kids?'

At this point I heard my mother bansheeing from the kitchen—

'The *car*, Maurice! The *car*! Have you gone stark raving *mad*! Say something about the *car*!'

At which point, and thus prompted, he remembered his two-ton present and waxed more fulsome than Sir Richard Attenborough being given an award. And you know how fulsome that is. I often wonder what would happen if you gave him a biscuit and a cup of Typhoo.

I suppose my most infuriating habit over the years has been my ability to shake my head and say 'Yes'. I've done it with jobs, I've done it with charities. Where it gets dangerous, of course, is when you do it with men. Years ago I was inveigled into a London hotel by an American who had phoned me out of the blue having seen me on the plane over, in a film. It was his masterful technique which lured me:

'Be at the Langham Hotel in one hour. Do not wear black velvet trousers.'

The latter was a relief as I didn't possess any. I shook my head, but over the phone it didn't register. I shared a flat with three girls in those days, so without telling them I was going on a blind date with an actor whose only confessed film appearance was in *The Boston Strangler*, I took a taxi into town.

Striding towards me was a cowboy who was very handsome, six foot four at least, and wearing fringed boots, leather jacket and ten gallon hat. I was, of course, 'dressed up', since I assumed trousers were not *comme il faut*, in long black skirt, white organza blouse and with some kind of dead animal around me. This was 1969 and I'd never seen anything like him and he'd never seen anything like me. Particularly since the film he'd seen me in was *Up The Junction* where I was dressed like a tart. I thought of walking straight past him but it was too late.

'Marine?,' he drawled. (They always call me that.)

'Er, yes, hello.'

'Hi.' He gazed deep into my mascara. 'I thought we could have a bite in my suite, so we can really talk.'

I shook my head again. And said yes. I was doomed.

We had cold beef and salad, and I was dessert. But, worry not, this is after all not the habits of Joan Collins and if the story ended any other way than how it did I wouldn't be telling it to you. Not at this price, anyway.

I saved my skin and several other bits of me by going into such a comedy routine that the gentleman concerned was first astonished, then amused, then hysterical, then incapable. I don't know where the jokes came from — That Great Comedy Store in the Sky, maybe — but were they thick and were they fast! Finally, I picked my way across his body, hitched up my skirt and went back to the Finchley Road Tube Station. After all he preferred me 'in flight' didn't he? All the way home I kept repeating, 'Aren't you a lucky girl then?' And shaking my head in reply.

Another man I never got to grips with was Mr Habit himself, a writer friend whose peculiarity was to do everything by the clock. And I do mean *everything*. (His life was so ordered that he actually had a chart in the kitchen listing the favourite beverages of all his friends. So it would say 'Jack — coffee — no sugar; Maureen — tea — one sugar; Denis — coffee — two saccharines'. Thus the appropriate drink would be placed on the occasional table directly your wellies hit the welcome mat.)

Morning ablutions were scheduled from 7.32 to 7.45. Press-ups from 7.46 to 7.59. Writing was from 8 till 12 and 1 till 6 . . . then came the evening! He would ring a girlfriend's number from a chart Buddied to the phone, and invite her round at roughly 7.24 precisely. At 7.24 precisely, the doorbell rang and the exquisitely-trained woman arrived. Seductive music played for exactly half an hour. After that, the bedroom door closed and, I am reliably informed, the real split-second timing began. Foreplay, 4 minutes. Earlobes, 3 minutes and 28 seconds. Left breast, 6 minutes; right breast, 8. It would make an interesting Olympic sport, wouldn't it? Synchronized sex. Particularly if you did it under water. With a peg on your nose. Smiling.

Finally, I want all Ye of Little Habits to step forward and confess. Raise your right hand — we won't look at your chewed nails — if going into a bookshop makes you want to go to the loo. Yes, I thought so. Too many to count. All of you sinners — all of you used to read your comic in the only private place in the house, didn't you? Well, the damage is irrevocable, I'm afraid. From now on the mere sight of a W.H. Smith bag will act on you like a bowl of prunes in a seaside hotel. I'd like to extemporize on the subject but — if you'll excuse me — I have to run.

Stories out of School

THE DEADLINE WAS up last week. Number One Daughter's next school. The decision, when made, was split-second. The build-up to the decision was just the ten years. It accelerated, of course, during the last few months. We began to bore for London and the Home Counties last February and have been emptying rooms at parties with unerring regularity ever since. Rather in the way I used to delve into people's kitchens to compare their fitted towel and tea-cloth-recess with mine, I began delving into people's educational experiences or what I larkily called 'Keith Joseph and his Quota Many Scholars'. Now this not only bores the bum off *you*, but it bores the bum off *me*. Until this present crisis, that is.

Now I'm hungry for details of Emily's mastering of the Common Entrance and Joshua's being offered the Chair of Divinity at Westminster aged eight. I crave the ratio of children to computers at one comprehensive, the number of cornets per orchestra at another, gasp with awe at tales of Remedial Maths and Social Studies.

What do I mean? In my day the only remedy for lousy maths was a lousy detention. The only social we studied was the Maccabi Club on a Sunday night. Wasn't life easier when you just accelerated to the Scholarship, put down your choice, sat the exam, failed it and went into the family business? None of this 'Open Evening' business then. Four hundred school-phobic parents on hard wooden chairs. As browbeaten now as the last time they occupied them a quarter of a century ago. The air thick with the smell of massed anxiety. Like tarts displaying their wares in the Reeperbahn — 'Hey, stranger, looking for a lovely time?' Hey, teacher, looking for a gifted child?

Sometimes you have a guided tour of the schools in your area to select your *first* choice. By which I mean your *only* choice. The schools regretfully make it clear that there's such a bunfight to get in, you'd better not shop elsewhere or you don't even stand to get a bun.

And this, mind, is your State education. Once you enter the private sector, the competition is so ferocious that ten-year-olds attend crammer courses in 'Exam Technique'! Can you beat it? Presumably this means simulating exam conditions. You know — the clock-ticking silence, the palm-sweating sickness, the pressure and sheer, bloody, blind panic. As my father would say, 'Listen... As long as the kids are happy...'

One Open Evening was due to begin at 8.30. I duly arrived at 8.25 to find that the headmistress had been in full throttle for several minutes. How's that for up-your-man-ship? The hall was jammed with eager parents, fresh from the strain of exchanging contracts to move into the catchment area. There were no seats vacant and the only way to catch any of the Head's heavily-cultured pearls was to mount the stage behind her and sit on the late-comers' benches. 'What a grand idea for a first night,' I thought, as I Marcel Marceau'd my way past the other sinners. 'Excuse me,' whispered one of them, 'could I have your auto-graph?' Ever seen a minor celebrity try to disappear down her own skin? Pity you weren't there.

Now, I could tell from the Head's back that I wouldn't like her front. Her patter contained such winning phrases as 'I'm afraid I'm unable to invite prospective parents to look around my school'... 'No child who excels at English will be considered if her Maths is weak'... and my all-time favourite... 'One might say you need us rather more than we need you'. Later, she exonerated herself totally by announcing that 'there is a strong emphasis on oral work in all French letters'. By the time she'd corrected herself, four hundred sharp intakes of breath had been quelled by four hundred sharp elbows in ribs, and the only sound in the hall was that of M. Lipman laughing in a manner first patented by one Sybil Fawlty.

So there we are. The decision is made. Needless to say we chose the school that means a sixty-minute round trip twice a day as opposed to the five-minute walk round the corner with friends. I keep waking up to the smell of burning boats. Alan Bennett in his play *Forty Years On* says (and here I misquote) 'Education is what we remember when we've forgotten everything we've been taught.' What do I remember?

Primary-ly the smell of the Headmaster, nicotine and sulphur from every pore and orifice. Tiny toilets and miniature milk bottles. Interminable afternoon rests that now I'd kill for. The mysterious 'fold your hands' dictum. What did they think we were doing with them in front of forty-nine other kids? Or did it just look tidier? More specifically, a whispered hooray at the end of a Double Sewing Period, owning up, getting the backs of my legs smacked and then calling the teacher a 'big fat bugger'. I don't actually recall saying it, well, not 'fat' anyway, but I recall being hauled back by my Dad to apologize, putting on my 'dumb insolence' face, refusing and being clouted all the way home.

Secondary-ly, I remember the bike ride to school and the bus ride home. No, it makes no sense to me either, but that's what I remember. School dinners. Each day I swapped my main course for my friend's puddings. I lived on treacle sponge, tapioca, sago and Fly Cemetery for eight years. Even today the skin on a baked rice pudding can fill me with nostalgic lust.

Wheeling my bike tyres over yet another appalling report to try and make it illegible: ' aureen is a t lly disr ptive fluence', and fooling no one. Smoking on the train to Wembley with the school Games Captain and others. Two puffs, seven coughs and they had us brown-handed. The interminable queue outside the Head's office and the Games Captain's brilliant alibi: 'Smoking is my only cure for period pains'. Brilliant because the mention of the word 'period' in any context other than 'Double' or 'Free' rendered the Headmistress comatose with embarrassment and we found ourselves dismissed in a puff of smoke.

The dear Geography teacher whose severe speech defect coupled with my natural indolence ensured that at the age of twenty-six I still thought China was an island. The eccentric seventy-eight-year-old gym teacher with a shock of white hair, navy knee-length divided shorts, beige floor-length divided legs and a skeleton in the cupboard.

The skeleton's name was Jimmy, and with his animated assistance she taught us Hygiene. And you know what that meant: s-x, pr-cr-ation and p-r--ds, on which subjects most of my gang could have given the Reith Lecture with illustrated slides. In fact, it's the 'gang' I remember most. Marilyn the artist, Ann the voice, Jenny the enigma, Paddy the innocent,

Kay the experience, and me, the court jester. By the time we were of an age to be revered by the Third Years, we'd already established an end-of-term routine. The school would 'surge' us on to the playing fields, make a huge circle, sit down and wait for the show. It was like Woodstock without the sex.

Once seated, they set up a chant — '*The* Horse! *The* Horse! *The* Horse!' And they were never disappointed. 'The Horse' was a poem my brother learnt in California. A very young child (me) is bullied by its pushy mother (Ann) to recite. She reluctantly comes on (i.e. is thrown) and proceeds with much lisping, stammering and hitching of knickers, to recite 'The Horse, by Maureen Lipman' — except it never gets further than the fourth line because she constantly gets the details wrong:

'Ve horth is ananimal wot lives in a field
And eatsth grath all day,
It has two ears, two eyes, two legth,
And a coat of pearly gr...

Oh, no. Two legth? Ve horth?' (huge raspberry, followed by much squirming and looking through legs upside down). Then ... 'The Horth, by Maureen Lipman ... Ve horth is ananimal etc. etc.' The audience-hysteria would build as the child repeatedly cocks up the poem, and it reached its peak as she begins to need the loo. Badly. Since the mother won't hear of letting her leave till she's finished reciting, the poem gets faster and more garbled than ever and is accompanied by violent squirming, knee and eye crossing and attempts at escapology. Finally, poem and contortions reach a grand climax and, midstream as it were, she quietly pees on the stage and watches its trail with silent fascination. Then, on a tremulously rising inflection — 'And that is the end of The Horth, by Maureen Lipman', she does unspeakable mime to indicate the state of her underwear, socks, and shoes.

It's not easy to describe (as if you hadn't noticed), but it was the crowd-pleaser to end them all. We added a few vicious impersonations of the Staff, including the Headmistress' habit of fiddling with the buttons of her blouse nearest to her... chests... (arf! arf!), topical jokes re Semolina v. Fly Cemetery school dinners and suggestions of where to put them, and ended with a song spoof based on current TV, *Double Your Money* or *Dr*

Kildare. Then, amidst stamping and cheering, we ran off leaving them wanting more. Afterwards mob scenes took place in the bike sheds, where we signed hundreds of tattered autograph books... 'If in life you want to make all/Deal the cards and shut your cake-hole'. Up school! Up school! Right up school! Howdy and Goodbye *[signature]*   , Lower VI and other major witticisms.

It all seems very innocent now when you consider we were about sixteen years old. I went to my daughter's last-day party at Primary School and it was very different. Many of the girls, at eleven years of age, looked like certifiable jailbait... Ear-rings, swinging mini-dresses and wild, fuzzy hair flying to the thud of the disco beat. All very well, I hear you retort, times change and you're a dreary reactionary. Except these huge, pubescent girls and some of their giant counterparts among the boys had spent almost the entire year bullying my child to the extent we couldn't get her out of the house in a morning.

It got so bad, that Jack spent one whole lunch hour crouched behind the railings watching two of these girls, described by him as resembling two nineteen-year-old hookers, tripping up littler kids and roaring their victories to imaginary crowds. He reckoned they just didn't know what to do with their physicality. I knew what to do with mine though. But I wasn't allowed near the place since it was assumed I would bang their dull, mean heads together as soon as look at them. I would have.

'The happiest days of your lives'. Whoever said that was either contorted by hindsight or hadn't had an afternoon rest since 1945. But, rest assured, that's what I'll be telling my daughter from now till next September. 'Don't let school interfere with your education,' said George Bernard Shaw. When will we ever learn?

2

Lipmanish Allthoughts

A Week in the Life

I'VE HAD A pig of a week and you might as well know it. It started well enough on the Saturday — oh, don't be so conventional, where is it written 'Thy week shall beginneth on the Monday and shall runneth until Sunday and on that day shalt thou defuzz thy upper lip and all that is good therein'? (I'm foaming at the mouth and this is only the opening paragraph.) So shuttup and listen.

On the Saturday we took the kids to the Adelphi to see *Me and My Girl*. It was a special holiday treat, by which I mean once you've paid for the tickets, the souvenir programme, cassette, T-shirt and supper afterwards, you've probably spent more than it cost to mount the show in 1930. All I can tell you is, it was worth every florin.

I had a little weep when the Cinderella story came out trumps — which is not as unusual as it sounds since I once began crying in the foyer as my husband purchased the tickets for *The Way We Were*. Anyway, we sang 'The Lambeth Walk' all the way to Joe Allen's where we met our friends, the Shindlers, and their kids, and after putting the four children's dinners into doggy-bags, having a screaming fight about who'd sleep at whose house (of all the combinations, it looked at one point as though the only sensible one was all the parents in one house and all the children in the other), we all went home en famille in deux chevaux.

During the night some governmental numskull decided to change the time. Bloody bureaucracy losing me an hour of my dwindling life — I know it's for my own good, so I'll get more light and stop committing suicide all the time like in Finland, but I resent it. Particularly when I'm woken at 9.05 a.m. by my son demanding to be taken to cubs five minutes ago at ten o'clock. Fast asleep, I peanut butter the outside of his sandwich, clingfilm a raw egg and watch his departing woggle in disbelief.

Later that day, after the Transport Museum had withstood the onslaught of Akela and his little green friends Dib-Dob-Dibbing the joint, he returned home with the contents of his tuck-box untouched but browner, and demanded a three-course dinner.

The diary then revealed that in forty-five minutes (their time!) I was to be snapped smiling outside my local cinema, The Phoenix, triumphant at having saved it from closure with the formation of a Trust (which seems to mean that if the cinema doesn't prosper, I get the bill). Anyway, it's a bloody good flea-pit, and I'm delighted to toast it with alacrity, while my fellow Trustees do so with champagne.

I arrived home in time to annihilate, during the cooking process, some rather pleasant-looking veal escalopes which had done me no harm at all. In the afternoon, I tried to work on my script. For this, read I rearranged the plants in the front room, adjusted the loose (for this, read baggy) covers, and played tapes to help me concentrate on the learning process (for this, read listened to 'Songs of the Auvergne') for an Alan Ayckbourn play. Meanwhile, the little girl who'd come to play with Amy had decided the house was too quiet (an occurrence rare enough to justify a place in *The Guinness Book of Records*), so she wrote on the blackboard erected for our French lessons (no, don't scoff, more of that later): 'Dear Amy, I am bored and I want to go home.' Her mother assured me at the door that it was only because she wanted to play with her new pink plastic handbag, but Amy needed a bit more reassurance than that. Full marks to the kid, though, for perseverance in the face of ennui.

Later that night, I am to judge the National Maccabi acting competition. To say the organizers had phoned me a few times that week is like saying Placido Domingo can hold a tune. I am to be there at six o'clock (New Time!). At 5.59 my Mother's Help is still out somewhere in Jack's car with the A-Z, my car is petrol-less and the bank machine has eaten my cash card again.

We bundled the kids on to the Shindlers, bless 'em, who kindly took them to Anna Scher's Children's Drama School. This had the result of turning Amy into Eve Harrington for the rest of the week and she's not stopped auditioning ever since. And I mean around the house. Meanwhile we set off in our juiceless car, praying, and lost ourselves hopelessly in the jungle of the West Hampstead one-way system. By the time we got there, me in my new trendy cricket sweater, I felt like an advert for Mum Rollette (before) and the committee had a look of the Simon Wiesenthals about them.

Actually, the plays were divine — in pidgin Yiddish with songs — in an intentional over-the-top style of acting. I had a ball, wished like mad I'd brought the kids, and judged the rightful winner joyfully. Then, arms full of silk flowers, and petrol tank full of fresh air, we limped to the all-night garage, dinner with friends and home. Once there, I wrote a filthy note to our Mother's Help about promising to come home and not doing so — using words like reliability, thoughtlessness and bending over backwards. In the morning she told me she'd forgotten to put her watch forward.

Why, on the few occasions when I let go my anger, is it always on the wrong person? Can you tell me? When I feel I've been carved up by a driver and I honk and yell, why does the sticker say 'Disabled: No Hand Signals'? When I scream at the check-out girl in the supermarket because my queue hasn't moved for fifteen minutes, why is it her first day at work and why has the computerized till packed up? Why? Forget the psychiatry, Bottling It Up Is Best. Every time. So you die a little younger, what the hell? At least you get a bigger crowd at the funeral.

But I digress, and it's only Monday. At ten o'clock I'm due at Dickins and Jones to buy clothes for the Ayckbourn play on BBC. At 8.50 I dip into a yoghurt, yes, a yoghurt, and the crown comes out of my tooth! The dentist fits me in, but the Wardrobe Lady is therefore unable to fit me out. I'm thinking of taking out a mortgage on a doghouse. I drive to the Rehearsal Rooms in Acton and spend a pleasant, uneventful time fumbling, like everyone else, with learning Ayckbourn's deceptively naturalistic dialogue. One 'but' instead of 'and' and your brain becomes a computerized till in your local supermarket.

Tuesday is distinguished by rehearsals being followed by the recording of a pilot for a radio show called *Hoax*. John Cleese, Jeremy Lloyd and I are to tell a story each. One of us is lying. I have chosen to lie. This is a foolish decision as it entails writing a four-minute story from scratch. I do this to the point of perfection and the audience guesses to a man that I'm the liar. I consider whether it could be my face. But on radio?

Wednesday is a murky day (as the French say) and I spend the morning at Channel 4 recording an interview for a women's magazine programme on relationships. Since what I know about this subject could be written on a Lil-let, I opt for comedy.

Q: What are the signs that a relationship is ending?

A: If he masturbates, then says, 'How was it for you?'

After half an hour of such intellectualism, the lady producer, puzzled, asks for more 'in depth'. I dive out, past the many macramé women on the floor of her office, and head for my relationship with Alan Ayckbourn.

Wednesday night is our French lesson. Me and Jack and Denis and Astrid are taught by the lovely Mireille how to stop humiliating ourselves abroad. We all behave like eleven-year-olds and cause Mireille beaucoup d'hilarity. Afterwards, outside a French restaurant, we are accosted by a gang of youths who ask us if we know the name of the small glands at the base of the neck! After endocrinal and rhomboid they seem satisfied with thyroid, thank us and leave. Astrid, who was brought up in New York, considers that back home your thyroid would, in all probability, have been lying on the sidewalk by now.

Thursday, however, is best. It begins at 5.20 a.m. when the children set off the burglar alarm trying to get into the garden to play dawn football. I don't have the space to describe my feelings. After a morning in Oxford Street shopping for 'tasteless' clothes for my character, i.e. insulting the manageresses of several department stores, I drive for one and a half hours in a traffic jam to the homoeopath who's treating my migraines. I arrive with the daddy of them all. The homoeopath gives me a pill and I drive home through another two and a half hours of traffic, where Chris, the painter, awaits me, shade card in hand. I throw up, choose a colour, lie down, throw up again and muse self-pityingly on the glamour of showbiz. The fireplace-tiler arrives, and I crawl into the hearth. Afterwards, Jack skims the chicken soup and I peel a horseradish root, for tomorrow is Passover and we have eight to dinner. I consider why He chose me.

Good Friday dawns and I'm resurrected miraculously. Rehearsals are rather tense and I arrive home at six p.m., in time to polish the fish-knives and scream like a fishwife. The guests and the time-honoured service arrive. We fill a cup of wine for Elijah, the prophet whom we await yearly, and then relax into the satisfying 'seder' ritual. Later I have to admonish the boys for drinking Elijah's wine. 'It's all right,' says seven-year-old David, 'she never comes anyway!'

On Saturday we all go to see *42nd Street*. The stars are sick and the understudies are on. Which is what the show's all about. Only in real life nobody comes off a star.

I contemplate asking the government to consider putting the clocks back a week.

Pumping Irony

I'VE BEEN THINKING lately about 'working my body'. Feeling that 'burn', perhaps even releasing the odd modicum of oxygen to what passes for my brain. It's mostly because when I go out people keep asking me what's wrong. I can't face my face first thing in the morning — so in order to avoid the confrontation I stagger out of the house looking like the Ghost of Christmas Past, and spend all day answering thoughtful queries from members of the public about how long I've got to live.

However, a change of rhythm is definitely needed, and I've nothing but praise for the power of physical exertion. At present my idea of a good work-out is a two-hour worry about the bags under my eyes, but in the past I have dabbled in legwarmer-land along with the best of them. In fact, many's the morning you may have glimpsed me on the way out of my Lotte Berk muscle-tightening class, blithely attempting to walk unaided to my car, both legs shaking so violently that I am forced to seek support from passing wing mirrors.

Before jogging gave you anorexia, I was out there on the Heath breaking in my track suit and hoping I looked as though I'd been doing it since the days it was called 'running'. I started out as the book sugested, at 15 minutes — worked my way up to 17, back down to 10, and packed in.

For a short spell I jogged around the park, with the kids, *before school*. How's that for one-Lipmanship? One morning we jogged down to the animal enclosure, where one of the llamas entertained us with the world's largest, loudest and most vituperative fart. It convulsed all three of us so much, that every other morning was an anti-climax, and we packed that in too. (I like to think that the llama was somehow expressing her subtle comment on the whole exercise boom.)

Then it was swimming. Just back from holiday with the right number of white stripes, I made the decision to keep up the swimming, ignoring the fact that it was not quite the same without iced coke, bougainvillaea and a language barrier. The swim itself was fine — it's the software which depressed me. The fight for supremacy between myself, a 5p piece, and an old tin locker. The 'OH, YES, YOU WILL GO IN.' 'OH, NO, I WON'T.' 'OH, YES, YOU WILL.' — Kick — OW! syndrome.

The changing cubicle with the curtain which just covers your thighs so you are forced to undress hunched into a figure of eight by shyness and cold. The journey to the aforementioned locker, re-arranging your pile of clothes into the order required for putting them back on again. The fight to open the locker. The fight to lock it. The fight to re-open it when you discover you've still got your glasses on. The shamefaced dodge through the obligatory shower. The chill of real fear when you discover the pool to be full of seven hundred post-examination sixth-formers who've been sent there to work off excess energy.

All this and nothing to look forward to but the return journey. An action replay with hypothermia. Finding the number of the locker without your glasses. Attempting to wrench the elastic band and key off your damp and deeply grooved wrist. And finally — the unkindest cut of all — apart from the one on your wrist — the inevitable fall of your knickers on to the sodden floor as you balance upside down on the cubicle bench, trying to put your socks on in private. Then it's a wet head hitting the outside air, and cellulite all the way home. Uphill.

There must be an easier way of dealing with fatty deposits. I like yoga. The people are nice, the pace is civilized, and nobody dresses like a shiny barber's pole, or yells, 'Hey there — stretch that tendon!' And karate was great. Once I'd got over the embarrassment. There's a good deal of bowing and saying 'oos' involved, you see, and my cousin Maurice's judo suit did tend to stay the same rigid shape with or without me in it. But nobody laughed at me. Nobody laughed at anything. The discipline is everything, and when thirty-five people all make the same movement and shout 'Ki-ay!' at the same time, it's as beautiful as any ballet. Of course, the first time I heard it I thought I'd been shot and fell over!

Why did I give up? I suppose lack of dedication and competitiveness, really. I felt the same way about ski-ing. Something to do with dressing up in funny clothes, dragging yourself and twelve pounds of equipment half way up a mountain, frightened to death and maroon-nosed, just to come down again. Too much like show-business for my money.

The best part of a 'long-run' in the world of exercise, is the weekly camaraderie. That brave bunch of faces, thighs and accents who give up their every Wednesday in pursuit of keeping, catching or betraying their man. How I loved the sessions of ruthless self-punishment, all done on automatic pilot, whilst the stories of sex in the suburbs poured breathlessly out. I always wanted to write a play about it: 'And stretch-two-three — *he didn't!* — Lift those buttocks — *so what did you say?* — *You didn't!!* And heels back over your head — *You know, if I were you, I'd write to Marjorie Proops about that* — And relax those legs-two-three — *I mean, it's not natural!*'

Still I can't help feeling that the bottom is about to fall out of the exercise boom, if you'll pardon the cliché. And the pun. It may be good for our self-esteem to have a body beautiful — but when you look around at some of the high priestesses, I doubt it. 'Britt Ekland's Sensual Fitness Programme' screamed a tabloid hoarding. I know — I shouldn't have read on — but once you've dirtied your hands and dressing-gown on a Sunday paper, you might as well dirty your mind. One of the pearls dropped by our comely Swede is that an all-over massage with warm oil is the perfect prelude for a night of love-making. I must remember that next time I'm cleaning out the chip pan. There are also exercises to firm and trim the 'muscles you need for love'. Like your brain, presumably. And others to raise the bottom. Alternatively you could just read articles like Britt's and have the bum *bored* off you.

Which brings me to Jane Fonda. To the feat of the Goddess. Fonda, a marvellous actress, a beautiful and interesting woman. She loves to dance and she finds a way of making a huge profit out of it. A profit which she then gives to the man she loves to further his political career. So far, so good. And if you can get through a chapter entitled 'Beginners' Buttocks' without cracking up, you're a better man than I am. Which brings me to the video. At the risk of bringing Miss Fonda's lawyer scurrying in, I found it a fairly spurious mixture of masochistic exercise and self-conscious sexual come-on. In close-up.

It's not just the 'You Marzipan — Me Jane' see-how-easy-it-is-to-look-like-me approach I question. It's the eyes gazing deep into camera, lips fully glossed and pouting, whilst wrapping a careless leg around a fully-flexed earlobe. The endless repetitive stretching of taut and flabless sinew in pursuit of the fearsome 'burn', and worst of all, the sound track. This consists of Fonda and her lissome cohorts — 'The Fondues', as I like to think of them — giving out with the 'Whhops' and the 'Weheys', and the multitude of orgasmic grunts which characterize all US quiz games, chat shows and political rallies.

In other words, it's just another psychological soft-sell. A part of the 'I'm OK, you're OK — I love my body i.e. I love myself, therefore I can give you L.O.V.E.' and other such self-congratulatory clap-trap. I mean, are we entirely what we look as well as what we eat? Sure it would be nice to look like Joan Collins at fifty — it would also be nice if it didn't matter if we looked like Sandy Gall! Look at Mrs Thatcher (it's all right, it's only for a minute, I promise). Look at that careful, combed, co-ordinated image. A calculated look for a calculating woman. And of course the public loves it! Because she's made the best of herself? Or because the Saatchi Brothers have made the best of Herself?

Equally, they revile Mrs Shirley Williams on the grounds that she has flyaway hair and dresses for comfort — i.e. she *is* herself. All I'm saying is — doesn't 'Body Consciousness' finally negate all the insecurities, eccentricities, charm and therefore humour which grow alongside dumpy defects? May I produce the evidence here, me Lud, in order to pour vitriol from a great height on to legwarmer-land and Fondaerobics. I took part in a radio interview not long ago together with an apostle of weight-training for women. She was gorgeous. She was glowing. She was fulfilled. (I know all this because she told us so.) She was also wearing a leotard. On radio? I heard myself getting cross and so did several thousand listeners. If only some fully-flexed, flawless, fatless proselyte would admit that the chief reason for their love of leaping into print on the joys of exercise was MONEY.

There's a bandwagon going round. It went around turning dance halls into Bingo halls and bowling alleys. It forced us all into wearing a hula-hoop instead of a waspie, it put us on skateboards, it fastened a yo-yo to our fingers and it forced the same fingers round a Rubik cube. It's very, very clever and a lot of people are getting very, very rich from it, and bloody good luck to them. I just don't happen to subscribe to a programme which is never going to turn me into Victoria Principal, thank the Lord, any more than I would subscribe to the Reverend Jim James and his cyanide punch. If it helps while away the hours, terrific! If it keeps a few kids by the barre instead of by the bar, even better. If it brings a sense of companionship and well-being to both housewives and sweat-band manufacturers — Hallelujah! Just so long as that's all, just so long as it ain't a new Messiah. Oh, please, not that. Don't let him come in footless tights and wristbands with an Adidas bag. That's all I ask — I never could stand organized worship.

However. Before some kindly soul points out that she saw me there, I wish to confess. I joined a health club last year. I did it partly because of the swimming pool, partly because in my new role as lack-of-exercise-pundit, I was hoping for a discount. Unfortunately, my punditry didn't reach as far as North London, and I jolly well paid what everyone else paid and lumped it. (Whatever does that mean? 'If you don't like it, *lump it*' — I've wondered for decades!)

My membership allowed me to swim, jacuzzi or sauna till 6 o'clock weekdays, and from 6 p.m. at weekends. This made me an off-peak member — which could hardly describe me better. The kids were extra every time. They loved it, pin-ball machines, video, food bar and all — and wanted to go every day. There was, however, a preponderance of women who swam in pairs in gold eye-shadow, who shouted at the kids for being there. Their entire reason for being there was to get away from *theirs*. Once, in mid-breast stroke, an elderly man swam up and said, 'I hope you don't mind my asking but I wonder if you could define the nature of good comedy?' I almost drowned. Then, treading water, I gave him a considered and rather erudite analysis of the whole business — which you'll find dried out in a later chapter. At the end of my diatribe he said, 'Because I'm the treasurer of the So and So Amateur Players group and I wondered if your husband could write a play for us?' On the whole though, I enjoyed the club and wish I'd had more time to use it and didn't feel guilty each time I did.

I think I really blew it with the 'Born Again Bounce Brigade' on *The Gloria Hunniford Show* last year. I was the first guest, followed by Frank Carson, the mad Irish comic, and a certain American movie star, Miss Raquel Welch, flogging her fitness philosophy and, incidentally, her book. We didn't meet before the show as she was late arriving from Manchester, but rumours filtered through that she had already astonished the researcher by demanding a hard-boiled egg. Then, it seems, they got her into the make-up room and Frank Carson accosted her with his own special brand of blarney.

'Oh, Miss Welch,' he crowed, kissing her hand and arm, 'I've loved you since I was a boy.' You can imagine how well *that* went down — I mean, you don't even talk to these people except through their entourage, let alone insult them and handle their limbs. 'I want you to be in my latest fillum,' he went on, 'it's called *The Wreck of the Hesperus.*' Well. Suffice to say she ran from the make-up room and hid in the toilets. Presumably they lured her back with fresh hard-boiled eggs because it was in the make-up room monitor that she saw ME.

'You keep very slim, Maureen. Do you have a fitness routine yourself?' said a well-primed Gloria.

'Oh, absolutely. I couldn't function without it,' I bare-faced. 'It's very arduous but I stick to it rigidly. What do I do? Well — first thing I do as soon as I wake up is have a total stretch. I stretch out my arm, like this, and wrap the fingers round a huge mug of tea — like this — bringing the mug to the mouth, rather like this. Here I exercise all the muscles up this arm and in the mouth, neck and throat. After this, I lie back in the bed in a curled-up position — like this — and represent a sleeping cat. Thirty minutes later I wake up again, fall to the carpet and crawl into the bathroom, making low groaning noises, which exercise the vocal chords. Once in the bathroom I look in the mirror and go "Yaaarghhhh!" which, again, works wonders in the chest cavity and waters the eyes. After this, I jog downstairs to the kitchen, stretch all the way up to the cupboard for a packet of salt and vinegar crisps and head for the front door. Then I just close the door behind me, breathe and just walk ... to the car, where I exercise the jaw and tongue muscles by screaming at passing drivers who try to carve me up. ...'

The audience were laughing and identifying away, as was Gloria, and a good time was had by all. Save one. Miss Welch was apparently apoplectic in the make-room room.

'Who is that woman? How dare they invite me on this show and make me follow that dreadful woman? I did NOT come here to be insulted, etc...' and out she stalked with her multi-coloured entourage in tow.

News travels fast in TV and within seconds the director, producer, researcher and probably the hard-boiled egg maker were pleading with her in corridors, assuring her that I was absolutely nobody, that they had no idea I was going to say those terrible things, and certainly she could have a transcript of Gloria's questions and my answers.

Meanwhile, safe in my innocence of all this, I finished my shtick, and sat with Frank and Sandra Dickinson off stage in a little hospitality section. As Miss Welch tottered by, clad in a brown jersey dress that appeared to be on the *inside* of her skin, I patted the empty chair and said, 'Would you like to sit down?' Well, if looks could kill, I'd be writing this chapter sitting on a celestial cloud with a harp on my knee and wings on my glasses. Still in my ignorance, I thought that was just nerves. She did her bit and tottered off. Whereupon I said 'Well done' or 'Jolly good' or some equally fatuous remark. 'Thayank you,' she spat, and departed for ever.

Why am I telling you? To illustrate, as if you didn't already know, that if you look like Raquel Welch the last thing you need to develop is a sense of humour. I mean, can you imagine the average man in a hotel room with Raquel Welch saying, 'So what's new? You heard any good jokes lately?' No, of course you can't. Happens to me all the time.

. I wonder if Golda Meir's life would have been more fulfilling if she'd read the chapter in Fonda's book on 'Beginners' Buttocks'? She might have lost her 'saddle-bags and falling butt' (sic) but would she have increased her charisma? I rest my face.

If Music be the Food of Love, I'm Dieting

AS I SIT here, clutching this feint and margin 10 × 8 refill pad, with a brainful of suet and a failing Bic, I can clearly hear the sound of my husband either playing his violin or having his back molar filled. If all this appears to be in code, well, too bad, so does Life sometimes. Particularly in our house. The point is that, to Jack, his violin is comfort and relaxation. To his inky wife, it's time to put her head down the waste-disposal unit again.

My introduction to classical music was watching my mother doing a robot-like impersonation of Shirley Temple singing 'On the Good Ship Lollipop'. I remember wondering, never having seen Miss Temple, why she sounded like a gnome with a speech defect. Mother also sang 'Oh, How We Danced On The Night We Were Wed', to which my father always added, 'We danced and we danced 'cos we hadn't a bed.'

We had a wind-up gramophone, four or five Edmundo Ros and Mantovani 78s, and 'Red Roses for a Blue Lady'. The number of 78s was severely depleted when my brother and I heard that you could make fruit bowls out of them if you melted them down. We then had four or five plastic bowls from which we expected to hear 'Ramona' if we held on to them and ran round the room very quickly.

For a while I was heavily into being Alma Cogan. In this I was gently encouraged by my mother, who forced me to sing 'Dreamboat' with a laugh in my voice. 'Now do Eartha Kitt' she'd heavily stage-whisper before a captive audience of neighbours and relatives, who all rolled their eyes relentlessly at the prospect of this performing midget.

At pantomime-time, I sat bolt-upright until the moment when Buttons or Wishy-Washee or some 'Dick' or other called out, 'Are there any children in the audience who'd like to come up on stage and —' Dig!! An Ethel Merman-like elbow went straight into my well-braced ribs and whoosh! I hit the boards like grease-painted lightning! Once there, and seat of smocked dress dislodged from knickers, I belted out 'Sugar in the Morning', lungs akimbo, eyes rolling apoplectically and voice choking with vivacity.

I'll stop writing for a bit now to give you time to go out, throw up and come back. There, feel better now? I know. Sometimes even I can't believe I'm still making a total tit of myself thirty years later, often eight times a week, and for money!

Schooldays and the sound of music was 'For Those In Peril on the Sea' which had special overtones if you lived in Hull, and 'Lord, Dismiss Us With Thy Blessing'. This last made me howl like a coyote no matter how much I'd loathed the term from which the Good Lord was dismissing me. Music Appreciation meant listening to 'Morning' by Grieg, in a supine position, slowly unravelling into a daffodil, heavy with morning dew and, in my case, morning mirth.

Recently Adam returned from school saying, 'Do you know a song called "Morning" by Greed?' 'Oh, darling,' I said comfortingly, 'Did they make you be a daffodil?' 'No,' he rejoined, obviously puzzled by the question, 'we just used our imagination and talked a bit about Norway.' And they say education's going downhill!

Music also had the power to soothe things a lot more savage than a breast. Take my friend Ann. As big and busty a villain as any of our gang, she knew all the rude bits of the James Bond books *by heart* and was given to lewd squirming noises when confronted by well-thumbed pictures of Sean Connery. But when she sang... when *she* sang, her pure contralto voice not only made your heart swell, it transformed her face into a Botticelli angel, and her body into angles of delicate grace. Then she'd hit a wrong note, say 'Oh, shit,' and we all knew it was Ann again and breathed a sigh of relief.

At home, our teenage years were symbolized by getting an extension. Built on. This had a big effect musically. It gave my brother and his friends a place in which to congregate and beat their suede shoes. It was about 12′ × 10′ and 'contemporary'. The chairs were strung with yellow plastic and the coffee table — coffee having just come into Hull as a means of communication — was also yellow plastic with black legs and was — wait for it — palette shaped! Every night, my sixteen-year-old brother and his friends tuned in to Joan Baez (or Wailing Winnie as my Mother, perhaps not unfairly, called her), Bob Dylan and Buddy Holly, whilst protesting, pragmatizing and putting the world to rights from the safety of a yellow plastic bucket-chair. Phrases like 'Yeh, but let's be really *basic* about this' and 'Let's face facts, man', were music to my ears, as I hung about the kitchen waiting for the right moment to saunter casually in, cheeks carefully pinched so's I shouldn't look sallow, and top two buttons of school shirt daringly opened to reveal eight inches of skinny neck. 'Anyone else wanna coffee while I'm making one?' I'd mumble vivaciously, whilst surreptitiously rubbing the glasses mark off my nose. 'We shall overcome' was 'Raining in my heart', as I spooned in the Nescafé, and the 'answers were blowing in the wind' as I carried the cups in singly to make my allotted stay aloft longer. Buddy's gone but I still love him and, in a way, he went out at the top with all that was dear and good to me about adolescence, whilst Bob and Joan seem like just two profits (sic) of doom with old voices and new noses.

The first time sex came into it, though, was the Beatles. I thought people were screaming because they liked the music. I didn't know it was their *bodies* they wanted! Well, I was a late developer. Still am. I was still getting over having a crush on the Games Captain — female — when most of my friends had already been through to 75, let alone 25 and 50. Those of you over thirty-five will know what this rising scale represented, and those under thirty-five will still be trying to find out who Bob Dylan was. Any-old-how, the Beatles came to Hull. To the Regal Cinema, now, alas, no more. I was, I suppose, sixteen and totally uninterested in the Beatles or any other form of pop music. My heart belonged to *West Side Story*, *Gypsy* and *Calamity Jane*. However, I was, by now, old enough for younger girls in the school to have crushes on *me*, and some of the Lower Thirds invited me to the famous concert. I sat back disdainfully in my balcony seat and watched the shenanigans going on. Girls were fainting, screaming, and gasping, and this was before the fellows had even come on! When they did, my entire head went into shock and my ears began to cry. The caterwauling was so loud that 'I Wanna Hold Your Hand' could have been 'When Irish Eyes Were Smiling' for all I knew. I surveyed the wild animals with every grain of cynicism in my unmoved body, *Juke Box Jury*-style. Quite suddenly, in what passed for a lull, John Lennon stepped forward. He hit his guitar with a jangling bass chord and paused for effect — then, head back, eyes narrowed, he looked down his nose, touched his lower lip with his slight overbite and hollered from his soul:

'The best things in life are free
But you can keep 'em for de birds and bees . . .'

Somebody very close to me let out a piercing and prolonged scream of ecstasy — I looked round to see who it was and the Third Formers looked back. It was me. 'Like — I got the message and it was very basic, man.' The next day I was hoarse and deliriously broke with every record the Fab 4 ever made. The Cinema Manager told my Dad they'd found forty pairs of knickers abandoned in the stalls. Makes you think about the journey home, doesn't it? Going upstairs on the bus? And Hull was so *windy*!

When I met Jack, he had three records. One was *Hair* which he played in his lunch-break at Granada TV every day. One was Morgana King, best known for her role as Mrs Godfather, singing 'I Can Do A Trick With My Heart', which was really rather beautiful, and one called something like 'The Complete Peter Sarstedt' which I swear only Jack and Mrs Sarstedt ever bought. I had a lot of Barbra Streisand and Dory Previn LPs which I used for weeping into, and a fair smattering of James Taylor, Leonard Cohen and other self-made saviours. And, of course, the Beatles. Nowadays I listen to opera cassettes and Radio 4 and find an equally wonderful outlet for my melancholy.

I'm not terribly good at going to the opera. It makes me want to wear a leather jacket and carry a copy of the *Morning Star*, but I have enjoyed the odd trip to Glyndebourne with my beloved cousin Maurice. Not last year, though. It was some dreary Strauss thing. In German with a very bland and boring soprano. I kept getting these involuntary twitches in my leg, and finally fell asleep, only to wake with a start to find it was not at an end. We all force-fed on cold chicken and an excess of pudding in the interval and I poured oil on a violent row about who had forgotten to pack my cousin Harold's lovingly-prepared gazpacho. With no one speaking to anyone, we went back for the Third Act, where a small stage-struck bat flew into the acting arena and hovered around the diva during the dénouement scene, apparently throwing its voice and undoubtedly stealing the show.

Recently, I awoke to the sound of my doorbell ringing and found an affable cabbie standing before my bleary eyes. 'Morning, Maureen,' he chirped. 'Taxi to Radio London, 8.15.' I prised my tongue from the roof of my mouth and managed to extract the information that I was due on a radio show in thirty-five minutes with my fifteen all-time favourite records. This posed several problems, few of which were solved by the time I reached Marylebone High Street with an armful of ball-point squiggles and a pain in my brain. During the recording of the programme, I began to grow hot with the knowledge that every record I'd chosen was by someone no longer alive. There was Alma and Buddy and Gracie Fields, Elvis and Lenny Bruce and Joyce Grenfell and Maria Callas, and well, it wasn't morbid or anything — it was just, well — nostalgic.

For another radio interview, I was asked to choose six favourite records. On arrival, I found they'd ignored all six in favour of such much-loved classics as 'Turn, Turn, Turn' by Dolly Parton. In vain I remonstrated that, if Dolly Parton turned once, let alone three times, she'd fall over. They had made my mind up and they were sticking to it.

There is a belief that the pop music of today has no content. I've just completed six of *When Housewives Had The Choice*, a retrogressive look at the most-played records of the '50s, and I'm here to dispute that. Popular music rarely has content except as a sociological guide to an era. Show me the content of 'I Tort I Saw a Puddy-Cat', 'I've Got a Luvverly Bunch of Coconuts' and 'Where Will The Dimple Be?', and I'll show you the door. Ronnie Ronalde — now there was a phenomenon. A man who could sing like a Viennese tenor whilst whistling like any known ornithological species — during the same song. Now, that's content!

And how about the television repeats of *Ready-Steady-Go*? Isn't it the most wonderful example of the temerity of yesterday's savage? I watched Mick Jagger being interviewed by a bespoke Keith Fordyce the other night, and he was so *nice*! A nice, accommodating, polite young man would have been my summing-up. So where was all the angst? Why were the Stones considered so dangerous? As for the Beatles, they seemed as well scrubbed and decent as an altar boy's cassock. It's the Waltz Syndrome again, isn't it? Don't do it! Don't even watch it! It will incite you to sexual activity! Like you needed inciting at *seventeen*! Just a jaded revolutionary, that's me. Is it time, I wonder, to hang up my leather jacket and start writing the pop music column in *The Lady?*

Minor Machinations

THE BANK'S CASH dispenser has developed megalomania. I mean, it's always been a little peremptory in its dealings with me. Never much of a one for small talk, but over the past few months our relationship has become strained and its tone indicates that it's definitely moving in for the kill. 'Please WAIT!' 'REMOVE CARD!' 'This number is no longer viable!' 'Wipe your feet! Don't slouch! Sod off!' It's beginning to get me down, I can tell you. It's past the stage where I can just take the money and run, for the vendetta has now entered a new phase.

A few weeks ago I 'inserted my card' as instructed and it refused to take it. It clenched its teeth and moved its head from side to side, like a kid rejecting Strained Baby Prunes. I tried it frontwards, backwards, even upside down — me, I mean, not the card — but with a firm hand it put its foot down and said 'No'.

I stormed the bank. The bank loves it when I storm them. They laugh a lot. It takes their mind off their figures. When they'd dried their eyes, they took my card and threatened it with being cut up. It wasn't remotely cut up, so they promised me a new one. That would teach it. It would also teach me, as I'd only just got its number so to speak by dint of writing it in Biro on my wrist each day for a month.

Anyway, a week and a half later, after spending an unusually large amount of time searching for my Post Office allowance book in order to rob the children of their birthright, my new card arrived.

Here, I must digress. I don't go in the Post Office much for the family allowance because the lady behind the till thinks I'm too rich to claim it. She also objects to my habit of letting it mount up so I can buy something useful with it. Like, say, a small tin of salmon. Consequently, she goes into a violent flamenco dance on my book with her stamping machine, each thud getting louder with each page turn. Then for an encore, she bangs down the individual notes on her side of the counter. 'Bang, thud, lick. Bang, thud, lick. Bang, thud, lick.' It sounds like the sound-track to a dirty movie. She then lowers the notes downhill through the tunnel in her counter. I force my hand into a position not unlike a Kathkali Temple dancer's in order to retrieve it and, on her orders, stage a recount. Then I smirk and grovel my way out. End of diversion. Please drive on. ,

So the card arrived. I learned the number simply and efficiently. No. 9 is two away from the age of my first child. No. 5 the birthday of my second child — all but two, and the remaining two numbers are the same as my mother's wedding anniversary minus one. See? It's a doddle, isn't it? I swallowed the paper it was written on and proceeded jauntily to the cash dispenser.

I inserted the card into the slot. It slid in. 'Wait!' it snarled (like I was about to leave). I waited. 'Enter your number.' I unleashed my powers of retention on its buttons. The machine retaliated. 'Do you wish to change your number?' Well, that flummoxed me. You could have knocked me down with a lavender bag! I was being offered a choice. Like a grown-up. It almost brought tears to my eyes to press 'No' and be unable to add 'But thank you for the offer, though. It was really very nice of you.'

At which point it did the only thing it could do without losing its character. It ate my card. Whole. Smacked its lips, belched discreetly and, with a smooth, gliding movement of its plastic panel, it bit my hand! Being a calm and mature sort of person I thumped it in the panel and called it two very rude words, citing both its parentage and its sexual activity at the time. The man standing next to me in the queue became quite hysterical with laughter. I couldn't help but observe that he was one of the bank's employees. I left him tottering back to the bank with explicit instructions as to where to put his computer — but knowing that it was really just a case of 'Hey, you guys, guess what Dispenser Tracey just did to Maureen Lipman's card again!' I could feel the laughter from two hundred yards down the road.

One of the things which banks share with supermarkets and airport duty-free shops is the queuing system. It works for me like this: first I get in what I think is the shortest queue. Then I wait whilst every other queue moves briskly forward. A glance at the front of mine reveals a gentleman depositing the cash earnings of a multi-branch business in twenty-four brown bags chained to his wrist. And he's mislaid the key. I move to another queue. Whereupon the original queue moves like the clappers and mine goes into action replay slow-motion whilst the teller counts out six bags of twopences for a lady who only speaks Icelandic. I move queues again. This time it moves forward at a regular rate until I reach the teller who, as I open my mouth to speak, places a 'Till Closed' sign over the counter and starts on a bilberry yoghurt.

The only variation on this theme is that if it's the supermarket, the lady in front has just done her eight-monthly shop and the cashier is holding up a packet of Minced Morsels with no price tag, whilst pressing a bell for the attention of the Manager who's in the stock-room with Miss Meredith from the vegetable samosa counter.

If it's a duty-free shop then the queue moves not at all, you are carrying six bottles of unwanted foreign liqueurs, several evaporated perfumes, four hundred Government Health Warnings, plus hand luggage containing three heavy terracotta pots, 'Fragile — With Care' glassware, and a Portuguese soup tureen. And, naturally, the computerized till has broken down. In a foreign language.

I wonder if the theory is true that some people's electric field is irregular and can therefore confuse machinery. I have a brand new washing machine, purchased four months after paying out the £70 which would keep the old one working 'For another five years, no problem'. The new machine is perfect — if you like wet lino and a jammed door — and the after-sales guarantee omitted to mention that the service man was in Benidorm and wouldn't be back till two weeks' washing had filled up the utility room and invaded the lounge.

I have defunct and, apparently, extinct Carmen rollers, an exploded pressure cooker (the recipe *said* use a tin of condensed milk) and a travel iron whose handle takes the skin off the palm of your hand — which is useful when you travel. I also get electric shocks from my car door. But only when I open or close it.

Sometimes machinery can make you feel so silly. There is a

car park in town attached to a radio station where I sometimes work, which employs a square box on the end of a short pole as a car park attendant. It's the same sort of thing as you see in the States when, God forbid, you drive in for a Wendy Burger, and the embarrassment starts when it strikes up a conversation with you. 'What is your name and to what programme are you attached?' it crackles unintelligibly. The silly part starts when you have to reply.

'Er — my name is Maureen, er — Whatsit and I don't believe I'm doing this — and, er, — I'm in Studio 4B working on *Afternoon Theatre*...'

Click, burr — strange microphone noise, static, crackle — then the parking barrier half raises, judders, comes down again and the box says, 'Please park elsewhere, there is no one booked in that name.' Clicks off. One day it will click on again, say 'Oh, and incidentally you were okay in that Ayckbourn play. Bit over-the-top, but okay. Have a nice day now.'

Travels With Me Aren't . . .

OUR FRIEND WILLIS can't wait for us to go on holiday. That is, he can't wait for us to come back. I can hear his little long-distance voice (live from Keighley) now: 'Well, go on then — what went wrong?' And of course, the more gruesome the tale, the more helpless the glee. And we never disappoint him. From the moment the post-Christmas palms and oil-skinned nymphettes start swaying across the corner of my living-room, and the voices of the richest actors in the land seduce me to foreign climes, I shut my eyes and think of Willis. Somehow this keeps me well clear of my local Travelorama. Like good wine, our family does not travel well.

It started long before I ever had one. A family of my own, I mean. As a Yorkshire child we invariably took our fortnight's jaunt in Bridlington, Hornsey or Scarborough — occasionally venturing down south as far as Tankerton or Margate. The familiar photographs of my brother and me in one-piece bathing suits — one piece each, of course — and wind-swept hair, brandishing spades and teeth, cover the fountain at Butlins as well as the Esplanade at Eastbourne. I don't remember much about these holidays except that the countryside never entered into them. There was sand, sea, ice cream, small hotels and amusement arcades in the rain. 'Give the kids five bob's worth of change, Maurice. We'll be having a cup of tea in the Palm Court lounge — all right? Just there, this side of the road, so don't cross. The Palm Court. Don't forget. Tuck your vest in, Geoffrey. Pinch your cheeks, Maureen. And don't talk to any strange men!' Geoffrey leaping off to get away from the child who'd foiled his life by being born. Me spending two shillings on the 'lucky dip' — a prize every time, and the rest on the Laughing Clown, loving the crowd which gathered round.

No camping, though; or climbing; or walking; or cycling. Not for a nice Jewish family. It was just an extension of home really, where Mother didn't have to cook — and boy, could we taste the difference. Or even oy, could we taste the difference. 'Do you know that's the whole pleasure of a holiday to me, not having to cook, just having it put in front of you and just getting up and leaving all the mess behind you.' Only thirty years later do I understand what she meant.

My strongest memory is of a Blackpool guest-house where our two holidaying families were served cracked cups of tea in the cramped and mangy lounge by a disreputable, greasy-jacketed waiter. It was on Day Two it became highly obvious that we'd made a bad choice. My mother, returning from the loo, stage-whispered: 'Those toilets are absolutely filthy.' The waiter, who actually had his thumb in the teacup when he filled it, looked up sharply. 'Oh, sorry about that, love, I'll go and see to that right away.' Putting down the cup, he left the lounge, returning minutes later to continue his pouring. 'Did you tell someone?' said my mother as he handed her a plate of sandwiches. 'Nah, there wuz no one about, so I just give it a quick lick over meself while I were at it. Do you want sugar with this, love?'

By the time I was a teenager, holidays meant gaggles of girls and 'Abroad'. By the age of fourteen my brother, as president of the B'nai Brith youth club, had won a trip to an American summer camp. He'd set off a callow boy and returned a Callowfornian. I was hoping for the same two years later, when I was elected to go to the same camp. I was jubilant when I phoned home the news, and positively distraught when they refused point-blank to let me go. One law for the son, another for the daughter. Sexism would never hit me so hard again. I was devastated, and still mourn the woman I might have been had I gone. Instead I stayed tied to those pinny strings and my teenage years were hopelessly shambolic because of it. The rebellion which hovered did not emerge for another twenty years. But that's another story. And another book.

In 1966 I travelled with a party of young things to Israel. I was sixteen years old, not particularly sweet, and as green as baize. None of which prevented me from becoming shipbound confidante for the sexual goings-on of the entire party. How wisely and with how much nodding of sage head did I advise one particularly enthusiastic participant of Deck Coitus to give her sailor the elbow, and how round were my eyes when she informed me she'd given him a good deal more than her elbow — 'twice' — on the maindeck — standing up! I learned a lot on that journey.

Once there and confined to a sort of kosher Butlins, I fell madly in love with a visiting actor chappy who didn't know I existed. The one overwhelmingly important conversation I had with him, seated under the high stilts which supported the building, was somewhat interrupted by the nightly camp ritual — when the entire area was sprayed with fertilizer — a rare case of the shit actually hitting the fan.

The return journey was by train and was dampened by Arthur, the organizer, a bizarre, red-faced little Scotsman who spent the entire three weeks trying (and failing) to get laid. In his pursuit of a spot of earth-moving he had omitted to purchase 'return tickets for his party', who, therefore, were forced to stand all the way from Athens to Calais. This would have been just about bearable had not my presents included a 4′ × 3′ representation of the Ancient City of Jerusalem (executed in fluorescent paint on black felt) with which I scarred the moving parts of every passenger who had the temerity to seek a way past me in search of the non-existent buffet car. 'My Israel' by M. Lipman!

I did other places in the same way. Rimini, Ibiza, Majorca — my album reveals the same shots of the same gaggle, or should I say giggle, of girls on identical beaches, in identical two-piece costumes, squinting into the sun, coke bottles held high and flanked by boys never seen before or since the photograph was taken. You'd think your whole life was spent on a beach, wouldn't you? Or blowing out candles.

It wasn't till I met Jack though, that I became a really seasoned traveller. Take our trip to the Dordogne — we borrowed a tiny cottage in Riberac and motored down there, stocking up on cheese and wine just as the colour supplements tell you to. The sun blazed down, the cottage was divine and I developed a sun rash which turned my skin piebald. I cut out the wine and cut out the cheese and finally, cut out the area — but not before we'd indulged ourselves in one really fine French meal in a four-star hotel picked from the Guide Michelin. The outside of the Hotel d'Whateveritwas was covered in badges,

crests, stars, awards, and the inside won First Prize for gloom.
We whispered our order to the maitre d' who appeared not to
hear in French. We accepted with alacrity (which means 10 per
cent) his suggestion, no, his command, that we start with the
famous spécialité de la région, a home-made 'rillette'. In time
(and by that I mean about a week and a half), a plate of axle
grease was placed in front of us — I had an unshakable desire to
be in the Golden Egg in Hounslow.

> *Me (sotto voice)*: 'Jack — we'll have to go.'
> *Jack*: 'We can't. We've ordered.'
> *Me*: 'It's all right, I'll be very ill.'

I stood up, swayed and reeled about in an over-the-top
fashion and clutched the air saying, 'De l'eau, de l'eau.' Jack
leapt to his feet, sending the priceless goose-grease flying in an
arc de triomphe, and with a wave of traveller's cheques, and a
flurry of 'pas necessaire', we found ourselves back outside the
badges, the crests and the stars. By this time I was green in the
face with the effort to be convincingly ill. 'Are you all right?'
whispered Jack, half in character. 'You look terrible.' 'I know.
Good, wasn't it?' I grinned and promptly threw up sur l'herbe.

Some months after the birth of our firstborn, we decided to
take a ten-day break in the sun. It being February (I find it's
usually February when there's a gap in our proceedings), we
settled on the island of Tenerife as being the shortest flight to the
warmest place. We packed the burn cream and the boiled sweets,
left Amy with doting grandparents, and flew off misty-eyed
at the thought of seeing her again.

We landed on the said rock through a set of cumulus and
nimbus that could maybe be described as Mancunian. Grey was
the day, wet was the weather, and on its merry way to Colombo
was the luggage. After a desperate search and the subsequent
filling in of many forms, we got on a bus filled with irate holiday-
makers who tut-tutted us all the way down the aisle, and slowly
bumped and ground our way to the hotel, which was full of
small green bananas and Jack's relatives sheltering from the
rain. (Apparently when the weather was going to be fine you
could see the top of the mountain opposite. We never did.) Once
there we discovered that the gourmet menu meant gourmet fish
(unknown variety) and chips, gourmet chicken in a basket, and

gourmet pizza followed by a small green gourmet banana. Beware of small green bananas, readers — they mean unjust desserts. We also had them for breakfast. After the third such breakfast of small green bananas, I noticed an alarming desire to hurl them at the wall. Which I gave vent to. The feeling was so satisfying, that I gave vent to it every morning of our stay. The weather only perked up for the last few days, and our phone bill was the price of a week in the Seychelles.

Portugal — in the Algarve — was pure pleasure. Willis was mortified, but we healed the rift with Florida — oh boy, and how! It started with the flight. Two kids under six, one au pair and a typhoon over Miami. The weather report said it was the worst February since 1946. The orange crop had been virtually annihilated. Fourteen hours and two identical styrofoam dinners later, we arrived at Miami airport having been re-routed via Boston. It was four o'clock in the morning, and oh wow, what a welcome! We stood for almost two hours in a slowly shuffling queue of Cuban immigrants and holiday-makers, whilst the Mafia-faced customs men barked 'Any plants, fruits or seeds?' into our fatigued faces. Once having convinced them that our last intention on earth was to smuggle aspidistras into their bloody country, we limped through the X-ray arch and all hell broke loose.

After our release and the confiscation of Adam's toy pistol, we drove through driving rain and actual hailstones to the hotel, and somehow got through the remaining fortnight. My most cherished memories are of shlepping the family around Disney-land with Joyce Grenfell-like enthusiam, trying desperately to ignore the feeling that I'd somehow wandered on to the set of *The Prisoner*. (You know the sort of thing — a soft voice over the tannoy as you leave your car, 'You have parked your car in Dopey 412. Please remember that you have parked your car in Dopey 412. There are over 60,000 cars parked here every day . . . so if you forget that you've parked in Dopey 412 . . . we will be forced to set fire to your leg.')

My two eccentric children found a plot of concrete with a flower bed in which to continue their imaginary game, and ignored their surroundings. 'But darlings *look* — there's Mickey Mouse' — the real thing was actually standing there, human-sized and waiting to be patted.

'Oh, Mod — don't spoil our ga-ame, I'm being the mean school teacher and Adam is being Heidi.'

Exit Mickey stage left. Piqued.

Then there was that last-minute hol in Ibiza. Ever slept on a foam mattress in 85°F? I had to hang them out each morning for fear the chambermaid would think we were incontinent! Ever slept on a foam mattress with the hotel disco playing inside the bedroom? It wasn't till I got home and was lying in hospital with pneumonia that I realized the never-ending tune was 'Last Night a DJ Saved My Life', not 'Last Night a Bidet Saved My Life'. My version would've sold more copies!

Once we went to Menorca for two weeks, after a hectic stint in a West End farce. We traded one farce for another. As the plane touched down, with me hysterically chewing gum (for my ears) and praying (for my life), the pilot announced the weather conditions to be cloudy, drizzly and more or less beyond hope. At the airport we were met by the representative of the travel firm. No name, but it should be written in neon. She gave car keys to the rest of the party and sent them on their way. Not so with us. 'I'll drive, you follow,' she said, gamely adjusting her sou' wester. 'Why?' I ventured. 'Oh, you'd *never* find it on your own,' she tossed back over a wet shoulder. We drove in noisy silence till she suddenly took a vicious left off the road and up a dirt-track of red earth, strewn with unfinished concrete newel-posts. 'No!' I whimpered aggressively. 'Turn back, it's no good, I'm not staying!' Jack was calmer. (What do I mean was? *Is.*) 'Wait,' he screamed soothingly, 'it may be a short cut.' It was. To *another* dirt-track. At the end of which was a villa and nothing else. I was out of that car so fast the rain missed me completely. 'No good, can't stay, too desolate, too far from beach.' In vain she extolled the virtues of the villa, dishwasher and all. But one look at the swimming pool, set neatly in a pile of red rubble and open drainage was enough to propel me straight into the car and back across the island to the only other available villa. No pool, but on the beach. We took it. Damp, cold and uninhabited as it was. We unpacked everything, wrung out the sheets and were attempting to ask the Spanish housekeeper, in flawless pidgin, how to l-l-light the c-c-calor gas s-s-stove, when the front door opened and two suitcases came in. They were followed by the owner of the villa, who'd arrived unannounced for his annual two weeks' hols.

Suffice to say, we decided to move again, the moment he threw us out. This time to an even damper and more pool-less and beach-less villa. The rest of the meteorological disaster was spent drying socks and knickers over the stove and rubbing butter on a stray dog's ticks. That made you prick up your ears, didn't it? It had much the same effect on the dog. It's an old Swedish custom, apparently, and one that seems to work. The tick, not being Swedish, is obviously shocked to the core when buttered, so that the mere flick of a forefinger sends it leaping on its way like greased lightning. A bit like us, on our way home. No more. No more holidays abroad. 'Jack,' I swore, 'if I ever mention going abroad again I want you to hit me on the head with a rolled up travel agent.'

Best hols I ever had was one week in St Tropez out of season. There was a gang of us. One couple had a flat there they'd rented each autumn for twenty-four years, they knew the place backwards. Every day we'd drive to a beautiful empty beach and bask there. At lunchtime we ate French fries au naturel, and I can still taste them. In the evening we strolled around the bars and shops, dined like kings and laughed till two. We almost managed the language, too, after a shaky start. My friends Julia and Jerry, Jack and I sat in a café debating who had the courage to ask for something to munch on before dinner arrived. Finally I called the waiter and said, 'We are hungry', in well-rehearsed French. He raised an eyebrow and left. 'Nous avons faim, s'il vous plait' had come out 'Avez-vous femme?' And even in France they balk at asking for a woman before dinner.

I must add a postscript to the tale of St Tropez. It was September when we were there, and the following February, Bobby and her husband, Derek, the ringleader of the expedition, asked us all round for a 'Paella Reunion'. We hadn't seen the old crowd since the holiday and, in a flash of foolishness, I suggested to Jack that we should turn up exactly as they'd last seen us. Now, it would have been a quaint idea in, say, early May, or even late December, but this was not only February, it was the coldest February since the Punic Wars, and the ground was frozen to a sheet of ice. Everyone walked miles to the tube station rather than taking their cars up the glaciers, and I remember with pleasure Jack walking me to Highgate Tube to record an episode of *Agony* at Waterloo. The reason I remember it so vividly is that it was our first chance to talk to each other alone and unexhausted for seven years.

But I digress, which at this stage of the book will not surprise you. I wore a blue and white bikini, a large sun-hat with cherries on, plastic beach shoes, sunglasses and a nose-guard. Jack wore trunks, flippers, a sun-visor, a beach bag and a large out-of-season water melon from Fortnums (which cost more than the holiday!) We applied sun-tan cream in zig-zag lines ready for smearing. We wore coats over this but we were less than comfortable and stopping at the off-licence for a bottle of Pouilly-Fuissé beggars description.

The car slowly crawled the distance to Hampstead and painfully slid up Parliament Hill. Then Jack uttered the fateful sentence: 'What number do Bobby and Derek live at?' It would take a whole other book to describe our knocking at all the basement-flat doors in Parliament Hill, and the numbers which slammed in our sun-creamed faces. We began by asking for Bobby's number, but after a while, we asked only for shelter from the blinding, freezing cold. When we reached their flat, we were speechless, blue and totally numb.

And the guests? They were too hysterical to ask us in! We stood at the door like two stalactites on vacation, whilst they hooted and pointed and wept and rolled on the floor clutching their innards. Of course, we'd forgotten to bring clothes and had to be kitted up in sweaters and pyjama bottoms, but it was actually worth it. As the dinner progressed, there was always someone who would look at us in mid-conversation, and explode all over again, till we all lay exhausted over the paella. It was a bit like a holiday, really.

There is a joke which goes: 'What's the difference between Los Angeles and yoghurt?' The answer is: 'Yoghurt has a live culture.' Los Angeles is the place Jack goes to have his hair greyed, his lines delineated and his cranium numbed. It's the place where the sky is always blue and so are the screenwriters. Where the storyline is accepted on Monday by the twenty-four-year-old head of a studio, and rejected on the Thursday by his sixteen-year-old replacement. It is the place where eye-bags are called 'allergy sacks', and *A Bridge Too Far* is the only person in town who hasn't had his nose fixed.

'In *Movie of the Week*,' said one pubescent studio executive, 'we work on three kinds of scenario — Heart, Stomach and Groin.' He paused for effect. 'Heart means love, Stomach means horror and Groin means sexploitation.'

'Really?' mused Jack, 'I'm afraid I only do elbow.'

Don't laugh. The next day the guy phoned Jack's agent and said, 'We have to work with this Britisher who only does elbow — sounds really interesting.'

Another time he went into an office and heard the producer speaking to his girlfriend on the phone. 'Come over and pick me up, honey,' he yawned, 'I'll be through in fifteen minutes. I just gotta see this schmuck from England.'

By the time she arrived, he'd discovered that Jack had written the Streisand film *Yentl*. 'Come in, sweetheart, I want you to meet one of England's greatest writers. This man is dynamite, he is responsible for some of the finest screenwriting...'

'Hello,' said Jack, 'I'm the schmuck from England.'

This trip I went with him. No one was going to treat my man mean without getting a couple of my fingers in the eyes by way of explanation. I determined to hate the place. I wasn't going to work there — not that I'd been asked to. No one knew me from Eve. Still, I thought, I might perhaps see a few agents while I was there, so before I left I phoned my agent and said, 'Whilst I'm there, should I, er, you know, should I do anything?'

'Oh, yes, darling,' she said, brightly, 'Could you bring me some Georgio perfume?'

I had a ball. We reached the airport to find that Jack's first-class seat had not been cashed in for two in club class as promised, but that *he* was in club and I appeared to be in a locker on Flight deck. Mind you, I was travelling as 'wife', which is Californian for hand luggage! That was easily solved — you just put your hand in your pocket and pay out more money than you have earned in six weeks, and the problem disappears like magic.

The flight itself was a lark owing to the fact that most of the stewards were fans of *Agony*, it was our twelfth wedding anniversary — the polystyrene one isn't it? — and they bombarded us with enough champagne and British Airways toilet bags to bath Cleopatra. We watched Ryan O'Neal in

Irreconcilable Differences, which should have won an award — for us, I mean, for sitting through it — and arrived in LA ready to do the town. At four o'clock in the morning, English time, we sat down to our evening meal, then strolled back to our hotel, which was swarming with large black bodyguards with walkie-talkie machines and large black transit vans, who were on guard for small black superstar, Prince, who was staying there.

Each day I met old friends and shopped. Since the dollar was almost at parity with the pound, a pair of dungarees for Amy cost £40. Still, when the guilt sets in because you're here and they're there, £40 is very, very cheap, especially when you get them home and they reach her knees — leading to more guilt because how could you forget the length of your own firstborn's leg?

I also encountered some unknown Californian relatives who were so thrilled to see us, it was both touching and embarrassing. For example, whilst shopping for a jacket in one of the big stores, my Auntie Gladys, a Californian for forty years, said to the salesperson, 'My niece from England wants to try on the blue jacket. She's just won the Laurence Olivier Award.' Can you imagine my face?

My incredible discovery was that my grandfather's brothers and sisters had been a famous Russian dance troupe called the Boris Fridkin Troupe, who had worked for George M. Cohan. The sepia-coloured pictures of my fabulous ancestors were a revelation to me, more so since I'd had no inkling that anyone in my family had ever been in the professional theatre. 'I don't know where she gets it from' had been the frequent lament in our house. Apparently, my great-uncle Sid had been on the stage at the age of two and a half, billed as the 'pocket George Landrush'. No, neither have I — but I bet someone reading this has... all contributions deliriously awaited.

I did go to see an agent whilst I was there. Jack typed out a résumé which was so impressive that even I wanted to take me on as a client. He carefully put all the awards nominations up front, followed by the most prestigious names I'd worked with, then a list of credits. I was embarrassed. He said, 'I promise you it's the only way — the slightest suggestion of British reserve, of self-deprecation and you're billed a *loser*.' I must say, the agent was apologetic for not knowing me, and really k-o'd by the résumé. He was also pleasant company and we had a really good laugh. But he hadn't the vaguest idea what he would *do* with me. I didn't fit into any known category. I had to agree.

I met up with another agent from England, my ex-agent in fact, Barry Krost. He's now involved in both music and film production, and heavily involved in running several gay banks. Yes, really. He and some associates realized that the ideal bank client was no longer a middle-aged, upwardly mobile family man with 2.2 children and a hefty mortgage. That same client now had 2.2 ex-wives, 4.4 children, hefty alimony and a pacemaker. Your average single parent or gay couple, on the other hand, had few dependants, a well-paid job and could not get a mortgage for money let alone love. The rest is future history. They now have six branches and are growing gaily. Only in California? I shouldn't bank on it!

Everyone went to bed very early. As soon as the decaff hit the table, everyone stood up to leave. At first I was convinced it was my jokes, but I was reassured to the contrary. They all have to be in the gym by 6 am in order to be showered and taking a business meeting by 7.30 am. Let's face it, they're all bloody mad. But then, who isn't? At any rate I enjoyed my week, miserable weather and all, and came back, for me, surprisingly refreshed. What does a Californian make for dinner? Reservations.

Hooked on Heroines

OUTSIDE, AS NIGHT falls, a coverlet of snow settles with silent intent over the landscaped lawns. The icy wind screams its pain against the casement shutters. Inside the chamber, a roaring log fire flickers and dances in every corner of the damask-covered walls. 'Next time, madam,' sighs the last fireman to leave, 'use the hearth.'

Damn, I was going to attempt romantic fiction and I blew it after forty-four words.

She gently sets down her glass of golden Calvados in the hearth to warm, and pushes back the tawny mane from her glowing face. Snuggling further down the pile of lacy cushions, she languorously opens the crisp covers of her new book. Alone with someone else's Muse, she devours the pages from first to last. With a sigh of pleasure, she closes the book and lies basking in a sea of stirred emotions . . . Happens to you a lot, does it? Me too. An uninterrupted good read is about as familiar as a course in religious scuba-diving. True, I sometimes dip into a book at bedtime, but, when I say 'dip', I mean as into boiling bathwater. One book can take me so long to complete that I often have no idea what happened in the first two hundred pages by the time I reach the second, and have to keep going back to Chapter One to see who the hero is. And as soon as I've finished it, however memorable it was, it's gone forever from my memory. There's a fault in my computer and one day I'm going to complain to its Maker. I've been known to get through three-quarters of a newly acquired book before realizing I've already read it. Which is okay in one sense, because it means I have a houseful of unread books waiting to be re-read.

Mostly it's scripts or letters or unlearned lines that I dip into these days in an attempt to allay the guilt of tasks undone. I've got to the stage where I automatically begin every letter with: 'Please forgive this unforgivable delay, but . . . the cat ate your address/I've had a terrible boil on my femur/or I had to walk a friend's gibbon for her.'

Holidays are a good excuse to read, and with my luck with the weather, I should in theory be able to get through the complete works of Barbara Cartland, God forbid. In practice, I don't pack anything except *Thspanish Made so Ridiculouthly Eathy, You'll Sink You Were Conceithed in Barthelona*, in a lame attempt to learn a language. *Any* language. Then at the airport I buy junky books by Jackie Collins and Judith Krantz, just to get me through the flight delay. That's my excuse anyway, and I'm super-glued to it.

The point about blockbuster, million-dollar, family and soft-porn sagas is that, to be grammatically precise, they are unputtable-down. It's like cream cakes, nicotine and bitchiness, you hate yourself but you can't stop doing it. And every book carries a Government health warning if you just look for it — *'She was a woman for whom the twin passions of love and revenge seared through three generations. Headstrong in her thirst for success, dazzling in her upwardly-mobile career, she abandoned the men who desired her with a stubborn ruthlessness. Until she met Dirk D. Studmeister III. Until she met her match . . .'*

The book weighs more than a baby. Once you've got to the hotel and read the precis on the inside of what you've just read on the outside, you are sinking. Once you're bending the book's spine inside out until it tears so's not to miss the last word of each line, you're sunk. You become a Closet Reader. Slovenly in bikini and dressing gown, you fake reasons to return to the bedroom after breakfast, sleeplessness until four in the morning, and headaches during mealtimes. As you reach the last chapter of the steadily-mounting pile of pillage and pudenda, you feel sick with a mixture of impatience, relief and, well, sickness. Your eyes feel like greaseproof paper, and your face is suntanned but for two round, white patches where your glasses have been. You resemble a raccoon on amphetamines — and for what? You're Hooked on Heroines. Someone should form a self-help group, and quickly, before my next vacation, please.

Hospitalization is a great cover for a guilt-free read. With nothing else to do but correct the dosage of drugs with which they attempt homicide on you each day, listen to the nurses' problems and avoid being mistaken for the patient with your surname on his wristband who's in for an amputation, it is more than possible to lose yourself in a book for, oh, minutes on end. I did the six Jane Austens at a sitting — well, a lie-in. (I know you thought there were only five, but there's an unfinished one. By her, not me.) Oooh, it was grand! Like being saturated in satire. I still rank Mr Darcy as one of the most desirable men in literature, but then I'm funny that way.

I was once given a book by my Auntie Rita when I was about nine or ten. It had been a favourite of hers and it became a sort of mantra to me. I read it and started it again literally hundreds of times and never got bored. It was called *Nicky — New Girl* by Irene Mossop and had an extremely old, faded blue cover sporting a line drawing of two girls in gymslips playing hockey with bobbed hair. No, they were playing hockey with a ball, but they *had* bobbed hair. And real 'twenties faces. It concerned young Monica (Nicky) Kenley who was sent to join her brilliant elder sister, Diamond (sic), at boarding school. For her part, Diamond wanted her crazy, tomboy sister in her House like she wanted a frontal lobotomy. She and her friend, Crystal (sic again), ignored her and continued their glittering pursuit of the inter-school tennis trophy, were prefects and fearless crackers-down of the mysterious 'Vikings' gang. Nicky was taken under the wing of one Lorice Laurence, who in the eyes of Diamond was a total slacker. I'm sure it won't spoil the suspense if I tell you Lorice turns out to be a 'real brick', and in her quiet, unassuming but steely-determined way she saves the day, the tournament and one of the sisters' lives. It is undoubtedly one of the finest books *ever written* and deserves to win the Booker prize every year. I don't know on what level of identification it gave me such pleasure, I'd never in my life met such ra-ra-up-school-anyone-for-a-tuck-type girls, but I knew them all intimately. And what fascinates me is that my daughter loves it now as much as I did, and reads it whenever her new books run out.

The first book I remember vividly was a large, brightly-coloured *Haggadah*, the Book of Passover, which appeared once a year, every year in our house. It had movable pictures — such as baby Moses in a basket which bobbed up and down on the waves when you pulled a paper lever. (Know the movie joke? Miriam brings home a baby and everyone says, 'Ugh, what an ugly baby!' She says, 'Funny that. He looked all right in the rushes.') It also had a picture of God with flowing white hair and beard, William Blake-inspired complexion, worryingly-stern eyebrows and flowing red robes. We've still got the book, Moses by now Sellotaped to his coracle and the ten plagues reduced to The Slaying of the First-born. Thirty-five years later I still visualize God in the same way, perched on a bunch of clouds with one finger pointed accusingly downwards. At me.

I also loved *Heidi*, though Clara was a bit of a drip and Grandfather's irascibility made me nervous. I loved the little straw-covered loft Heidi slept in and cursed my own divan with its nylon-quilted bedspread for not smelling of 'sweet fragrant hay'. (The name Fräulein Rottenmeir always intrigued me as I imagined Fräulein to be the German equivalent of Pauline.)

The Famous Five rated very highly too, though on re-reading them with Amy I find them wetter than a liquid lunch with Francis Pym. Julian, of course, was always racist, sexist and just right of Oswald Mosley, and Anne didn't bear mentioning. She made Clara in *Heidi* look like Mommie Dearest and didn't even have the wheelchair by way of compensation. George, however, was favourite and Dick was okay, for a *boy*! What a life, though. Adventure after adventure, each one punctuated by a never-ending stream of meals, picnics, snacks, suppers and farmhouse teas. Those four kids must have been as fat as pigs with what they put away in the course of a normal day's solving and snooping. And Timmy must surely have spontaneously imploded with all that licking clean of four plates and polishing off twelve-course snacks. 'I say, Anne, I'm feeling pretty peckish after that shin up the cliff-face and digging up all that buried treasure, what have we got in our kitbag, Old Thing?'

'Well, there's not a great deal, Jules,' grovels Anne, 'only a whole boiled ham, some cold new potatoes, a freshly-baked loaf I picked up from the baker's at six o'clock this morning before we started the adventure, lashings of crispy, English lettuce, a couple of pounds of firm red tomatoes, some tinned apricots, a pot of home-made jam, six or seven bars of chocolate and a wonderful-smelling seed-cake which I baked in a brick in the noonday sun when you wouldn't let me join you on the deserted oil rig because I was only a girl.'

'Oh, well, I suppose it'll have to do.' This from a stoical Julian. 'Come on, Old Girl, get it laid out on a crisp white cloth, while Dick and I do some body-popping on the shingle...'

The books I strive to avoid are those compilation jobs — particularly those in which I'm featured. These are the result of a letter saying, 'I'm writing a book with my friend Derek called *Funny Things That Happened To Me In A Month With A Y In It* so could you please...?' Or 'Do you have any funny knicker-elastic stories?' If it's for a charity, then it's okay, but mostly it's just for 'me and Derek's' old age and a nifty way of getting the world and his mother to write your book for you.

So, gentle reader, for so you are, I will leave you with a word of advice. Or 106 words.

Tonight, when you return home from a hard day at the Sexual Harassment Centre, throw off your parachute silk jumpsuit, fill to the brim your cast-iron claw-footed bathtub, sprinkle some random rose petals on to the surface, and ease your town-dusty limbs into its caressing depths. Let the pressures of the day flow from your shoulders out into nothingness, and the lines of tension melt away from your face. Give yourself permission to be at peace. Slowly, effortlessly, pick up your long-desired new book. Place it firmly in the bathrack and open it at Page One. Breathe in deeply through your nostrils, smile, and as £9.50 worth of hardback crashes through the soapsuds and sinks without trace, never to be recovered except as papier-mâché, consider the advantages of a simpler pastime. Like knitting a car.

Games For a Laugh

SHOULD IT BE true that the human race is subdivided into givers and takers, active and passive, extrovert and introvert, then we should also add game-players and non-game-players. I'm a games player by nature. Don't get me wrong. Nothing that involves movement. Like leaving my chair. Oh, no, *party* games, I mean — like Treasure Hunt, Yes, I Am Not Botticelli, In the Manner of the Word, Charades. If I played my cards right I could be North London's answer to Gyles Brandreth. Even my husband has, over the years, evolved from smiling bystander to over-enthusiastic participant.

Organized sporty games leave me cold. Literally. School games from my point of view looked like a John Betjeman parody: 'The thrust and the threat and the thunder of sticks, The twenty-one women, scarlet-faced and Aertex-vested, Forging their destinies as the field rings again and again.' From the thunderers' point of view it must have looked pure Dylan Thomas: 'Weary-worn and wrong-ended of field, Blue-lipped Lipman, Left Outside, white of knuckle, knock of knee, trampled terribly underfoot by the tramp of the twenty-two men. In her head a different scenario of single-handed salvation. A sweep of her avenging stick as she saves the school, the day and North Humberside.'

Why the message, so strong in my head, never got through to my legs is a mystery to me still. My elder brother was a natural athlete who excelled at anything from alleys to rugby union. In fact, he had his nose broken so regularly in the scrum that he ended up with a retroussé. No mean event in our family.

My daughter shares my enthusiasm for turning out in weather that would make Sherpa Tensing tense. Wearing navy knickers and toning lips, she has all her mother's natural affinity with a locker-room radiator. Meanwhile, back in the back patio, her brother leaps constantly into thin air and crashes to the concrete shouting 'Aaand another miraculous save by Rosenthal, and the crowds go wild!' Thus history repeats itself. Or is it conditioning? Or just something in his hand-me-down genes? Whatever it is, I expect it's my fault.

But what of the other kind of games that people play? Parlour games, board games and quiz shows are quite another kettle of poisson altogether. Give me a Scrabble board and I'll give you a seven-letter word faster than you'll give me a four-letter one. In our house we've indulged in Scrabble, Junior Scrabble and even Dirty-word Scrabble for some years. A friend of mine used to play Scrabble with a confirmed cheat. This clean-living citizen when confronted by a bag of plastic squares saying X^8 and A^1 turned without further ado into Richard Milhouse Nixon. His rules included looking up words in his dictionary before putting them down, swapping all his letters if he picked up three the same — without losing a turn — and acceptance of such well-known expletives as OB, YP and FRNST. The challenge for my friend became beating him in spite of the cheating, particularly when he found (whilst clearing up) four or five useful letters secreted down the folds of the armchair.

Trivial Pursuit was hot favourite this year and I too blew warmish for a while, after attending a TP party at Stringfellows nightclub. Here fishnet-tighted hostesses showed various minor celebrities the subtleties of the game. At my table was the ebullient and computer-brained Fred Housego, who showed his superiority by smirking as we stumbled over the longest river in Papua New Guinea. 'Come on — you must know that! — Think!' he beamed in a manner reminiscent of my brother when confronted by my Maths homework. I even found the 'World of Entertainment' questions weird, not to mention ungrammatical i.e. 'Who did footballer, Billy Wright, marry one of?' Yes, I *know* it was a Beverley Sister — God, you're as bad as Fred!

The kids love it. Here is a typical exchange:

AMY: 'Which Rev-ol-ution-ary group had a leader called DART-AGN-NON?'

ADAM: 'Er-ooo-ah-don't tell me — (*violent banging of head on table*) it's on the tip of my — (*grasps tongue*) oeerghaw!'

AMY: 'Shall I give you a clue?'

ADAM: 'Aw, all right, then.'

AMY: 'The Three Musket— (*gestures to ears*).

ADAM: 'Er-oo-ah-don't tell me, it's on the tip— aargh' etc.

Occasional impromptu games parties and festive occasions have been phenomenally successful, but have you ever tried organizing one in advance? 'We'd love to. Games, ah, yes, super. Oh, wait, did you say Saturday 8th? Oh, God, I've just seen it in the diary, it's, it's Armistice Day, isn't it? Oh, God, I'm so sorry, it's just that Dee and I sort of promised to take this party of—er—maimed veterans to Ardennes for a sort of Hovercraft and brunch thing to commemorate — oh, hell, I just *don't* see how we'd get out of it—' It is at this point that you dig up the Treasure Hunt clues, eat the *Call My Bluff* definitions and order more tequila.

We once had a terrific New Year's Eve party. It was impromptu. A get-together for those who hadn't already been got together. As I was putting the finishing touches to something gourmet — like a bowl of hedgehog crisps — Jack came down dressed in black tuxedo, bow tie, no shirt and light-brown hiking boots, complete with red carnation. Obviously something had snapped. Not to be outdone, I went upstairs, changed into black, strapless dress, striped leg warmers, running shoes, Manchester United scarf and brown leather hat. We stood there looking at each other in disbelief as the doorbell rang. We opened the door and the guests slapped their hands over their mouths — 'Oh, God, we didn't *know*!' 'Know what?' we blinked. 'That it was black tie,' was the response.

Now, you might think it amazing that two people could be dressed as idiots in every colour under the sun and still have that effect, but the proof of the pudding was in the greeting, because every guest who arrived had precisely the same reaction. They saw only the black and white, and assumed the rest. It was a rare do. We played games in a highly unorganized fashion, wished we had a piano, but sang in the New Year with the requisite emotion and hardly saw each other again till the following year, when we tried to do it again. Fatal. This time we did it at a friend's house — with a grand piano. Invited several people who played instruments, and organized the games. Did it work? If I tell you that there were four of us left to sing in the New Year, would that answer your question?

There was one memorable Christmas when telepathy games were all the rage. I remember stunning a room into silence with one wonderful piece of chicanery. Whilst I was outside the room, the guests chose the name of a famous person — Cassius Clay, to be precise. When I re-entered, Jack said, 'I went for one day to London, and stayed three.' And I said 'Cassius Clay.' Well. Were they flummoxed. The point about tricks such as these is that they are *such* fun when you know and so bloody awful when you don't. Immediately, they sent Jack out. This time they chose the name Jack Rosenthal. The subject returned, and I said, 'I was in Yugoslavia for four weeks, five days.' And he said, 'Oh, it's me, isn't it?'

By this time several people were working out that R is seven letters away from Y and J is eight letters earlier than R, etc., but to no avail. 'Go out again!' was the cry. I went. When they called me back, Jack said 'I was in Quebec for five months, two weeks and two days, Niagara and Seattle, then I went to Saratoga for three days and back to Seattle.' I knew immediately it was Princess Margaret — but also thought it would give the game away because of the length of the clue. It didn't. No one's ever tumbled it, yet everyone groans with ease when they're told. Stand clear for groaning — I'll tell you at the end. That'll make sure you don't skip-read.

The other hot favourite was The Wizard. I have the feeling this is illegal, but I'll tell it anyway. So, British Telecom won't answer my calls for another twelve months. Why break the habits of a lifetime?

There are several wizards of my acquaintance around London and Manchester. Whilst sitting with a group of people, preferably including children, ask them to pick a card and say you'll ring the wizard to see if he can guess what it is. You dial and the following conversation ensues...

You — (or if entertaining royalty — *One:*) 'Good afternoon, may I speak to the wizard, please?' (*Pause*) 'Yes. Because there's someone here who'd like to speak to him.' (*Pause*) 'Thank you, sir. I'll just put him on now, shall I?'

You then hand the phone to the child and watch with glee, as first the eyes widen in disbelief and then the child says: 'Thank you... er... Mr... Wizard... very much,' or 'How did you know that?' or, in the case of some slightly more worldly children, 'All right, clever-dick, when did he tell you?'

Now, as Raymondo would say — *This* is what you *do*...
Suppose the child has chosen the seven of clubs. First dial your
known wizard. When the voice says 'Hello', the following
conversation ensues. Only this time, I'll also tell you the wizard's
half...

> YOU: 'Good afternoon, may I speak to the wizard, please?'
> WIZARD: 'Spades. Hearts. Clubs—'
> YOU *(firmly)*: 'Yes. Because there's someone here who'd like to
> speak to him.'
> WIZARD: 'Ace. Two. Three. Four. Five. Six. Seven—'
> YOU: 'Thank you, sir. I'll just put him on now, shall I?'
> WIZARD: 'The seven of clubs?'

Assuming he's got it right, you hand over phone to child, and
the wizard says in dark purple tones: 'YOUR CAAAARD IS
THE SEVEN OF CLUBS!!' and rings off. Simple when you know
how, but very impressive.

Occasionally it can play you at your own game. As, for
example if the wizard is a) asleep, b) on the job, or, in the case of
a good friend (then) and accommodating wizard of ours, in the
middle of the row which finally led to his divorce. She had just
thrown the wedding plates when the phone first rang, and
immediately before the fourth phone call, he had kicked straight
through the kitchen door — 'THAT'S IT! WE'RE FINISHED! IF
YOU THINK—'... Ring, ring... 'HELLO! SPADES! HEARTS!
CLUBS—'

I'm not taking the blame entirely, but somehow I don't think
we helped.

Talking of wizards. *Call My Bluff* is a wizard game, as Arthur
Marshall might say, both on telly and off. Actually, of all the TV
games shows *Call My Bluff* is the most civilized. This is mostly
due to my being in Arthur's team, since he's the sort of person
whom, as the Lithuanians are wont to say, 'You could lay on an
open wound'. Our team doesn't care a fig (Arthur's expression)
whether we win or lose, so long as we have a jolly good hoot (also
Arthur's expression). And as I am a bugger (my expression) for
the double-bluff i.e. striving to present the true definition with
such truthfulness that the opposition feel you would surely have
sent it up more had it been true, it makes for a wizard evening.

Give Us A Clue, charades by any other name, is a great game for
TV and real life alike. Although it's amazing how blank your
mind can go when confronted by a card saying *Yentl*. It's all right
doing 'Sounds like "lentil"' — you try and mime a lentil. Una
Stubbs's greatest nightmare is the introductions. 'My first
guest,' she beamed to camera, 'is the comedy actress whom we
all remember in *Agony*, will never forget in *Outside Edge*, will you
welcome — aaargh, I've forgotten.' But the greatest of these
blanks was perpetrated by my other pal, Julia McKenzie, on
her own *This Is Your Life* when Eamonn said, 'It was at this point
in your life you first heard this voice.' 'Hi, Julie,' came a
Canadian-accented voice. 'Do you remember that first evening
we went out to dinner after the show—?' Julia's face was
contorted with panic. 'Yes, it's . . . Gosh, I know that voice. Oh,
it's . . .' Seeing no way out, an ever helpful Eamonn was forced to
say, 'Yes, it's your husband, Jerry Harte.' I know familiarity
breeds contempt, but amnesia?

Then there are the TV game shows where you are called
upon, by dint of your intellect, to help someone lose a thousand
pounds. This conclusively proves you to be as big a blockhead as
the public always suspected. And proves, after the show, why
the hospitality room at the TV studio is always known as the
hostility room. As for *Blankety Blank*, well, I don't do that one
any more. It's too hard. Oh, you may scoff, scoff away but you
try sitting in the ageing comedienne's seat and working out the
missing word in a sentence like — 'Stone me,' said Sir Gawain of
the Gusset, '"I've got my blank stuck in the grapefruit
segments."' Brain immediately goes into early redundancy,
Wogan approaches with gleaming eye, acerbic wit poised to
spring. 'Roight, let's see what our *distinguished* panel has got —
Yes, rapier, sword, dagger, and what about old Maureen
O'Lipman skulking behind her card? Ah, Maureen has written
"woggle".' (Much laughter and pointing ensues.) 'Woggle,
Maureen? Well, at least she's well prepared—'

Of course, nothing but nothing holds a candle to what the
Americans get up to on their quiz shows. Firstly, they obviously
hold auditions for the contestants. 'Wanted: Aggressive and
moronic hysterics for TV game show. Hyperactives and thyroid
cases only need apply.' The selected few are then tutored in how
to leap in the air screaming 'God Bless America!', clap

themselves at the drop of a floor manager, and clasp rapaciously to their bosom the bottle of vegetable oil masquerading as a compère. All this at nine-thirty in the morning, seven days a week. Alone in a hotel room in Los Angeles, I went into solitary spasms watching a team of three try to answer, for $60,000, the following question: 'The King of England, Edward VIII, abdicated for the love of an American woman. What was her name?' Came the tentative reply, 'Edith.' 'Hello, room service, can you send me up some dry knickers, please, I've just watched a game show.'

Talking of taste, the British can sometimes excel too. I was once unfortunate enough to be on the panel of a TV version of *Quote, Unquote*, called *Cabbages and Kings*, to make it more accessible — to vegetarians and monarchists, presumably. An undiscernible squiggle appeared on the screen, resembling a worm leaving an apple. 'Can you identify this signature?' leered the compère, who could. 'Er, no,' leered I, who couldn't. 'Too bad, you'll kick yourself when you know. Yes, it's Stevie Wonder!'

Think about it.

For all you people who followed the clues in *Masquerade* and can play *Dungeons and Dragons*. Here is the explanation.

1   The numbers of days/weeks/months equal vowels A=1, E=2, I=3, O=4, U=5.
2. The initials of the place names are the consonants.
3   You never spell the name. Instead you spell a clue.
4   '*And Then*' means a new word, i.e.:
    1) One day in London and stayed three = A.L.I. — I knew it was Mohammed Ali. I also know Jack wouldn't have spelt the name itself.
    2) Yugoslavia for 4 weeks and 5 days = You — easy one.
    3) Quebec for 5 months 2 weeks 2 days Niagara and Seattle *and then* Saratoga for 3 days and Seattle = Queens Sis, i.e.: Princess Margaret. The clue could have been Smoking Princess or Mustique Lover — whatever is shortest and least obscure.

Where it fails is when your partner gets over-enthusiastic and screws up the clue, as with a dear friend of ours who couldn't wait to have a go, was landed with Idi Amin and quite laboriously spelt out Kenyan Colonel as opposed to Ugandan General — or even, 'I went for 3 days to Denmark and stayed 3 weeks,' which although breaking the rule about not using the name itself, would have worked because the first letter is a vowel and would not therefore have aroused suspicion — Four days in Karachi?

Eating the Hand that Bites You

NOW LET'S TALK about oral gratification. There. That made you sit up. Thought you were reading Claire Rayner for a minute, didn't you? I'm referring, of course, to food. Throughout my memorably unmemorable life, I've often stumbled upon scenes of anger and chaos whilst attempting to put fork to mouth. I don't just mean family weddings and Boxing Day lunch, either. Though where TV drama would be without such round-the-table carnage, I don't know. Take *Dallas*. (Please!) How they manage to force down so much brunch whilst thinking up so much fratricide, genocide and, no doubt, insecticide is beyond me. I reckon the ranch should be called 'Mouthfork'.

Many hundreds of years ago when Jack and I first met in Manchester, we decided to discuss our common grounds over Jewish food. The large restaurant was deserted, save for one man and one waiter. They were screaming abuse at one another. As we walked in, the customer rose to his feet, and purple in the face, and arms at right angles to his body, he shrieked in our direction: 'Tell me — if you order braised steak, does it *necessarily* mean you've got to have *gravy*?' We stammered in unison: 'Er — er — *yes*', thus proving that one of the things we had in common was the knowledge that in Jewish restaurants the waiter is always right.

It's not as though I'm argumentative by nature. Oh, no, I'm not! Take the little Chinese restaurant in Hampstead we used to frequent. The Proprietor was warm and welcoming, the ambience amicable and the food piquant — well, Peking to be perfectly accurate. One night the service was unbearably slow. We didn't complain to the owner, however, as his utterly inscrutable expression revealed he was as worried as we by the ominous crashings and hissings emanating from his kitchen. Finally our food arrived. We leapt at it. Three minutes later, two Chinese chefs leapt at us. Screaming Oriental expletives at one another, they circled the tables brandishing matching meat-cleavers and emptying the restaurant in two shakes of a bottle of soy sauce. Only Jack and I continued eating, more concerned with losing our appetites than the sides of our ears. We paid our bill as the police removed the battling bantam-weights, and we assured our shaken host that our enjoyment of numbers 43, 17 and 91 had in no way been diminished by the novel floor show, and we would be back to see him very soon. We never returned and I feel a cleaver-like stab of guilt every time I pass.

After all, it can't be easy providing the perfect ambience for a diverse and disparate group of diners every night. I've been totally defeated by fish fingers for five. In the '60s, when there was only one of me, I used to frequent a fashionable 'tranny' in Battersea, where the large and colourful Polish owner would serve up the nectar of the gods for the price of a tin of creamed rice. Here, long distance lorry drivers would nestle up against Chelsea 'lardies' for the chance to sample Stanley's duck in orange sauce — price 7s 6d., served by his wispy and drily sexy Irish wife, Vera. Believe it or not I used to do a cabaret after dinner consisting of a pantomime striptease, and a long-winded joke about a lady with an over-developed right breast. The high point of the evening was when Stan reeled vodka-strewn from his tiny, torrid kitchen, place a heavily tattooed arm around your shoulder and launched into show-business: 'Dere's dis Eskimo — he got a penis this big...' Mid-demonstration, Vera would flit effortlessly past, balancing twenty plates and breathe: 'Will ye cover up yer sinful mouth this instant, Stanley.' Every meal was an experience, every night a party. Like the '60s, it expanded into twice its importance and suddenly disappeared. I've missed it and them ever since. (Since writing this a plump little bird has assured me that Vera is back in business — must dash...)

Mind you, I don't have to *sit down* in a café to incite aggro. Rehearsing in a draughty barracks in Camberwell, five of us decided on a hot Indian take-away. We waited the obligatory four hours and Took It Away. It was Liza Goddard, a genuine animal-lover, who discovered the first creepy which crawleth on its belly on the face of her lettuce. 'Oh, dear, livestock,' she said

cheerily. Then, 'Oh, another. Different colour.' By now all five of
us were spitting, yucking and generally over-acting to a degree.
I spent the following hour combing through every leaf with
David Bellamy-like intensity until I'd discovered an
entomologist's paradise. What to do? Should I phone Channel 4
and suggest a small documentary for *Wildlife on 4*, or should I
arm myself with fellow actor, Christopher Timothy, and take
all the creatures great and small back to the take-away? We
chose the latter.

The man behind the counter gave a performance worthy of
Ben Kingsley's Oscar — he would lose family, friends and job if
the manager found out. Mortified, we offered to accept half the
refund and handed over the bugs — at which point he foolishly
admitted he *was* the manager, and offered us a free meal instead.
With the grace of a grasshopper I leapt over the counter,
retrieved the evidence and fled in search of the telephone
number of the nearest Health Department.

After twenty minutes and numerous wrong offices, I spent a
full half hour explaining the event to a sympathetic lady at the
other end of the line. 'Ugh, there wasn't! . . . Urrgh, how awful!'
she exclaimed. 'Well, where do we go from here?' I asked her. 'I
don't know,' she confessed, 'This is the casualty department at
King's College Hospital.' I crawled away to look for a piece of
lettuce to lie in.

Then there are the places which specialize in gimmicks but no
food. 'Hi, there, I'm Martha, your waitress for tonight,' said a
mouthful of orthodentistry in a downtown Florida cafe modestly
called 'Old Possum's Famous Fabulous Olde Worlde Eatery'.
(It's my favourite name — along with 'fishtique' and 'Shish and
Donerama!) As the iced water hit our root-canals, Martha hit
the table with either the complete works of Dickens or an 84-
page leather-bound menu. It was the latter, and contained prose
as purple as the face of the man who didn't want gravy with his
braised steak. 'Succulent, sizzling super scrumpy Burger,
nestling on a savoury sea of crispy frozen-berg lettuce with
breath-bating blue cheese and Possum's famous boysenberry
dressing . . .' We ordered an omelette and agreed to sample a
plate of their Famous French Fries. They came in a basket. Hot
potato crisps accompanied by two dips. One maple syrup and
the other sour cream. Being British and loath to be 'Uncle Dick'

in a famous Eatery, we left. 'Have a nice day now,' cooed a bewildered Martha.

One night in downtown Key Biscayne we went to a kosher restaurant. There was a marvellously laid-back waitress, the sort played by Patricia Neal in movies of the early 'seventies. Very thin and dry, her chest caved backwards and her pelvis forward like an out-of-condition mannequin. She scarcely looked up as we placed our order. 'Uh-hu .. uh-hu .. uh-hu.' As a postscript, she murmured, 'Ya want soda water with this?'

'No, thank you,' Jack replied. There was a pause. She looked up. She regarded us blankly. Then she said, 'You Jewish?'

'Er . . . yes?' We were pretty sure on that score, but failed to see the connection. *Now* we had her interest. 'You Jewish and you don't want soda water?' 'Er . . . yes. No. We don't. Why, for heaven's sake?' She let her pad drop, sat down at the table and regarded us with the mixture of sorrow and pity usually reserved for cannibals by a missionary.

'Well, howya gonna eat it all? Ah mean, if yu Jewish yu come in heah, yu drink the soup, y' eat the liver, y' eat the kishkes, you swaller some soda water, yu burp, yu eat some more, yu drink some more, yu burp some more so's yu can eat some more. Now. Are y' absolutely sure yu don't want soda?'

She was wonderful. A complete character. Throughout the dinner I absorbed her like a Vitamin C capsule, and she's still in there, waiting to be unleashed on the right part.

Of course, working in a kitchen is hell. No one knows that better than me — except maybe Arnold Wesker. After a childhood spent reading in the loo every time there was table laying or washing up to do, I spent one summer holiday begging my parents to allow me to join my schoolfriends who were working in a Bridlington café. They finally acquiesced, a wise move on their part. I packed a huge trunk, waved a tearful farewell, travelled the fourteen-mile journey snivelling, and was back home within one week. Fired. For total inefficiency. I'd soon learned to belt out the vernacular 'One Sos Tom Streaky Without', but so clumsy, disorganized and exhausted was I after two days, that the boss demoted me to the toffee apple stand outside. There I cocked up the money, jammed up the toffee machine and was sent home, lugging six weeks' luggage by taxi. Later, my friends told me the boss had said if they ever brought that bloody disaster with them again, he'd fire the lot of them.

Nowadays my food tract describes raised voices, but these are mostly at home. '*Will* you take that knife out of your mouth!' 'Cut it, don't *tear* it — God, it's like eating with animals!' 'Yes I know Daddy's elbows are on the table but . . . he's tired!' And, 'There will be no pudding unless you at least *try* the mange-touts . . .' And 'Yes of course they make you see in the sodding dark!'

Of course it was never like that in my day. Mealtimes at home in Hull meant a very hot dinner on a very cold plate. None of this helping yourselves to vegetables from a casserole business — it all came in a delicious, but compact mass, followed somewhat later by my mother, who threw down her food fast enough to be up to serve dessert the second her last potato disappeared. 'Why don't you sit down, love?' was the constant enquiry, though it never occurred to the enquirers to stand up and give her a hand.

Incidentally, and here I lower my voice, what do you reckon to this 'barbecue' business? No, go on, I won't say anything. Everyone keeps saying 'Have you got a barbecue?' Rather in the way they used to say 'Have you got a wok?' or even 'Have you got herpes?' And lately I've taken to dropping large barbecue-shaped hints in the direction of my husband, who hates them — the barbecues and the hints. His claim is that, with the exception of Astrid's marinated lamb, every barbecued meal he's ever had has been cold and black and tasted of worsted. I'm sure he's wrong but there is a morsel of truth in his barb. *Do* we really like standing on a chilly patio with a plate full of cole slaw and a rapidly-cooling baked potato, waiting for the next batch of lamb chops to be singed, whilst making devastating small talk to the man from next door who's only been invited because of the wind direction. 'Oh, mercantile shipping? Gosh, how unusual! Do you see many of them? Ships, I mean.'

There's a lot to be said for beans on toast and a fried egg, whilst watching *Film '85*. I'm sorry to 'producer-and-saviour-drop,' but we once cooked dinner for David and Patsy Puttnam — it was fish and chips and rice pudding with a skin on. It really went down better than three weeks with Anton Mosiman.

Actually, my best-ever dinner party conversation went like this:

> *Me (after an animated twenty minutes to the man on my left, to the man on my right):* And what sort of work do you do, er — (glance at place card) — Jeremy?'
>
> *He (after gazing morosely into my face):* 'I study the corneas of chickens' eyes.'
>
> *Me:* 'Oh super! A little more Coq au Vin?'

I've just read Jack the last page, and he said that's all right, but everyone who's ever given us a barbecue will be insulted. I then counted them up on two hands and agreed to cut out the paragraph. He then said, 'Well, I suppose it's OK. I've nothing against barbecues really, it's just that ovens are so clever, aren't they? I mean, you don't drip it all down your trouser-leg when you're trying to talk. If I want my dinner burnt on the outside and raw on the inside, I can have it in the comfort of my own home.' Thank you and goodnight!

As far as being a good hostess myself, I can honestly say that I am unique. I owe half of London dinner, and large chunks of the Home Counties, too. In my defence I must point out that I am an excellent guest. Witty as all get out, wildly appreciative of décor and cuisine, abstemious yet high as a kite on other people's lack of sobriety. I also give myself total nervous exhaustion when I do have what my mother calls 'an evening', by over-shopping, over-cooking and overdoing it all to a ridiculous degree, so that by the time the guests arrive, I'm hyperactive and bloated with testing, tasting and sampling. And, like an opening night, it almost always goes well and I'm smug enough to plan the next one whilst stacking the plates from the current one into the dishwasher.

My most enduring restaurant memory is of a stony-faced American couple who ate a three-course meal in total silence in a West End bistro. Very occasionally she would sigh heavily. He would glance up, then quickly avert his eyes. Too quickly. Once or twice she, too, pointedly shifted her position between courses or studiously adjusted her make-up in a small gold hand-mirror. Once he put down his wine glass with unnecessary vigour and ground his crowns. The silence was more highly charged than the customers. Finally, it broke. Leaning tentatively across, he made some inaudible enquiry. She straightened her spine, placed her fork on her plate, fixed him with her astigmatism and growled with great deliberation, 'It's not the boeuf bourguinonne, Henry — it's the last twenty-three years!'

Hair Today

LAST WEEK JACK went for a haircut. He came back looking as though he'd had his head sharpened.

'It'll settle down,' he said, gamely, plucking frantically at his empty head in an attempt to lengthen the remaining hairs.

'It's nice,' I lied, as we headed towards the kettle in search of comfort. Later, over a two-day-old custard tart, he confessed rather wanly that he'd been waiting forty-five years for a haircut like the one he had in his mind. He added that he remained optimistic up to and including this very day. I don't.

Every time I enter a hairdressing salon, be it Mr Damien of Dalston or Lord Sassoon of Sloane, I get the same feeling. It's not exactly 'sinking' like 3.30 pm when the dentist will see you at four, nor 'elated' like the sight of a loved one at Euston, but with its mixture of fear, hope and blind faith, it bears more than a passing resemblance to the feeling you get when your waters break.

It's a very emotive subject, hair. If you saw the television documentary *Mothers By Daughters* you'll know that it was the single strand that bound together the likes of Elisabeth Lutyens, Barbara Windsor, Bernadette Devlin, and — well, me. Though our backgrounds were as different as our mothers — and though we all were interviewed quite separately — it seemed there came a point in each programme when the inevitable happened — 'My mother was always messing about with my hair' — 'Whenever I see my mother, I always have to make sure my hair is perfect...' — 'She wasn't just forever brushing it — she was forever worrying it!' We collectively remembered the aggravation of being perpetually primped and permed and plaited, as though the tops of our heads were symbols of their dissatisfaction with the rest of us.

'What did you think of the programme, Mum?' I really wanted to know and was frightened to find out.

Jack and I attending a wedding. Ours, in 1973. *Inset* — my mother at same wedding. You can't see, but she is carrying five hundred fishballs!

'Our Lady of Muswell Hill' or 'Halo, halo, halo' — with prodigal daughter.

Babes in the garden. Or, Adam and Madam.

Outside the school gates. Or, 'Who's that woman with Adam Rosenthal?'

A typical bath night *chez* Rosenthal

Try-out in our kitchen for this book's cover photograph.
Would you believe the phone rang?

Let me make one thing perfectly clear, the man on my left is *not* my husband Denis.

Jack and I going out for a stake.

Gentlemen prefer wigs. Understudying Diana Rigg in *Jumpers*, 1973.

'Your hair looked nice,' was the innocent reply.

At least now, when I tell my daughter that she looks like a drowned rat, I have the advantage of knowing that the primaeval echo is a primaeval echo and not just nagging.

I wonder, does the colour lilac have a strong effect on you? Does it remind you of Elizabeth Taylor's corneas, or like me, does it transport you back to the salon where you had your first perm? After years of rags, pincurls and the fearsome wave clips which attacked plump little fingers at the drop of an elder brother (and all this before I was on solids), I emerged in photographs a button-eyed child on a Bridlington beach with one startled curl in the middle of its head.

Bathnights were followed by a ritual head-toasting in front of the electric fire — and a night's sleep rendered impossible by virtue of my scalp being quietly acupunctured by its surrounding hardware. Which could account for a lot.

But back to that salon. Along with the lilac claustrophobia came the lilac smell. Thick, sticky, heady, hot and sweet like the tropical house at Kew. It hit you in waves as you went in. Hours later it was superseded by enough ammonia to bleach tar. And finally the nice natural smell of lacquer sprayed on — straight into the eyes. Which at least prevented you from seeing what two mirrors would have you believe. Then you prayed. Shut your eyes and prayed — it was all an optical illusion. 'Thank you. It's great. Really. Great.' (This to a murderer.) Then you paid your money and cried for a week with your school scarf wrapped round your head.

Every perm I ever had turned out the same. Flat on top like 'Her Majesty', then erupting around the ear region into a mass of chipolatas, bearing scant resemblance to either the hair I had before or the hair of any living creature save a dromedary. Back home in the bedroom, I'd pull it, stretch it, bend it in a reverse direction and occasionally iron it in brown paper. But in vain. Nothing, but nothing, has the resilience of a recently permed head of hair.

'It'll soon drop,' my mother would helpfully remark.

'I wish it *would* — out,' I wailed. 'Look at it, it's like a woolly hat — and it stinks!'

'It's nice.' The final insult — 'It makes your face look fuller.' This was the one which engineered the head into a basin full of water — a kamikaze gesture if ever there was one. For it was only then that the full extent of the damage could be seen.

Still, it only lasted six months. And somewhere in the sixth month it suddenly looked good. Bouncy, loose, soft — you know, like — hair. That stage lasted a week and during that time you relented entirely on your campaign against the permanent wave industry and started wearing your lilac waspie again. Six hours later you were the possessor of the same lank, lustreless disaster area that drove you salon-wards in the first place. Plus split ends and rust.

All of which brings me to my text for the day. Hairdressers and why I wish I could dress my own. I'm forever changing my crimper and wishing I hadn't. I've been head-hunted off the street by an ex-stylist, actually, while perfectly happy with the one I've had. Once in there he lifted the odd colpoon of my hair as though retrieving a diamond from a dog-turd and said 'My dear — who did this to you?' Immediately I became a supergrass and quite rightly got tarred and feathered for it. With the new haircut I was too embarrassed to return to the old hairdresser and too cross to remain with the new one.

I wonder if it all dates back to the lilac salon, and the occasion of the nits. It's one of those moments which are emblazoned on my heart like a suburban version of 'Calais' on Mary Tudor's. I remember sitting in the leatherette swivel, a bri-nylon cape swathed around my pounding heart and a copy of *Modern Screen* on my lap. 'Is Liz Infanticipating? Only Eddie knows and he ain't tellin',' screamed Louella. A pretty stylist, with freckles I'd have killed for, was combing out my wet hair when she suddenly and inexplicably left. Never to return. The minutes passed. I'd said nothing to upset her, my conscience was clear, and I'd never felt guiltier in my life. Several more minutes of stage whispers later, the owner of the shop, a lady well known to my mother and her circle, came over and without a word of explanation took over my head. If ever I knew I was lousy, it was then.

I must be honest, if only for a paragraph. I've been very pleased with my hair on occasions. At least it doesn't usually give me cause for abject despair as the rest of me often does. Possibly because by the time it's grown, it's dead.

I have a photograph of myself back in the heady 'sixties where my hair is shoulder length, copper red and cut in the 'new' shaggy, layered long back and sides look. I think at that moment I peaked — coiffure-wise. It's too late to recapture the hairstyle — no offence to Linda McCartney intended, and the glow was as much to do with youth as it was to do with being a redhead. At the time, it gave me a certain 'Dotty-glamour', enhanced the wardrobe and made the wisecracks seem wiser and more cracked. Too much autumnal hue, however, can make one head for a Fall! And all that bleach every six weeks! By the time I'd had Amy I'd come to a crossroads of decision — Red Hair or Disposable Nappies. Head you lose — tails you win.

As for blondes having more fun, well, let me dispel that rumour forever. They do. On the occasions when I've been blonde in TV plays, the difference in the amount of fun I had was so marked that I'd gladly trade in my Moulinex to be permanently platinum of hair, eyebrows and other pertinent bits.

These days I've taken to sending Jack to Sheila down the road. He comes back a very happy man. I presume it was because of the haircut. Then I sent along my brother, who had flown in with a thatched head from Geneva where he lives, and flew out again as svelte as a Swiss sea-lion. Now I go along too. It's great to have your hair washed in the kitchen sink and cut in the conservatory, then to have a really good moan about almost everything. Cheaper than an analyst and you come out looking less streaky.

There was, in the 'seventies, the real epoch of the hairdresser as self-styled psychoanalyst. This peaked with Warren Beatty's film *Shampoo* which, although well 'over the crown', was often very accurate. Certainly Ricci Burns would give me wonderful advice whilst teasing my roots: 'Don't make a daughter out of Amy — make a friend.' This when I was having troubles with Number One Daughter. 'Take your old man on holiday — tomorrow!' when I was bleary-eyed and weepy. And 'Don't do a thing to your nose, you'll ruin yourself!' This from a man who sees more of his plastic surgeon than he sees of his milkman. Bless him, he's always right, damn him! Or maybe I'm just so grateful for a chance to sit down and a captive ear that I just blurt till I feel better.

Even Adam, when forced into the Cypriot barber's on the

Broadway, behaves accordingly. It's a real *man*'s barber's, you know, with a pole and Durex and copies of *What Car?* He sits on a wooden plank over a maroon leatherette swivel chair and honestly, no sooner has his bum hit the plank than he starts with the man's talk. 'So how's your team doing, then? You still supporting Tottenham, are you? Why don't you try a decent team like Manchester United? I mean, who have they got apart from Hoddle? No, but did you see us murder Videoton and with only ten men — Oh, what a referee . . .' Etc., etc., just like a little old man at the barber's.

Actually, I have noticed the appearance of some strange, wiry, irregular-shaped hairs — in my head, I hasten to add — leading to the purchase of a home henna kit. I now have strange, wiry, irregular-shaped yellow hairs, a magenta-coloured sink and slimey green bits on my dressing gown. A delightful Glaswegian called Thistle at Maneline has promised to rectify this. By the time you read this, I may have a blue Mohican and a bin-liner over my head. Hair today . . . none tomorrow . . .

Let's face it, dead or not, your hair has a life of its own. It's forever scheming how it can droop on you once a month just when you need its help. How it can send out scouts to spring out of what you thought was a beauty spot — how it can alarm you by turning grey or standing on end, given the right set of circumstances. How it can stand the combined onslaught of rain, chlorine, ultra violet rays, leather Fedoras and even those rubber caps through which strands are pulled in order to be high-lit — so giving the wearer a strong resemblance to those pieces of cress you grew on blotting paper.

I imagine it will continue growing long after I am underground or in the kidney repository — so perhaps it's time I awarded it the respect it deserves. Say kids — we could even do a musical about it — *oh no*. Perhaps I'll just clean out my hairbrush.

Dressing Down

I BOUGHT THIS leather suit for *Give Us A Clue*. It was five to six on the evening before the recording when I discovered my wardrobe was full of nothing to wear. Now, I don't like leather *per se*, except on a cow or the sole of my shoe — it's too prone to Ribena stains and squeaking — but charades players can't be choosers and even downtown Muswell Hill is closed by six o'clock.

So I bought it. The jacket was cornflower blue with padded shoulders, voluminous pouches and an odd aertexy-texture here and there. The skirt was straight and dangerously split. The shop girls pronounced it 'reellynice' and I happily paid up more money than I earned for three editions of *Give Us A Clue* and lugged it home in a plastic portmanteau.

Later that night, I had a 'try-on'. Jack and the au pair looked horrified, and Amy pronounced it 'fat'. Fat was right. It was huge on top and sort of tapered from the hips. It was also very blue. All in all I looked like a burning gas-jet. Glumly, I packed it back in its plastic, wore a well-worn favourite on the show and collected the biggest credit note I've ever possessed.

This meant, over the next few weeks, I could buy *free* clothes. At least that's what it felt like. The piece of paper made me feel quite light-headed. 'I'll have one of those, two of these, a pair of those, now, how much have I got left?'

It's always a mistake to spend a lot on clothes. I remember buying a silk gypsy dress trimmed with antique lace for the premiere of the ill-fated musical version of Jack's TV play *Bar-mitzvah Boy*. Someone sprayed a little champagne on it, so I took it to a high-class cleaner's who turned three spots into a Rorschach test. The dress lasted slightly longer than the show — about ten weeks. And neither of them will ever be revived.

Most of the parts I play on stage or TV require either appalling taste or a trip to the Oxfam shop, and the only time

117

I've ever worn designer-clothes was for the series *Agony*. The costume lady and I would wander down South Molton Street saying 'We'll take these shoes in the blue, the brown and the yellow, with matching tights, the mustard-checked trousers with the Missoni cardigan and throw in two silk shirts, one burgundy and one cerise.' All the clothes were slightly dotty (slightly? Most of the time I looked like Pass the Parcel) But I loved them, and they never dated or fell apart, unlike their wearer, who, throughout three series, did both.)

As teenagers, my friends and I used to dress like forty-five-year-olds. I have pictures of myself, back in Hull, wearing a navy two-piece suit (with pleated skirt and lacy collar), a dog's dinner hat, white gloves and clutching a clutch bag. I looked like something on its way out of the Conservative Party Conference. In this erotic ensemble we would visit the synagogue on a Saturday morning, where we'd giggle disgracefully, ogle the talent below, then repair to the local expresso bar for a — wait for it — frothy coffee. Well tanked up we'd march round the two department stores buying American Tan stockings and a $33\frac{1}{3}$ rpm. Cliff Richard, then straight to the Fourth Floor for — AFTERNOON TEA! WITH CAKES! Am I shocking you? I also possessed a pink puff-ball evening dress with a boned top and a skirt of increasing hoops, ending with a tiny one which just circled the knees. It was fine till I sat down, whereupon the whole skirt rose up and covered my head, exposing much American Tan-covered white thigh.

By the time I hit Drama School, I dressed entirely in mix 'n' match. For my first day I wore a green woolly dress, emerald-green tights, dark green boots (painted), a grey-green hat with a pom-pom and lurid green eye-shadow to the brow. My fellow-student, Philip Sayer, told me later that I looked like a big blade of grass. As the term progressed, my gear got more and more way out, venturing into floor-length coats, old theatrical costumes and floppy Fedoras. It got so bad that, at holiday times, my mother used to wear dark glasses and a beard to meet me off the train.

I still adore dressing up. A couple of years ago, our friend Astrid had her American parents to stay and wanted to introduce them to her nice English friends. I suggested to Jack we dressed as Beefeaters. As always, and to my amazement, he agreed. I hired the outfits from Bermans, and they threw in a free pike. The costumes were glorious. That scarlet suit really suited me, and you should have felt the quality! I don't think I shall ever see a sight to equal that of Jack struggling into a pair of red tights. 'How do you *do* it??' he implored, heels over metatarsals and crutch by knees. 'Shut up and keep still while I put your rosettes on,' was my wifely response. 'Do you realize,' I added, 'that somewhere in London, right now, a real Beefeater is stepping into this garb, and saying to his kids — "Goodbye Darren, goodbye Wayne, Daddy's off to guard the Tower. Be good boys for Mummy."'

Sandi, our Australian (then) au pair, took a photo of us. Previously we had taken one of her in the outfit. She sent it to Sydney with a one-line message: 'Dear Mum and Dad, I have changed my job. Love Sandi.'

After popping next door to borrow a cup of sugar, which left them roughly as hysterical as we were, we drove to Hampstead. I won't try to describe the faces of the other motorists, nor the struggle to get an eight-foot pike into a Ford Escort. Suffice to say that when we arrived, Astrid was watering the window-boxes and she almost broke the World Free-Falling record. 'I don't believe what I'm seeing! Honey, there are two Beefeaters parking outside our— Oh, my Gaaaad!!' I mean I don't want you to think we do this sort of thing a lot — just because we do — but it was truly worth it. If only for the length of time we all spent lying about on the stairs with our knees crossed. Crying.

More recently, we went (normally dressed) to a friend's barbecue, where the lady making the salads turned out to be a part-time prostitute. I might tell you the subject only came up during a discussion about the televising of the House of Lords. You may draw your own conclusions as to how one topic led to the other.

Now this lady was plump, bonny, well-balanced, witty, down-to-earth. Like your husband's sister or the lady on the cashpoint in Fenwick's. 'I can't take my clothes off in front of anyone — not even another woman,' she said. 'I get there in my jeans and T-shirt as average as a Persil mum, but from the moment I put on my two layers of make-up, my six-inch heels and my leopard-skin top, I *am* the part. And when the door bell rings and I hear the clip-clop of my stilettos on the wooden floor, well, dears, I'm anything they want me to be.'

I expect that's what they mean by Clothes Maketh the Man.

I've just remembered, I once had another leather suit. It was a trouser suit and it was made by some mad Mexicans I'd encountered in the Kings Road. They 'sculpted skin to match your soul'. I almost died when I saw their interpretation of my soul. The flared leather trousers were bottle-green and had a luminous orange panel starting at the stomach and tapering into the crutch. The top was cut under the bust and fastened with a silver brooch. When I asked Miguel what I should wear underneath it, he grinned and said, 'Honly ze breasts!' 'Not *zese* breasts, Chutney,' I replied and set off in search of a polo neck up to the ears.

In an ideal world, I'd have only one style of dress. But I'd have it in scores of different materials. Silk, denim, taffeta, tweed. I know the style of the dress. It's the Fifties Look, with a cinched waist, raglan sleeves and crisp white cuffs. (David Shilling made me one for a Variety Club lunch. I kept telling people who admired it it was really a big hat.) It's the sort of dress that was worn in the movies by the wise-cracking girl in the office who never got the man. In fact, this wise-cracking girl wore it for *Give Us A Clue* instead of the blue cow. Tune in and let me know if I should proceed further with The Look or whether you prefer me bovine.

Ladies, Excuse Me...

'DANCE/IN THE old-fashioned way/Won't you stay in my arms?/And let the music play.' Charles Aznavour, back to camera, hugging himself, hands moving suggestively over mohair jacket, microphone cradled lovingly between head and collarbone. Noxious, wasn't it? Narcissus raising his ugly head.

Or was the lyric-writer right? Is dancing the true expression of happiness and, if so, when did you last get happy? Now I am a genius on the floor — but only the floor of my head. My dearly beloved partner is one of the 'shifting-his-weight-from left-to-right-while-moving-in-a-southerly-direction-back-to-the-chair whence-he-came' brigade. This necessitates a choice. I can either shift with him, my hands draped lovingly around his neck, talking animatedly away as if to suggest we have more important things to do than *dance*! Or, I can prance and strut alone, my outstretched palms climbing imaginary walls and my hips rotating relentlessly while he continues his aimless shift work. Only this time, with a radish-coloured face which he tries to hide in his breast pocket.

My first memory of dancing in public was on my father's feet. It was no doubt a family wedding or a barmitzvah, because I dimly recall a lot of beaded dresses and painful cheek-pinching from on high. I was at my most stunning, in smocked Viyella with just a hint of protruding teeth peeping alluringly through protruding lip. The music was probably 'I'd like to get you on a slow boat to China', my father's shoes were black and shiny, and throughout it, I trod, slid off and generally massacred them while clinging tenaciously to his thumbs, until I fell asleep and was carried home.

Every Saturday, my friend Bernice and I would attend the Muriel Riley School of Ballroom Dancing of Anlaby Road, Hull. Once there we paid our half-crown and changed into our silver-strapped dancing shoes. The floor was a sea of sliding, skidding, shrieking children until such moment as Miss Riley Herself — ''Er indoors' if ever there was one — 'she who must be displayed', even, and her partner came on the floor to dazzle our ten-year-old eyes with their virtuosity. Quickstep, Foxtrot, Waltz and Samba — me and Bernice taking it in turns to be the man. No wonder, twenty-eight years later, I keep putting my arms round men's waists as soon as the band strikes up. Not to mention standing on their feet, grasping their thumbs and falling asleep on them.

Anyway, after the interval and its obligatory vat of Vimto (never try to recapture the flavour of Vimto. Either it's changed, I've changed, or it always tasted like scented Harpic), we resumed the floor for the Palais-Glide, the Gay Gordons, the Polka and la pièce de résisdance — the Cha Cha. This latter was regarded as slightly naughty, with its Latin rhythms and its suggestive hip movements. Me and Bernice managed to keep our animal instincts under control though; an unremarkable task since there were at least twelve women to every man present.

'Anything funny happen to you on the dance floor?' I asked the butcher in Market Place today, by way of a change from 'How's the liver looking?' and 'Can you pluck its legs, please?' The reply was instantaneous. 'Never use one, love, not since I tore me two-tone Tiger Mohair trousers doing the Twist.' (You couldn't write a line like that.) 'Left standing in me Bum Freezer for all the world to see.' The Twist! Have you ever looked at all that footage of the beehived, miniskirted, stovepipe-trousered aliens that we were, screwing our right legs into the parquet whilst ferrying our upper bodies in an opposing direction and our elbows into each other's navels? It's as archaic as the Minuet and as foreign as Queen Salote of Tonga's tribe singing 'Blaze Away'.

Mind you, it takes a lot to topple the 'Birdie Dance' for sheer inanity. I once watched Jack being dragged on to the floor by an overbearing Entertainments Officer in a holiday hotel. She was a big girl, from Amsterdam, known to the residents as 'Dutch Gilda'; and when she shouted 'I need volunteers!' you knew to get the hell out. At least *I* knew. Jacko just thought he was having a quiet coke by the bar. Next thing he knew he was being yanked through the air by the scruff of his windjammer and was frenziedly flapping his fingers, revolving his torso and sinking to his knees to the most tuneless tune ever known to man or bird, while the audience bellowed their approval and his wife hooted so loudly she wet herself. 'Anglaterra huit points,' howled our dear old Dutch, and presented him with an Ibizan Biro for effort.

Can you imagine the terror and sheer ignominy of the time when a girl went to a ball dressed like a box of Quality Street and had to get her card filled up with prospective partners for every dance? I know exactly where I would have been. Up in the powder-room with 'the vapours', forging the names of every man I knew who couldn't make it that night.

Jack says his trick at the Palais de Danse was always to unbutton his jacket before embarking on the three-mile walk across the floor to ask a girl to dance. That way you had something macho to do with your hands on the way over, i.e. button it up again. And by the time you reached her and were told 'Ask me friend, I'm sweatin'' you could suavely unbutton it again on the way back. It worked for Victor Mature, he claimed. The funniest pick-up line I ever heard was ''Ere, my mate thinks your mate's f---ing excellent!'

We once went to a famous Palais to research a play about ballrooms, and it was one of the saddest evenings I can recall. There were all the fellas, dressed to the eights, standing round the bar in faceless clumps as though their one interest was to gerra few in. There were the women at the tables, smoking Bette Daviesly and gazing resolutely anywhere but at the men. It was all a bit too late — it was the scene of my youth with the same cast twenty years later. Same suits, same faces — just older and shinier and more hopeless. Perhaps we just picked a bad night. Perhaps they did.

As for discos, well, frankly, my dears, I've had them up to here (gestures to ear level). The invention of strobe lighting finally finished all hitherto-unfulfilled aspirations to be a jet-setting go-go dancer. Physical symptoms seem to set in and my tendency to attempt *speech* above the tremolo can result in unattractive vomiting over partners' Pina Colada. Two experiences stand out. One was the opening of the new Hippodrome when I was squired by designer David Shilling. He decided to dress as Bonnie Prince Charlie that night. It was not a fancy dress ball. I was wearing a couple of very expensive handkerchiefs, and in order to avoid seeing each other, we danced like demons possessed for hundreds of hours and came out feeling purged. The following day most of the skin fell off my feet. It was, I think, nature's way of telling me never to startle the ends of my legs without prior consultation.

The second occasion was with the hairdresser Ricci Burns in a now defunct club called Del Aretusa, when the music changed, unannounced, from Rolling Stones to Richard Strauss. Hypnotized by its power and no doubt stoned out of our tiny trees — we began to whirl. And spin. And whirl. And spin. The last thing I remember is the sound my head made against the wall, and as I lost consciousness, I was vaguely aware of the Blue Danube closing over me. Oooh, that Mr Strauss — he was a knockout! At least Disco has got rid of the wallflower. Except in the garden. By the wall. Actually it was probably wartime which did that, by women dancing together in armies, while the men did it for real. But your partner was basically a substitute for a man. Nowadays, anyone can dance with anything, since everyone is actually dancing alone. And it's men who've been released. Free now to preen and prance and strut and astonish us with their breakdancing and body-popping routines — surely the most exciting dance advance for years.

When Jazz Dancing first hit town, I went to the Dance Centre in Covent Garden. It felt a bit like walking into an all-Black, anti-Semitic, gay club. In Argentina. I was hopelessly conspicuous, as though my legs had 'Pure Cellulite' printed on them, and my feet, 'Les Grands Bateaux'. I intended to attend a class held by the legendary Matt Mattox — affectionately known to those who stood behind him in class as Butt Buttox. I managed to make it to the changing-rooms quite uneventfully by keeping my eyes crossed every time some pale-faced, huge-eyed, leotarded nymph pattered past me on points, and was just about to unravel a pair of support tights when I saw a dancer, standing in front of the floor-to-ceiling mirror. I could tell she was a dancer because she was stark naked but for one pink ballet shoe. She was crying large, silent tears which made her meticulous mascara run in rivulets down her beautifully ravaged face. She watched herself in the mirror as she cried. It was a poignant scene which not only summed up the Dance

Centre, but drove yours truly so fast into the street that you couldn't see my toes for twinkling.

I did tap dancing once, and that was heaven. I couldn't pass a piece of lino or a slab of concrete without launching into the old 'shuffle, hop, step, shuffle, hop-step' routine — to the consternation of passers-by, most of whom were my family. More recently, and now it can be told, I have appeared on *The Anita Harris Show* in a singing and dancing sketch. Since it has not yet been shown, I have no idea of how I fared, but I've never worked so hard in all my born puff. Why did I do it? Because it was there.

We have the most wonderful Greek family living next door and I tell you, when those fellas feel the spirit moving and they get up and dance, you really know where music touches you the most. It all seems based on some kind of endurance as they stoop down to the ground balancing on one leg, then spring over the leg on which they're balanced. Often it's very slow too, which makes it even sexier, if you follow my drift. And it's nothing to do with age — in fact, the older they are, the more meaningful the dance.

As for the ballet, well, aside from reading endless Lorna Hill books as a child, and fantasizing that 'Maureen of the Wells' would sound as romantic as 'Veronique at the Wells', I have never had much experience of the art. I'm told by them that know, naming no names but follow my glance, that they're all at it like rabbits or knives or whatever, and that for most dancers sex is something to be taken like food or breath or vitamin pills. I expect if you are physically as perfectly tuned as is your average common or garden sylphide, one's senses are equally heightened, or am I talking through my tutu?

I remember a friend of mine who was 'courting' a ballerina being so overwhelmed by the sight of her body falling into the most incredible poses and attitudes whilst they were making love, that it completely and humiliatingly put him off his stroke. 'It's all right, love,' she purred, stretching herself languorously, 'it happens all the time, don't let it worry you.' It took him months to get his confidence up, so to speak.

My overwhelming ballet memory is of a moonlit amphitheatre in Haifa, Israel, with a backdrop of the star-studded Mediterranean, and the tiny figures of Margot Fonteyn and Rudolph Nureyev spinning in space below my seventeen-year-old eyes. Throughout my childhood, whenever a male dancer leaped across our Bush 18-inch telly (usually during *Sunday Night at the London Palladium*), my mother would groan, 'Ugh! I can't bear to look at them in those tights. Ugh! I think it's *revolting*. Ugh!' until the sheer obscenity of it drove her out into the kitchenette, where she would bang about until Norman Vaughan came back.

This rarefied atmosphere, you'll be surprised to hear, produced few balletomanes. But in Israel that night, one was born.

Quite the best memory I have of dancing was a couple of weeks ago, whilst driving past Great Portland Street tube station. There on the pavement was a scruffy old man, bald, toothless and extremely plastered. To the music of the spheres (one supposes) he was breakdancing and body-popping with great concentration and even greater joie-de-vivre. I stopped the car, contemplated giving him Charles Aznavour's phone number, gave him a quid instead and sashayed merrily home.

Abscess Makes the Heart . . .

FROM AN EARLY age, well, roughly from the moment the placenta hit the pedal-bin and my mother found there was no way she could return me for a credit note, I realized I needed help with my looks. It was 1946, and the Korean War was news. I had a sallow skin, dark little currant eyes, straight black hair and the refugee jokes flew thick and fast.

My brother, who was described at birth as a 'nose on a pillow' had developed into an infant prodigy with golden curls, courtesy of the 'Twinky' lotion and his mother's rotating finger, and a nose which was normal but pink — with being pushed up into a retroussé by the same finger.

Old Chu Chin Chow's hair resisted everything but gravity and my skin grew used to the ritual torture involved in entering anyone else's home. 'Pinch your cheeks, Maureen,' came the hissed command.

'Why?'

'You look blech' (Yiddish for pasty).

I was eighteen before I dared enter a room without thumbprints on my face.

The second teeth, of course, came out horizontal, and by the age of twelve I'd broken my nose falling down a disused, ornamental well, and my front tooth falling off my bike. I confess to being a dentist's dilemma. They dread seeing me, and the feeling is entirely mutual. The minute I enter the room with the horizontal chair and the red water, I take on a marked resemblance to an Edvard Munch painting, and have been known to scream in an insane fashion when asked to fill in a form. This dates back, like most things in life, to early childhood. For some unaccountable reason, I have always disliked having a big, hairy hand in my mouth, hurting me like hell. I know it's foolish, but there you are. It's not for want of trying. I've endeavoured to come to terms with this prejudiced view of

127

dentistry since I gave up having Bonjela rubbed on my gums.

Teeth are a pain in the neck from cradle to coffin (that could have come straight out of *The Penguin Dictionary of Quotations*. And probably did.) Dentistry is a very high-risk occupation. To me especially. I left my last dentist because he believed that Mahler played very loud was an excellent anaesthetic. It obviously was. For him. Towards the end I began fainting as a means of drowning out all three of us.

I blame Him upstairs. How can thirty or so distorted pieces of enamelled ivory thrust their way through the nerve-ends of your skin in a pleasant way? Think how they would feel coming through your feet. Mind you, they'd get about the same wear and tear, but marginally less sugar, I suppose.

I don't remember much about my first teeth, but I vividly recall the permanent (ha!) ones. One day I just looked down and saw two flat, white surfaces looking back. Close scrutiny showed them to be my front incisors which had chosen to grow at an angle of forty-five degrees from their more retiring relatives. To these offending tusks I now realize I owe a debt of gratitude. They taught me to be funny. Ever noticed how many comics have an overbite problem? Make 'em laugh before they punch your teeth in.

For the next ten years it was a question of bracing myself against the world. My mouth looked like the inside of a Sinclair Spectrum. The teeth retreated, paused, fortified themselves and lunged out again, like the Charge of the White Brigade. I even sported a brace when my first boyfriend came home from university. He was awfully understanding, but I only hung on to him by the skin of my teeth.

Nowadays dentists believe in gentle pressure, particularly on the parents' bank account. One of my children models a night-time appliance which goes round the head, looks like a cross between a chastity belt and a BMX biker and appears to work by means of two rubber bands. In the era of the silicon chip, that's progress?

At the age of twelve, demonstrating the non-existent six speeds on my bicycle (Arbonate by name — Bike-Arbonate, geddit?), I jammed on the brakes, transcended the handlebars, and landed on one tooth. I counted to ten and then got up, but the tooth stayed down. And out. Since then my mouth has remained a mystery to me, and every dentist I visit gives the same sharp intake of breath which usually characterizes a visit to a new hairdresser. 'Who *did* this?'

My first dentist had halitosis. Now, as my mother was always saying, 'Breathe on me' before we left the house, in case there was a use for the Milk of Magnesia she kept in her clutch bag, I naturally assumed it was *my* breath that smelled, and consequently tried to hold it for as long as his face was near mine. This led to regular bouts of hyperventilation which were explained away by my being 'highly-strung'.

Another one gave me gas for an extraction. The next thing I remember was the ghastly hissing sound followed by a blood-curdling shriek as the dentist leapt about the surgery, clutching his bleeding hand and screaming 'She bit me, the little shit bit me!'

There's a certain time of day inexorably associated with dentistry. It's about 3.15 in the afternoon. It stems from the middle of Double Geography, when you remembered you were leaving early for 'just a check up' i.e. four hundred fillings and a twenty-minute wince. The feeling was as if a piece of dry cardboard had been inserted in your diaphragm, and it stayed there until you reached the smell of surgery, where it began to thud. Once in the waiting-room, you placed a nine-year-old copy of *Dandy* over your whole face and tried very hard to transmogrify yourself into a rubber plant.

Coronation Day came twice on the days I had my front teeth crowned. My front teeth have been crowned more often than the Habsburgs. The first time was after seeing myself in the film *Up The Junction*. I decided I looked a dead ringer for Arkle, and fled the cinema in search of a tooth-carpenter. The bit I like best in what follows such a decision is the 'shade card'. (This is where your particular shade of tooth is matched up against a chart to avoid the Mix 'n Match look). The expert flicks past all the whites and creams and settles on mayonnaise yellow as your best blend. Smile, please, you're on yellowvision.

Some years later, I noticed the precious porcelain was on the advance again. Several hundred pounds later, I re-emerged as snow-capped as an Alp and ready to out-dazzle the cast of *Dynasty*. My next offer of work was to play Rachel in a masterpiece of a play called *Messiah*. Rachel possessed the most protruding teeth in Poland. Believe it or not, I had to go back to the dentist's and ask him to fix false buck-teeth over the top of my straight new crowns. My greatest fear was that during the most emotional scenes of the play I would spit the teeth out into the eye of *The Times* critic, who no doubt would've given his eye-teeth for such a happening.

I recently worked with a wonderfully funny actor who occasionally, inexplicably, over-enunciated certain words. He would say, 'She was stretching out for the crisps' (pronounced 'Krrisspps'). We roared with laughter at his characterization. He protested it was the fault of his dodgy teeth. After the show finished he confessed he was going to a Harley Street dentist to have them all crowned. Wickedly, I found out his dentist's name and placed a discreet phone call. Oh, to have been a fly on that spittoon when he emerged from the anaesthetic and heard the dentist say, 'Could you just try to say "She was stretching out for the crisps"?'

When Jack and I first met we were immediately drawn to each other's overbite. Apparently he used to box at school, and since his long left ensured he was never hit in the face, he couldn't understand why he always left the ring with his face covered in blood. Until he realized his defensive right glove was constantly beating a tattoo on his buck-teeth and buck-lip. The only boxer disqualified for punching himself to a pulp.

Even now, the merest kiss en passant often results in such a clash of glasses, noses and teeth that it's really safer just to blow one. Kiss, that is. During a memorable period, when we were both visiting a dental hospital for gum treatment, the nightly flossing, single-head and double-head brushing, plaque-disclosing and mouthwashing took so long it became a whole new form of contraception. University College Hospital should have a plaque for it.

My latest dentist spends his mornings in the surgery, his afternoons in the House of Lords, where he is an hereditary peer, and his evenings playing in a jazz band. Don't say I don't introduce you to interesting characters.

Do you wonder why the Tooth Fairy continues to be the only growth industry in Britain? Fifty pence a tooth and double if you forget to let her in. I'm thinking of asking ACAS for a meeting with her. To discuss role-reversal... if I leave a new pound piece under my pillow, will she leave me a new tooth?

I saw my dentist only this week. He stuck back part of a crown with superglue. It had come out whilst I was eating a natural sea sponge at a dinner party. It was Annie's idea of a joke. All the other guests had a baked cheese thing covered in a tomato sauce. Knowing I don't eat cheese she'd thoughtfully prepared me an alternative. After trying to cut it, I put the whole thing in my mouth, and chewed away, laughing, till my crown fell out.

I've asked the dentist to cook the bill and send it to her.

A Joking Aside

YOU KNOW ALL those people who say 'Oh, I can never remember jokes'? Like most women for example? Well, I'm not
one of them. No, given the right opportunity and a captive
audience, by which I mean nailed to floor, I could happily bore
for Europe on the subject of clean ones, rude ones, some as
shaggy as your dog. Has this woman no shame?

The first joke I remember was, of course, 'Why did the
chicken cross the road?' I didn't get it but I laughed like a drain
to show that I did. Later I heard the answer given as 'To see the
Duchess lay a foundation stone'. And, this time, I laughed like a
sincere drain. '*Lay* a foundation stone, Mam... lay... oh,
forget it...' I packed my satchel and chortled all the way to
school.

Now I love it when the kids tell me a joke — the more
laborious and convoluted the explanation, the better. 'There
was this man and this lady. NO, WAIT — *I* WANT TO TELL IT. And
this baby. Er... well. Anyway. The plane crashes [*what* plane?]
and the baby says "Me not daft" — 'cos the others died, you see
—"Me not daft, me not silly, me hold on to Daddy's willy!"
Collapse of stout eight-year-old, clutching stout stomach, and
much repeating of punchline in sing-song voice.

Their favourite to date concerns a small squid with a tummy
ache lying at the bottom of the ocean. A shark approaches and
announces his intention of eating him. 'Please don't!' begs the
squid, 'I'm not very well.' 'Come with me,' says the shark, and
takes him to the cave of a killer whale. 'Who is it? Whaddya
want?' booms the whale. 'S'only me,' says the shark
ingratiatingly, 'I brought you the sick squid I owe you.'

All the animals in Jokeland have totally human
characteristics. The gorillas talk like Ronnie Barker and the
parrots philosophize like E.L. Wisty. No one questions an
erudite conversation about sex between a man and his dog on a

desert island. As in Disney films, we empathize with their dilemmas despite the indisputable evidence that they have long ears, wet noses and halitosis. Mind you, so do many of the people with whom I hold my most erudite conversations.

Anyway, the dog and the man have been on this desert island for months. They have plenty to eat and drink but their love-lives leave a lot to be desired, and they discuss their frustration over many a hot coconut soufflé. One day, while out marmoset-bagging, they chance upon the most gorgeous lady sheep, and both fall passionately in love with her. In order to be fair they toss a coin for who shall court her (that's not how I heard it described, but I have a delicate reader to consider), and the dog wins. Each night after supper, the dog excuses himself and goes off somewhat sheepishly to his lady-love (no doubt singing 'When I'm calling ewe'), and his human friend languishes alone for hours. One day, however, he discovers a beautiful, naked girl washed up by the ocean. She is half dead through exposure and starvation. Gently he wraps her in a blanket, carries her home and slowly and devotedly nurses her back to life. Overwhelmed with gratitude, she gazes at him through sweeping lashes and murmurs, 'Is there anything, ANYTHING, I can do to thank you for saving my life?' Shyly he demurs, but she persists. '*ANYTHING?*' 'Well,' he says, gazing at her longingly, 'well, after dinner tonight... would you... would you... take the dog for a long walk?'

Still on the subject of man's best friend — a scientist was carrying out an experiment to see if animals really took on the characteristics of their masters. The experiment involved putting the dog by an enormous pile of bones to see what he would do with them.

The first was the dog of a mathematician. He studied the bones, separated them into neat piles and finally arranged them into the equation of Pythagoras' theory.

The second dog was the dog of an architect. He piled the bones into a representation of the Pompidou Centre.

The third dog was the dog of an actor. He ate the bones, screwed the other two dogs and asked for the afternoon off.

The most enjoyable jokes are the shortest: 'What's the definition of a Jewish nymphomaniac?' 'Someone who will make love on the same day she's had her hair done.' Boom-

boom! What's the definition of Jewish foreplay — three hours of begging. A good Jewish wine? 'Oh you never take me anywhere...'

I've never had much time for the Shaggy-dog Tale. Too much depends on the phone not ringing during the build-up, and your mother not demanding the potato-peeler during the punchline. Actually, my mother once gave me the perfect intro to a lengthy joke which I'll tell you about. Shortly. It concerned a man having an audience with the Pope in a massive cathedral. He kneels before the altar and a mighty sepulchral voice intones to the tune of the 'Te Deum'. 'What is your na-a-ame?' *Man*: 'John Entwhistle, your Grace, your Holiness, Sir.' *Voice*: 'Where are you fro-o-om?' *Man*: 'London, England, Sir, Your Grace, Lord.' 'What is your business he-e-ere?' 'I dearly wish to convert to Catholicism, your Holiness.' *Voice*: 'What is your occupa-a-tion?' *Man*: 'Please, Sir, I'm a talent scout.' *Voice*: 'Moon River, wider than a mile...' It's the way you tell it, of course. Particularly after your mother has just said 'Ooh, Maureen, tell them all the joke about "Moon River".'

Have you noticed how jokes always come in batches of three? Like comic business in a farce? Or bad news? You hear no jokes for weeks, then somebody tells you three. Apparently, the real comedians seldom laugh when they're told a joke. Like doctors, they nod, say 'Ah, ah' and mentally file it away until they can convince themselves they thought of it in the first place. Almost every ethnic minority has a mythology of jokes on its back, and all is fair, I feel, provided that everyone gets lambasted. I once went on *The Parkinson Show*. Michael, I mean. (Mind you, *there's* an idea for an enterprising producer. *The Cecil Parkinson Show*. 'Live from his constituency, he-e-e-ere's Cecil! And tonight's star guest — Victoria Principal!') Sorry, bad taste. Where was I? Michael asked me beforehand to tell my favourite joke. It was, and is, the two Jewish ladies discussing their husbands: *Minnie*: 'Don't talk to me about my Benny. He makes me sick.' *Bella*: 'Why?' *Minnie*: 'Because yesterday he brought me home a dozen long-stemmed red roses.' *Bella*: 'So what's wrong with that? Very nice he should bring you home roses.' *Minnie*: 'You don't know what I have to do when he brings me roses.' *Bella*: 'So tell me.' *Minnie*: 'Well, *first* I have to go into the bedroom! And *then*, I have to take off all my clothes. And *then*, I have to dance around the bedroom. *Then* I have to lie on the bed. *Then* I have to put my legs in the air—' *Bella*: 'You don't have a *vase*?'

As I told the joke the audience gasped. There was a tiny silence of about a week and a half. Then they erupted with a laughter which I thought would never end, and which bubbled up repeatedly throughout the rest of the interview. I had been a fraction worried (a fraction? I bit through the inside of my mouth and was about to bite through Michael's). Most people don't like women telling jokes, particularly risqué ones. Joan Rivers and Marti Caine get away with it by being extremely glamorous and feminine and pretending to be neither. Only Bette Midler really lets it all hang out, and says, 'I am lewd, crude, outrageous and as funny as any man in the joint.' And why not?

Of course, in Liverpool every sentence you hear sounds like a joke. And in Dublin you really understand that Irish jokes are not a form of prejudice, they are everyday language which just happens to be perfectly-scripted dialogue. TV director Bill Hays was in the bath in his Dublin hotel room, when there was a knock at the door. 'Telegram for you, Mr Hays,' said the bellboy. 'I'm in the bath, just push it under the door,' called Bill. 'I can't do that, sor,' said the philosopher on the other side of the door, 'it's on a tray.'

One of my favourite stories concerns an interview for the job of lighthouse-keeper, where the applicants were asked to bring a hobby to counteract the boredom of the job. The Englishman produced Scrabble and a book of crosswords. The Scotsman brought darts and a pack of cards. And the Irishman placed a box of Tampax on the table. The panel expressed amazement and demanded an explanation. 'Well, now, see here,' said Patrick. 'Sure I'd never be bored. For look what it says on here. You can swim, you can go horseback-riding, you can play tennis...'

And now, ladies and gentlemen, at *enormous* expense, the silliest one of all. This one made Christopher Biggins and me fall into a swimming pool, which is a foolproof way of emptying it.

A Martian goes into a pub, and orders a drink for himself and one for everyone in the bar. The publican refuses to serve him, but the Martian just grins affably and repeats his request, adding 'and one for yourself, sir, of course.' Again the publican refuses and again the Martian most reasonably repeats his request (Rule of Three, again, see?). Grudgingly, the publican finally complies, then presents him with a bill for fifty-three pounds. 'Certainly, sir,' beams the Martian, 'I wonder... do you have change of a *zoink*?'

Similarly, do you recall the cerebral masterpiece about the two cockney cowboys in the desert — doncha just love the likeliness of all these premises? — and one tells the other he's very hungry.

'Aw, well, partner,' replies the other, 'if you ride a few miles further through the desert, turn right at the cactus mound, you'll find a BACON TREE.'

'Stone me, amigo, 'ave you gone bleedin' mad? There's no such thing as a BACON TREE, yer baccy-chewing twerp.'

'Course there is. I know this desert like the back of me Germans!' (Simultaneous translation: German bands — hands. Cockney rhyming slang/see chiming clang.)

First cowboy rides off into distance. An hour later he returns shot through from stetson to stirrup with arrows.

'That wasn't a BACON TREE, you berk, that was an AM BUSH.'

Mrs Goldblatt in Fortnum and Mason's food department is approached by a liveried floor manager in top hat and tails.

'May I be of assistance, Mrs Goldblatt, Madam?'

'Gimme a qvarter of chopped liver.'

'Certainly, Madam.' He calls out — 'A quarter of a pound of our best French pâté de foie gras for Mrs Goldblatt. Thank you. Will that be all?'

'I vant a half a pound of worst.'

'Certainly, Madam — a half a pound of our finest German salami for Mrs Goldblatt. Will that be all, Madam?'

'No — I vant you should gimme a box lockshen.'

'With pleasure, Madam. A box of our best quality Italian vermicelli for Mrs Goldblatt — and will that be everything, Madam?'

'Dat's all I vant.'

'Thank you. And would Madam like it delivered or will you schlepp it home yourself?'

That one you have to say out loud.

This is no joke — the gardener who had worked for the previous owners of our house was working in the garden one day. He called to me, 'Mrs Rosen— er Mrs Ronel— Mrs er' — my name would forever elude him — 'I've moved that large clump of er— er— whatsits — round to the front bay — the — er — thingummy jobs — you know — the — oh blimey — what are they called? — oh lord, it's on the tip of my tongue — the howsyafathers — doubreys — you know which ones I mean, don't you, Mrs Rosserall — anyway, I've moved them over to the bay — the er—ooo— yes that's it! The forget-me-nots!'

A scriptwriter's dream!

Gorilla jokes are legion. Three elderly Jewish widows, Minnie, Bella and Miriam decide to take a 'vacation with a difference'. Instead of a four-star at Fort Lauderdale, they will go to Africa on safari. All goes well until nightfall when they pitch camp. Without warning, a huge, black, hairy arm comes through the tent flap, picks up Minnie and carries her off through the jungle. Once in a clearing, he throws her on the earth and has his way with her. Once through, he picks her up and charges to the water hole, throws her against the bank and has his way with her. After that, he throws her over his back and thunders through the undergrowth, throws her up against a tree and, would you believe, has his way with her again, ad infinitum and through the nightum.

The next day a search party finds the exposed, exhausted and comatose body of Minnie in a clearing. In a specially chartered ambulance plane they fly her back to the Cedars of Lebanon Hospital where she is placed on an intravenous drip and a life-support machine. Into this scene come Bella and Miriam. To visit. Bella holds Minnie's hand. Miriam weeps. After some minutes, Minnie opens one eye, sees her friends and through parched lips croaks: 'Thoity-three times he had his way viz me. Thoity-three times. In a clearing. On a mud bank. In a tree. In the undergrowth, backwards, forwards every hour all night thru. Thoity-three times. Already. And since then — not a letter — not a postcard — does he call?— Nothing—'

I know it's horribly sexist but, it has to be said, so are gorillas.

Then there's the lonely gorilless whose mate has died just before breeding time, leaving both her and her devoted Irish keeper desolate with grief. The board of directors call a meeting and decide that, to save the zoo the embarrassment of all the advance publicity over a new baby gorilla, they will make Paddy the keeper an offer he can't refuse.

'Paddy, you love that gorilla like a friend.'

'That I do,' replies the keeper.

'Could you see your way for the honour of the zoo, for the future of the Gorilla House and for two hundred and fifty pounds to perhaps making love to that lady gorilla?'

'Can I think it over?' says Paddy.

They agree to reconvene after the weekend.

'Gentlemen,' says Paddy, 'I've decided I'll do it. But only on three conditions. Number 1: no foreplay. Number 2: any children of the union to be brought up Catholic. And Number 3: the two hundred and fifty pounds, could I put down twenty pounds now and pay the rest in instalments?'

Finally, and with ape-ologies to anthropologists and people of delicacy everywhere, I shall tell you of the randy gorilla who, on failing to find local crumpet, sees a lady lioness bending over a water hole and, unable to contain himself, leaps upon her and does his thing. Then, terrified of the consequences, he hurtles panic-stricken through the jungle, pursued hotly by the righteously indignant lioness. Breathless, he comes upon a clearing where a black missionary in a clerical suit is sitting reading *The Times*. The gorilla knocks him out, dons his suit, dog-collar and hat and just grabs the paper in time to be reading nonchalantly when the lioness thuds into sight. 'Have you seen a gorilla running through these parts?' she growls. To which the gorilla replies:

'Do you mean the one who screws lions?'

'Strewth,' cries the lioness seizing *The Times*, 'do you mean it's in the paper already?'

Before I leave the animal kingdom for ever, I must tell you about a man who stopped for petrol in a remote farm in a remote part of New Mexico. The farmer, with his great hospitality, showed him around the farm, where he was amazed and intrigued by the sight of the very friendly turkey who sported a wooden leg. 'What an amazing bird!' he commented. 'Tell me, how did it get its wooden leg?'

'Aw well,' said the farmer, 'that is no ordinary turkey. That turkey saved my life. I was down by the creek one day when I was cornered by a rabid dog snarling and foaming at the mouth.

That turkey heard my cry, came running five miles from the barn, leaped for that dog's throat and ripped it apart. Saved my life.'

'That's incredible,' said the traveller, 'but how did it get the wooden leg?'

'And that's not all,' continued the farmer. 'I once got my shirt-tails caught in a threshing machine. Another minute and I'd have been shredded to pieces. Suddenly the turkey stuck its neck round the barn door, saw what was happening, picked up an axe in its beak, hurled it into the engine and jammed the mechanism. Sure saved my life, I can tell you.'

'This is unbelievable!' marvelled the traveller. 'But — how did it get the wooden leg?'

'And that's not all,' the farmer went on, 'I went down to the ocean for a swim one day. Now, unbeknown to me, there was a killer shark lurking round that stretch of water. I was alone when I felt a tug in the current and there on the surface of the water I saw its fin. I was paralysed. Suddenly, from the beach came a strange gobbling sound, and the next thing I saw was the flailing wings of that turkey as it skimmed the water and, with a terrible screech, intercepted that shark's progress. Well, it thumped and it pecked and it scratched and it worried that critter so hard that it turned tail and swam clean off in t'other direction. Damned turkey saved my life again.'

Once more the traveller was overwhelmed with amazement at the turkey's heroism. 'But still,' he insisted 'still— you haven't told me how it got its wooden leg.'

'Well,' retorted the farmer, scratching his beard, 'if you had a turkey that useful you sure in hell wouldn't want to eat it all at once!'

Now, this is verging on the shaggy dog story and could, indeed has been, stretched out for as long as your patience could take it. I generally lose mine unless one is really wonderfully well told. My mother once fooled me totally with a 'true' story about going to see a Paul Daniels show in a Leeds nightclub with a couple of friends. She described how Leslie, the husband, had given Daniels his brand new gold and platinum Rolex for one of his tricks, and smiled confidently whilst Daniels smashed it to bits. However, as the show went on and his watch failed to materialize, he got somewhat worried and by the end of the

show they were all anxious enough to demand to see the
Manager. He seemed terribly nonplussed and took them
backstage to meet Daniels' manager. He was profoundly
apologetic, thanked them for coming and explained that
something had indeed gone wrong with the substitution of the
real watch for the fake and as a consequence, Leslie's watch had
been smashed. 'Well, you can imagine how we all reacted to
that,' said my ma. 'Anyway, his manager was very nice and said,
of course it would all be sorted out and the insurance would pay
up whatever was needed and intimated possibly more, and
would we be so kind as to have tea with Mr Daniels who was
very anxious to explain and make further amends.'

She then went on to tell me how very kind and apologetic he
was and how they were all served tea and plates of doughnuts in
his dressing-room. All of which she said was most enjoyable.

'Well. [Long pause.] Oh, well, we were all listening to Paul
Daniels, when Leslie took a bite of his doughnut — and he
suddenly stopped — and you'll never guess what was *inside it* —'

'The watch!' I yelled as though I suspected all along.

'No,' she said, flatly. 'Jam, you silly bugger!'

Ever been thoroughly had? By your own flesh and blood?
Talking of which leads me to the ultimate, the shaggiest, the
veritable yak of stories which I will and must, compress for the
sake of the conservation of trees used for paper making.

It concerns a very old American woman of nearly ninety-
eight who decides to take a vacation in India. No, not a single
gorilla in the story, I promise. Of course, everyone from family
to travel agent tries to discourage her, but she is adamant. She
will take the flight and what's more, while there, she will take
the mystical path to the mountains of Nepal. She arrives at the
airport after eighteen hours in the air. She then takes a train
right across country for many days, travelling with peasants and
chickens and young Americans and Sikh Holy Men, until at
last, dirty and exhausted, she arrives at the tiny town at the base
of the Nepalese mountains. Here she is once again dissuaded on
all sides by hotel managers and tourist operators alike from
proceeding further, for the journey will surely kill her. However,
the little old lady is adamant and after one night's sleep, she
hires a party of Nepalese bearers and an interpreter and sets off,
borne on high by the natives, up the winding mountain trail;

pitching camp beneath the stars and setting out again the following day for five gruelling days.

Finally, they reach a plateau in the mountain and her interpreter tells her they have now reached the last spot through which non-members of the mighty and now Holy Swami Banderaneckti's cloistered sect may pass. Undeterred, she spends the night in the tiny, whitewashed church and pooh-poohs the protestations of the priest that the rest of the journey to the Temple of the Swami is perilous, beset by dangers, and only possible travelling by a solitary donkey, then by foot, and then the Swami only appears once a month and scatters rose petals from a window. No one has seen him in person for many years.

At the crack of dawn she sets off. [You can spin out the perilous journey as much as you like — only until your listeners show signs of possible boredom, i.e. one guest manicuring the other's ingrowing toenail!] By some miraculous feat she ascends the remaining twenty thousand feet to the gardens surrounding the temple. Here the Swami's devoted followers tend her, bathe her and express their amazement at her achievement — but firmly assure her that the Swami's next appearance is not for another three weeks and that he sees no one in private, having taken a vow of silence many years ago. Undaunted, the exhausted, travel-worn old lady announces that she intends to go on a hunger strike until he sees her.

After a fast of several days, she is very near death and somehow word must have reached the Holy Man, for he relents and a shaven-headed devotee in saffron robes comes scurrying to her bedside to say the Guru will admit her to his presence. However, she may only utter four words, no more. 'Four words will do,' croaks the triumphant woman.

The following day she is bathed and robed in saffron and anointed with sandalwood and her forehead is daubed with scarlet. Twelve devotees escort her to the door of the Guru's cloistered temple. As they retreat, bowing, through the corridors, they reiterate, 'Four words only.'

She enters the sepulchral doorway. The room is impressive and its religious splendour and opulence overwhelm her. The air is filled with the heady fragrance of incense. Tapers burn, throwing flickering shadows on the silken tapestries which cover the hundred and fifty steps which lead to the altar. Strange, tinkling music of tabors and flutes fills her ears as she slowly and laboriously mounts the hundred and fifty steps leading to the tiny figure seated cross-legged on a priceless Indian carpet. She finally drags herself before him. He is making a low, repetitive, monosyllabic sound low in his throat, and appears to be in a deep trance. His hair and beard are streaked with white and touch the floor and beyond. His body is so thin you could see through it but for the thin, silken cloth swathing his loins. After an endless silence, he opens his startlingly piercing eyes and stares levelly at her. With difficulty she kneels before him, breathes deeply and long, and says, 'Sheldon. Enough is enough.'

Incidentally, before your corsets split — what's the worst thing about Oral Sex? The View.

Don't you ever wonder who it is who's sitting somewhere under an Anglepoise, chewing his Pentel, and trying to think up the definitive funny joke? All the time waiting for the phone to ring and Bernard Manning to bark, 'Well, have you done it, I'm on in an hour!'

Whoever he is, I'll bet he's hell to live with. Comedy is, after all, no laughing matter. Aristotle was wont to say, 'Tragedy is an imitation of an action which is serious — with incidents arousing pity or terror — with which to accomplish its purgation of emotions.' Now Ari was a hoot around the Parthenon and a terror with the taramasalata as you all know, but I wonder if he realized that, if you substitute the word Comedy for Tragedy, exactly the same rules apply.

Comedy, like its posh elder brother, is all to do with the purgation of emotions. An element of 'Thank God it's him and not me' coupled with 'That could be your Auntie Edna talking' makes an audience laugh not just with recognition, but also with relief. So often after *See How They Run* people came round wiping tears from their eyes and saying variations on 'I've been completely taken out of myself — I'm exhausted from laughing' and, in the case of a friend who almost cancelled because of an illness in the family, 'We forgot all our worries and just rocked!' Laughter, like tears, is therapeutic and yet an actor who plays mostly comedy is regarded with the same faint contempt as, say, a doctor who decided to specialize in Aromatherapy. Why?

My theory, for what it's worth, is that we laugh in public but we grieve alone. There! That riveted you in your seats for sheer originality, didn't it? Let me expound. Everyone knows a comic — the fellow in the fruitshop, the lady in Lurex on the 49 bus, the second eldest son with a gap in his teeth. How many times have I heard 'You want to come round our factory/dress shop/hairdressing salon. You'll soon have a new comedy series'. And it's probably true. We see laughter used all the time as a device to comfort, to diffuse, to cover embarrassment, to seduce or reject.

How often, though, do we *see* the actual occasion of grief or sin or pain in the everyday tragedies of life? We only see its results and sympathize with the attempts to return to normality. So when Shakespeare, Strindberg or Ibsen shows us the moment of passion or pain we are not only moved — we are *amazed*. How could that writer know what I felt when my daughter rejected me? How could that actor see into my emotions when my wife left me? Very few people can actually feel another person's experience, so when they are *shown* it, it's a revelation. It looks like sorcery, it looks like genius, it may well be both. Whatever it is, it looks a hell of a lot more difficult than a Neil Simon boulevard comedy.

Walpole said, 'The world is a comedy to those who think, a tragedy to those who feel'. *I think* he may be right. I *feel* he could be wrong. And there's the rub. All our laughter has an element of pain, and all our pain an element of laughter. Farce, even. I know. I had cramp during labour. I was the only woman in the delivery room shouting, 'My foot! My foot!'

Believe me, I'm not asking for Comedy to be *superior* to Tragedy — just equal. If there's to be a special award for Best Comedy Performance as distinct from Best Actor or Actress, then let's also have an award for Best *Serious* Performance. Because, make no mistake about it, an actor approaches all parts in the same way. The comic ones are more difficult because one must allow for various degrees of laughter each night whilst retaining the concentration of the character.

Every couple of years, some woolly academic gets the bright idea of casting a real 'comic' in Shakespeare. He does this out of desperation with the material in the low comedy scenes. Thus Thora Hird, Dora Bryan, Irene Handl, Max Wall are re-discovered by the Press and Public. And the implication is always the same — 'My God, these comics can actually ACT!' What's more, they can make inferior, dated tosh zing with freshness and inventiveness. Why not? They've been doing it all their working lives and, quite frankly, after single-handedly saving Summer Seasons and TV Sitcoms, *Pericles, Prince of Tyre* is just a piece of Brie.

Knight and Dame the lot of them — that's what I say! As we should have honoured Alastair Sim and Margaret Rutherford and Joyce Grenfell and countless others. And while we're at it — let's give our comic writers the same recognition. And while they're alive for a change.

All I'm saying really is when God said 'Let there be light', He meant it. Light doesn't mean insubstantial. No play has ever changed Society. But if you change the attitudes of enough individuals, you may eventually improve it. If you leave an Alan Bennett play feeling warm all over and are a mite kinder to your Auntie Edna because of it, then you've got the message. Whether the play had one or not.

By the way. Did I tell you about the elderly Jewish couple who retired to Brighton? They were sitting on the pier when a flasher in a long mac came running up, opened his mac, exposed himself to Leah. She remained totally impassive. Unable to believe it he returned, re-flashed, and received the same lack of response. The third time he was determined to provoke her. Inches from her nose he whipped open the mac, and stood rigidly before her. After a long pause, she turned to her husband and said, 'You call that a lining?'

Now there's a funny thing. . . .

You're Driving Me Crazy!

JACK ONCE BOARDED the Manchester train at Euston, settled down with a cheese and polystyrene sandwich, a copy of *Punch* and a packet of Government Health Warnings. As the train pulled out, the man opposite leant forward, tapped him on the knee and said, 'Don't talk to me about Cortinas!' Jack had no intention of doing so. His fellow traveller then bent his ear for the next two hours forty minutes — the length of the journey.

Funny thing about cars. They get you that way. I remember my mother taking lessons in her forties. She'd had sixty-three lessons to date when my brother took her up the street for a practice. As they reached the end of the street, Geoff said, 'OK, Mother, change down.'

'What?' she exclaimed, 'on my own?'

Geoff expressed some disbelief.

'Oh no,' she rejoined firmly, 'Mr Middleyard always holds my hand!'

Some years later she was fully weaned and passed her test. Alone. She still, however, drives as though waiting for Mr Middleyard to help her change gear.

I don't have a relationship, as such, with my car. I mean I call her Wanda, but that's purely 'cos she's a Honda and my mind works that way. Wanda is small, silver and automatic and as I regard myself as tall, dark and manual we complement each other well enough. Over the past five years Wanda has taken me to practically every studio, theatre and surgery in London. Through her I learned 'The Knowledge' and she knows it. Now the back streets of this beloved city are as familiar to me as the back of my son's neck — and as grimy.

Which is not to say all is perfect. Far from it. It has long been clear to me that Wanda is eccentric and I'm now beginning to think she has to go. It's not just her refusal to start unless the temperature is in the eighties and the palm trees are in blossom,

145

nor her endearing habit of cutting out her engine on the Archway roundabout — a kamikaze gesture worthy of her origins — it's really more to do with the fact that Wanda drinks. A lot. Oh, let's not beat about the bush — she's an alcoholic on whom even the AA have given up. Her petrol gauge has two levels — 'Full' or 'On Tow', and quite frankly I'd had it up to here.

Then, one day last year, tootling through a short-cut behind Camden Town, a parked Fiesta pulled out suddenly in our way and gave Wanda a nose-job. (To say I was jealous of it is an understatement.) The driver was sullen and unrepentant and when Wanda returned from our local garage, so was she. Every time I got in, she 'kvetched' (I know it's Yiddish but it's also onomatopoeic) and her alcohol consumption went up to compensate for her depression. Some time later, whilst my mother's help was driving her to school, someone did it again and Polly Paranoia really set in. You could actually feel her flinch as you started her engine.

It was at this point that the Press Officer from the Theatre of Comedy stepped in. Wearing her 'I'm sure you won't want to do this but it's my job to ask' face, she asked, 'Would you test-drive three cars for the *TV Times* next week and be photographed doing it?' I glanced at Wanda sulking outside the stage door and thoughts not entirely unconcerned with greed passed over my windscreen-eyes. 'Are they automatic?' I ventured, mentally waving Wanda goodbye. The reply was negative, but by now I was convinced that one of them could ultimately be offered to me for a song. Presumably, 'You, You're Driving Me Crazy' would do.

The first car arrived at 9 am and Paul, the photographer, at ten. I'd slipped into something snappy and prepared for action with a slice of cucumber on both eyes and the white of an egg all over my face. He accepted my appearance with equanimity — the first of many such mistakes — and refrained from saying that he'd never photographed a human salad driving a Ford before. I dressed the salad, poured in the Polyfilla, and we left the house having decided to head for Alexandra Park, where I would frisk and gambol around the solid but sparky vehicle for the benefit of his lens. We sat in the car and one of us gazed uncertainly at the manual gears. It wasn't Paul.

To allay the panic I reminded myself that I'd passed my driving test in a manual car. Being eight months pregnant when the test had finally come up and the examiner having no secret aspirations towards midwifery, I was not called upon to do the emergency stop. Otherwise, I'd passed with gliding, if not flying, colours. I knew I could do it. The last five years on automatic pilot were a mere hiccup in a career devoted to the use of the gear stick. Ten minutes later I was still trying to get out of the drive. The traffic was at a standstill and I'd exceeded the Olympic record for hopping to a height of six feet in a metallic blue vehicle.

Paul the photographer's expression never changed. I've rarely seen such raw terror at such close quarters, as we slowly ground our way towards Wood Green in first gear, any attempt to change into second on my part causing a noise reminiscent of the climax of *Clash of the Titans* and the disappearance headfirst into the hedgerows of the entire population of N10.

Somehow, with many an unexpected stop as I raised my foot from the clutch to emphasize a point, I managed to make it to the park, and even managed a twitchy smile or two for the camera. Paul's hands were a bit unsteady but I soon relaxed him with a joke or two and the promise of a ride home.

Things looked up after this. Like getting back on a horse I began to master the beast and was soon in the heady heights of gears two and three. After a drive in and out of town to the theatre and back, I was even able to curse other drivers for their appalling manners again. Just as I'd become really comfortable in the car, they came and took it away. I gave it eight marks out of ten for fortitude.

The following day I resolved to take a swim to ease the stabbing pain in my gear-changing arm. I donned my costume under my clothes, put my towel and underwear in Wanda, who now sat pathetically sulking in the drive cross-eyed with paranoia. Before I could set off, the VW Golf was delivered. Paul was arriving a couple of hours later, presumably wearing brown trousers and protective headgear — so with the confidence of the foolhardy I studied the manual for a while and set out poolwards in the Golf. It felt like sitting high up in a sturdy tank of Germanic extraction, which it was. I made mental notes on its performance and cruised down to the pool in a somewhat blasé fashion. I'd just completed a seven-point turn, or parked — whichever way you care to describe it — when I remembered the towel and the underwear were still sitting in Wanda. Rolf the Golf and I drove home drily. Wanda was smirking. Inscrutably.

Paul and his seventeen cameras awaited me. I'd got the time wrong. Hastily I put a trouser suit over the bathing suit and we set off for Hampstead Garden Suburb's shopping area to shoot me and the car having a perfectly normal shopping spree. We parked outside the kosher butcher's on the old A1, and Paul risked his life dodging the lorries to capture yours truly piling a basket of rye bread and salamis into a hatchback. At this point the story takes on a Truffaut-like quality as a huge pantechnicon, thoughtfully labelled 'Long Vehicle' for fear you shouldn't notice, sliced into a small red car and forced it on to the island.

Within minutes both drivers were racing towards us for corroboration of their innocence. The driver of the short vehicle was Irish, and the other was French. Not a great deal of progress was made.

I exerted my flawless French: 'Er, Monsieur, pardon mon interruption, mais il must téléphoner au police — er, parce que . . .' Overjoyed at my mastery of his native tongue, a torrent of Basque was directed in my direction. 'Er, lentement, s'il vous plaît,' I squeaked in heavy Yorkshire, 'je ne speakez pas all that bien . . .'

We retired — the three of us — to the delicatessen to téléphoner. 'They won't come unless there's a body,' said the delicatessant cheeringly. Both men began to expostulate as to the need or otherwise for the Force to be with us. The delicatessant wanted none of it. 'If you want to have a row — would you mind having it outside?'

I heard my voice speak: 'It's not a row — he's French — er, Monsieur — en Angleterre nous avons this rule . . .' By the time the police arrived the couple were getting on famously in sign language with flapping sheets of paper and I was getting in and out of the Golf with my baguettes. The police were suspicious of my role in the affair but once they realized I was that fruitcake from *Agony* they told me I looked better in real life than on the telly — a dubious compliment if ever I had one — and left me to say 'fromage' in peace.

Later, much later, I dropped Paul in town, in hysterics. By now just the sight of me made him helpless, and I shot off to keep a five o'clock appointment with the osteopath before my evening contortions in the farce *See How They Run*. I excused my lateness to him whilst shedding garments right down to my bathing suit. He looked surprised but the explanation was too tortuous to attempt. By now even I thought I was a fruitcake and it was confirmed in the theatre when I played the part of Miss Skillen, the village spinster, in twin set, pearls, tweed suit and Lycra swim-wear.

The final car, the Maestro, arrived two days later. It was round, shiny and green and immediately became 'Granny Smith'. Paul and I, dab hands by now, actually discussed Life and Art on our way to Hampstead Heath, or 'Hampstead Underneath' as my son was wont to call it, and I merrily stuck my head through the sunroof and waved camera-wards till the job was done. Once home again, I found that my au pair had gone to Sainsbury's in my car taking the house-keys with her. Undeterred, I picked up the kids from school in the Maestro and returned home, in time to see Wanda the Honda being ferociously rammed from behind by as mean and ugly a lorry as I've seen outside *Duel*. It was pitiful. I raced across the road like a mother-hen and screamed at him, 'What the hell do you think . . .?' He got down from his lorry. He was nine foot twelve high. 'Is your lorry all right?' I grovelled. Five hundred pounds per annum insurance I pay for Wanda. At least she's never hit back. She's just a masochist. One of nature's losers.

A point of interest to would-be actresses: You are a very high insurance risk. Though, like me, you don't drink, don't speed and don't claim every time a lorry sheds its load over your bonnet, your very profession puts you up there with the musicians and, God help you, the journalists. If you have aspirations to be all three, buy a pogo stick and hop it! Or just insure your legs.

Apparently we owe it all to Merle Oberon — good old Merle. My Dad always had a soft spot for her. It seems she had a car crash and needed expensive plastic surgery — all on the insurance bill. Ever since, regardless of whether, like me, you'd pay a high premium to look like Merle Oberon *after* a car crash, we're all lumped into the same astronomical category.

So there we are I then started taking *What Car?* and *Which Motor?* with the same dogged enthusiasm I used to buy *Homes and Gardens*. Jack keeps forcing British cars on me — which all feel like tins of sardines on wheels. Mr Taylor from the garage brought round a Subaru (I know it sounds like a fart in the bath but it's a car!). It was a shiny red with power-steering and apricot-lit dashboard and it was love at first sight. It had been around a bit — just the 3,000 miles on the clock — but I wasn't going to hold this past against him. I had a strong feeling that we were meant for each other. As I purred around the park, woman and machine in perfect harmony, I felt more than a little like Mr Toad sitting glazed-eyed in the middle of the road — 'Poop Poop! It's the *only* way to travel!'

In any event, I ended up with Maud the Ford as my new Escort, but not without a ferocious struggle on Wanda's behalf. Four months after she first found out about my infidelity, I was still driving her round and she was still driving me barmy. The only change, apart from her oil, was my insurance premium which mysteriously leapt after I wrote an article about Wanda and her adventures in the skid-trade.

The postscript to this saga is that I sold Wanda to the Clarendon Garage round the corner. The kids were distraught that they hadn't said goodbye to her. Pete from the garage sold her to a lady. The lady seemed pleased with her and Wanda went off. A week later, the lady returned brandishing the article I'd written about Wanda's malicious streak and thankyouvery-much, the lady wanted none of it and her money back. Wanda was a genius.

In conclusion, I bought a bike. A very pretty, flowered, burgundy coloured bike. It sat in the porch and I sat in a lot of taxis. Till Maud.

So far I've got nothing but good to say of her. Which is more than can be said about her feelings towards me. Last week at the shopping centre I left the ignition keys locked inside the car with the engine running.

The Security men were all out arresting a youth. 'What's he done?' I asked, as they returned with him in tow.

'Breaking into cars, Madam' was the stern reply.

I could hardly control myself.

'Can you possibly let him break into one more?' I pleaded,

'just to make sure you've got the right man...' They were not amused.

One of them accompanied me back to Maud who sat there hyperventilating, as the man in the next car tried to slide his American Express card into her lock. Naturally enough, it wouldn't take it.

Finally our trusty guard ripped off her rubber seals, slid a large wire into her private parts and released her for ever.

She's been huffy as hell with me ever since, so I've been out and bought her a new two-tone stripe which she thinks is an award for valour in the face of attempted rape. And I'm certainly not going to be the one to disillusion her.

3

A Broad On The Boards

They Also Serve Who Only Wait and Stand-in...

THE ACTOR'S NIGHTMARE is entering a theatre to be told by a departing back 'Good luck tonight.' No one listens to his protestations that he knows neither the part nor even the play and the nightmare continues until he is dressed in a period costume and pushed centre stage to face a faceless audience of thousands with his mouth open and nothing coming out. At that moment you wake up, change your pyjamas and, if you're sensible, your career.

I once dreamed I was playing a principal boy in a Victorian-type pantomime with raked (sloping) stage and footlights. In mid thigh-slap and just about to launch into a spirited rendition of 'On a wonderful day like today', I felt an insistent tugging at my tabard. Glancing down briefly, I saw my son's upturned face and heard the words, 'Mod — I want to wee-wee.' Momentary pause, then 'I defy any cloud to appear in the sky (psst — go to Daddy) — defy any rainbow---'

'But I need to wee-wee.'

'Geroff!'

Finally, of course, as I sang, he peed. It ran straight down the stage and fused the footlights.

Classic anxiety, of course — I've read my Kitchen Shrink — but in real life the role of understudy can be just as alarming. I once 'covered' Diana Rigg in Stoppard's *Jumpers* at the Old Vic. Mostly, I just slunk around the rehearsal room, admiring the verve of her performance and convinced that she would never be 'off'. Once the play had opened I had the happiest few months of my life in the understudies' dressing-room, giggling myself stupid and learning to crochet. What we found to glue us helplessly to our chairs long after the curtain had come down I'll never know, and, since I never learned to cast off, what started out as a cushion cover was soon big enough to carpet Versailles and so heavy it had to be transported to and from the theatre by taxi. It's been slowly unwinding itself ever since (well, who hasn't?) and will quietly become an egg cosy quite soon, but God, I wish I could encapsulate the amounts of laughter crocheted into its woolly being.

Before I become hooked (sorry) on the subject, I must tell you that the dreaded night arrived. Diana hurt her back. I tried to hurt mine and failed. Still, I was cool (at twenty-four, who isn't?). I knew the lines and had actually had a couple of rehearsals. The dress was taken in and let out in the relevant places, I had a new blonde wig in which I intended to have a lot more fun, and I sat making up my face in Diana's dressing-room mirror surrounded by Interflora. My heart appeared to be beating *outside* my body — but I was cool. Then, over the tannoy, I heard the announcement to the audience — 'Owing to the indisposition of Miss Diana Rigg —' there followed the loudest and most concerted groan I've ever heard. The Manager strove to continue. So did I. 'So — so in tonight's performance the part of Dottie will be played by Maureen Lipman.' Maybe they didn't all say 'WHO? WHO?' but that's what I heard. Maybe it was just an owl!

The next thing I remember was my first entrance. Seated on a crescent moon Dottie glides in, mike in hand, and sings 'By the light of the silvery...' She then forgets the next word. Then 'Shine on, shine on harvest...' she forgets again. Naturally the audience thought it was the understudy who had 'dried', not the character, and for a minute the place felt as dangerous as a bull-ring. Very Good Theatre, I suppose, but not so good for the rapid ageing process. That night I grew up fast.

More recently, in Philip King's vintage farce called *See How They Run* in which I was appearing, the leading lady lost her voice three days before the show opened. We were playing to preview audiences of over a thousand people, and without a single rehearsal, in a huge and complex part, the understudy, Diana de Nimes, got through the whole show without a prompt. Afterwards, she confessed that every time a bell rang, a door opened or a set of French windows parted, she had absolutely no idea who was coming through them. As a diet, an experience

like that has no parallel save acute dysentery. She dropped half a
stone in forty-eight hours and gained, I like to think, a foot and a
half in stature. In the same show, the part of Mr Humphrey —
the timid vicar who arrives in Act III, witnesses a scene of four
vicars in various stages of undress, and quietly steals the show —
was played by Derek Nimmo. Now Derek is a well-known social
butterfly, entrepreneur, dilettante and general good liver who
likes to put in a full day about twice as many appointments as
you or I might have in a Boots year-ahead-planner. The night
we opened the curtain went up at seven o'clock. No sign of
Derek. By five to eight his understudy had a lime-green skin and
was vibrating like a cricket. At eight Derek arrived, leaving
himself hardly more than a few minutes to slip out of his dinner
suit into his dog collar and saunter into Act III as the doorbell
rang and his fellow actors said, 'Who can that be?' It transpired
he'd been doing two episodes of *Just a Minute* at BBC Radio: one
just as our curtain was rising in Shaftesbury Avenue, and the
second as we were crawling for our interval cuppa.

The point of this story is that Derek's sang-froid was
everybody's sang-chaude. Now me, personally, I have to be
inside the theatre an hour and a half before curtain up or my
eyes start to twitch. Once in the sanctity of my dressing-room, I
don a dressing-gown, take my make-up off, read my mail,
arrange flowers, lie down, do deep-breathing, sing a little, warm
up my voice a little, finally, stand on my head against the door in
the belief that the rush of blood will make my brain agile. It is at
this point that somebody like the wardrobe mistress comes in and I
fall to the ground and play the performance with my head on my
shoulder like a budgie.

Quite seriously, I can't bear my routine to be altered even by
a visitor an hour before the show. Liza Goddard, with whom I
shared adjoining dressing-rooms in *See How They Run*, is totally
imperturbable and entertained her mother, her eight-year-old
son and her Golden Retriever in the dressing-room till ten
minutes before curtain up on the first night. I was a vicarious
nervous wreck, stuffing 'Quiet Life' tablets into my mouth and
deep-breathing into a state of hyperventilation. Meanwhile,
back at the Beeb, Lord Derek of Nimmo was doing battle with
Nicholas Parsons and his understudy was doing battle with the
kaolin and morphine.

The popular view of understudying is based largely on Ruby Keeler taking over from Bebe Daniels in *42nd Street*. Do you remember wicked old Warner Baxter as the director coaching Miss Keeler for the role?

'Say, Jim,' she stammers in a high-pitched monotone, 'they didn't tell me you wuz here. It's gra-a-nd of you to come.'

Baxter goes berserk. 'Where's the passion? Where's the heart? Wassermatterwithya — gimme some feeling!' (I'm paraphrasing, you understand.)

Gulp. She tries again. 'Say, Jim' (once more it sounds like she's reading the lines from *Architectural Digest*), 'they didn't tell me you wuz here. It's graand of you to come.'

This time Baxter takes her roughly in his arms, pulls her to his chest and with his snarl just a centimetre from her cupid's bow: 'Have you never felt a man's breath on yours, a man's body against yours, a passion surging through you...? Gimme that and more.'

The briefest of pauses while she pats her hair. Then, in precisely the same tone, 'Say, Jim. They didn't tell me you wuz here. It's graand of you to come.'

Unaccountably, or perhaps accountably when you consider how many takes they must have done to get *that* far — he yells — 'That's it!' and exhorts her to go on there a NOBODY and come off a STAR. She complies, and the audience, naturally filled with Broadway Big Shots, rises to its spats. In reality, Ruby would have thrown up in the wings, had no time to invite her mother, let alone her agent, and probably fallen through a trap-door in the Busby Berkeley routine. The following day it would have been a timid check to see if Bebe was better and back to the understudy's dressing-room and her crochet hook.

Julia McKenzie tells a story of touring with *Rose-Marie* with David Whitfield. The leading lady was taken ill, and the understudy didn't know the words, and Julia swears she heard this voice say 'I'll do it', looked round to see who said it, and found it was her. She was nineteen, full of confidence, not a nerve in her body and with a voice that could shatter a chandelier. She went on that night and played the romantic fur-trapper's daughter with every fibre of her being. After a week she was cooing the Indian Love Song with such passionate abandon, that she knew that her future was inexorably tied to romantic operetta. When the show was over, in a rosy afterglow she received the producer in her dressing-room, eyelashes fluttering in expectation. 'Julia,' he said, looking deep into her eyes, 'you've got a great future. In comedy.'

Even in real life I've occasionally found myself playing the understudy part when billed as myself. I once opened a charity bazaar in a London synagogue somewhere. I was billed on all the posters as a comedienne, and announced from the podium as 'that extremely funny lady' (the kiss of death for any speaker), and I spoke from the stage for long enough to realize that if I didn't shut up soon, the customers would break down the barricades. After the applause and in order to appear ordinary and approachable, I walked about the stalls. (Actually I was quietly stocking up on home-made cakes in order to appear a proper wife and mother should guests arrive unexpectedly.) I was eyeing some macaroons when the stallholder eyed me with that by-now-familiar look: 'Haven't I seen you somewhere before?'

I laughed painfully. 'Er, yes, I expect so — I just opened the...'

'You look so familiar!' she persisted. 'Where do I know you from?'

Before I had a chance to cast her mind back a full minute and a half, she grabbed her fellow salesperson by the angora, yanked her round and, 'Millie, look at this girl — who does she remind you of?'

Millie looked superior and aghast at the same time. 'Have you gone *mad*, Sissy?' she expostulated. '*She's* just opened the bazaar for us. *She's* just made the speech for us. *This* is Miriam Karlin.' I didn't contradict. I just lowered my voice an octave and bought a madeira cake.

I noticed in *American Buffalo* that Al Pacino (be still, my heart!) doesn't have one. An understudy, I mean. Without *him* the show doesn't go on. Having seen him, I understand entirely.

Recently, at a London Club, I met the Bogus Prince Charles. He makes a very decent living, thank you, with one hand behind his back, his teeth clenched behind his vowel sounds and his ears, believe it or not, plugged from behind to make them stick out like his Royal Counterpart's. I still felt slightly overawed meeting him, which says a lot about the times we live in when the notoriety value of a good fake is almost as powerful as the real thing.

Probably the world's greatest understudy was Old Mother Riley's. Arthur Lucan, who played the old washerwoman for most of his life, was fond of a drop or two of gin to drown his sorrows. He'd have done better to drown his wife Kitty, the cause of most of them. If Arthur was too 'tired and emotional' to appear on stage, then Roy Rollande would go on, unannounced, to play the part. And no one ever knew the difference. So perfect was the impersonation in every detail that thousands of people who remember seeing Mother Riley live on stage, will never know whether what they roared with laughter at was in fact the perfect double. Last year I played Kitty McShane, the wife of Arthur Lucan, in a stage and ultimately a TV play, called *On Your Way, Riley*. In the act, Kitty played Old Mother Riley's wayward daughter, but in life she ruled him with a rod of iron. She kept the money, dealt with the contracts, made the bookings and gave him his bus fare, whilst swanning around with a fur coat on one arm, and her lover on the other. It was almost impossible to find anyone who'd known the couple who had a good word to say about Kitty.

But I liked her. If you're playing a villain you have to. Often when I drove to rehearsals and someone carved me up in the traffic, I would scream at them in a brogue as 'tick as treacle'. The play was a great success for Brian Murphy, who played Arthur, for the production and for the play. Oh, and me. She was so different from anyone else I'd ever done — so big and so vulgar — and finding the reasons for her awful, bullying behaviour was intriguing. She had been one of a family of eighteen children (wrap your mind round that one, Mrs Gillick) and married Arthur at the age of fifteen. It seemed apparent that the hardness was a cover-up for the ensuing disappointment and the anger was misplaced vulnerability.

On the last night of the show, Jack and I were wanly clearing the eight weeks' worth of life that had been stored in my cupboard-sized dressing-room, when there was a knock at the door. It was two of Arthur Lucan's great-grandchildren, who were avid followers of the show, and we welcomed them in for a drink. There was another knock. It was the ex-Rabbi's daughter from Hull and her Iranian boyfriend. We cleaned out more glasses and tried to ally the two worlds, whilst still packing the bags. At the third knock we were pleased to see two gay friends who were still mopping up tears from the death of Arthur. By now, we were raising our elbows in turns, and as the next knock came, we all swayed to the right in order to prise the door open.

The couple were strangers. He was very tall. A big man. She was small and distraught. They were both Irish. 'We're relatives of Kitty's,' she blinked, 'and I've just come to say she wasn't like that at all. She wasn't vulgar at all, and she didn't use that kind of language, and you've no roight...' At this, the tall man leant over, slowly jabbed his finger into my chest. 'Your actin' was great, but your accent was f---in' doiabolical!'

'Oh, thank you, will you have a drink?' Suddenly I was Katie Boyle. 'Have you met er, Arthur Lucan's great-grand-daughters? This is...'

No sooner were de words out of me mooth, than the wailin' started. 'Oh, will you look at this one, sure, isn't she just like me mother's sister, and how old would you be? So your father was Donald's...'

A twenty-year-old family feud was being healed in my eight-by-six-foot dressing-room on a Saturday night, after two shows.

'Has anybody not got a dr—' There was a knock at the door.

'Yes?' I screamed.

'Hello, Maureen? It's Sir Bernard and Lady Miles — can we come in and say hello?'

Well, it was as motley a string of introductions as ever I'd had the pleasure to make. Somehow we all oozed out of the dressing-room and into the green room, and somehow we all stayed friends.

Meanwhile, back in the eight-by-six, Jack packed up the remnants, pulled down the telegrams and loaded up the car. They also serve...

After the transmission of the television *On Your Way, Riley*, Roy Rollande phoned me up. He was very moved, and said repeatedly, 'It was her. It was her. I lived, worked and slept with this person, and it was her. I'm ringing up with sincerity, and there's not much of that in this business. Wonderful.'

To all intents and purposes, Roy Rollande and Arthur Lucan were the same person; it had to be the highest compliment an understudy ever paid to a 'stand-in', and I was banjaxed with it all.

Occasionally I have 'stood-in' as that other great British villainess, Margaret Hilda Thatcher, a task which gives me even more malicious pleasure. I have my own navy suit, tie-neck blouse, court shoes, brooch, pearls, bag and wig, and am available for weddings, barmitzvahs and hooplas. No, seriously, the surprising element is that I'm nearly always booed as I enter, and on one occasion, at Stratford Theatre East, had a boot thrown at me. With only moderately quick-wittedness I boomed: 'This is typical left-wing hooliganism, when in doubt, put the boot in.' That shut them up. Once the sense of humour was revealed, they knew I wasn't she.

I start the act by saying graciously: 'No, don't get up. Stay kneeling exactly where you are,' and continue, 'No, times are hard. I've seen to that. But it's no use tummy-aching about unemployment. As I said at the start of my reign... (*roars of approval*)... it's never too late to start your own family business. All you need is drive, initiative and bloody rich parents.' More roars. Soft, feminine voice and deep, searching look into camera, noting where the key light is... 'I was asked recently if I would care to patronize the Arts. And I said, "Why, I'll patronize anybody..."'

Once, on a live *Russell Harty Show*, I was pacing backstage, going through my lines with Bob Sinfield who'd written my Thatcher piece. The idea of the show was that people should do 'turns' with which they were not normally associated. Thus Raymond Baxter sang 'I've Been To A Marvellous Pahty' in full drag, Bertice Reading sang on roller-skates, and a choir of politicans, from all parties, sang Xmas carols. During rehearsals, the MPs had been an enthusiastic audience for my Thatcherisms. They particularly liked the bit where I wished everybody 'both rich and starving, a merry Christmas and a Happy and Prosp... no, a Happy New Year.'

With twenty minutes to go before the show went on, the producer came scurrying up with a furrowed face, saying 'I'm afraid we've had a complaint.' 'Who from?' I gasped. The reply couldn't have amazed me more. 'From David Steel.' 'David Steel?' I rapidly fast-forwarded through the sketch... '*Michael Foot has absolutely no one behind him — which is why he keeps falling off the platform . . . Shirley Williams may have Crosby under her belt — or is it simply the way she dresses? . . .* But I don't mention David Steel!' I protested.

'No, I know. That's what he's complaining about. He wants an insult, like all the others.'

Well. You try and think of an insult for David Steel in fifteen minutes, in a tight wig and court shoes. Finally, I said, 'David and Shirley, or "Sapphire and Steel", as I like to call them,' and that seemed to do the trick. Rule No.1 in Politics and Show business: Doesn't matter what they say about you, as long as they say it.

Another masquerade happened after 'doing the lady' for an OAP Labour Rally at the Festival Hall. Neil Kinnock was there. Originally he was going to do a bit of a skit with me on the platform, but I think he was still struggling with his image at the time and decided against it. Afterwards I packed up the wig and clothes in a large bag and sped off to King's Cross to catch a train to Hull where I was due to meet my folks for some kind of family 'do'. I was being met in Hull by my Uncle Louis, who's a Labour Councillor, and it occurred to me that it might amuse him to see Margaret Thatcher step off the train to greet him. So, round about Brough or Goole, I nipped into the Ladies, put on all the gear again, jammed on the wig with a little soap round the hairline to keep the dark hair back and painted in the droop-lines round the eyes. I stayed secreted in the loo for as long as I dared, then hovered in the corridor, ignoring the suspicious looks of fellow-travellers till Paragon Station.

First off the train, I walked briskly and purposefully towards the ticket-barrier hardly able to keep my face straight for thinking of his. Being myopic (for that, read 'Bag-Over-the-Eyes case'), I couldn't actually see him, but about fifty yards from where I thought he might be, I started with the ''ere's-me-'ead-me-arse-is-followin' walk, the sick-as-a-parrot smile and the 'Sincerity-is-my-middle-name' angle of head.

I need hardly tell you he wasn't there. Sheepishly I handed in my ticket and bravely hung around the newsstand for all of twenty seconds before making a bolt for the telephone kiosk, where I kept a hunched vigil while phoning his home. Naturally enough, the times of the trains had been confused and it was a sadly-chastened leaderene-clone who ultimately crab-walked to the taxi-rank. Once within the bosom of my family, the joke went down very well when I told it how it was... but, quite honestly, you really had to be there.

The ultimate stand-in story, which may be apocryphal, stars that veteran actor and imbiber Wilfred Lawson, getting steadily stewed with a stranger one lunchtime in a Shaftesbury Avenue pub. After closing time he insisted his new friend accompany him to a matinee in a nearby theatre. They crept noisily to their seats whilst the first act was in progress, and after a few moments elapsed, Lawson tapped his friend on the arm. 'You see the fellow in the armchair?' He did. 'Well, in a minute there'll be a knock at the door and he goes to answer it, see?' He did. 'And do you know what happens?' He didn't. 'The door opens and I come on.'

I like to think of that story purely from the point of view of his understudy.

Literary Pretenshuns

THIS YEAR I started understudying for myself. Which isn't easy. A magazine called *Folio* asked me to write a 1,500-word parody of *Gentlemen Prefer Blondes* by Anita Loos. It was an impossible brief. How do you parody a parody? And a brilliant one at that? I had a year in which to do it. Just the *one* year. A piece of pie! Thirty words a week. Four a day. Three hundred and sixty-two days later, I began. An illiterate, charming, fatuous blonde from Doncaster emerged (thank God!) with an 'artificial-sweetener Daddy' and a shrewd best friend. I liked her and was sad to see her go. So. Having only a few days left to write my regular column for *Options*, I decided to let 'Marianne Plume' write it for me.

For those of you who, like me, wouldn't know an anagram from an Anna Karenina, Marianne Plume is Maureen Lipman — or Liane Manure MP, Murial Pen-Name, Marina née Lump...I'm hoping this creation is one giant leap for Lipmankind into writing a play. A part for myself? Oh, certainly. A short, dumb, busty, blue-eyed blonde with an empty brain and no neuroses, who does it for diamantes? Potential casting directors look no further. I'm perfect for it. Say, we could do the show, right here...

1

Hi there, readers! This is Marianne Plume and I am your new columist for this month, standing in for Moreen Lippman whom has gone off. She is aparently in Isreal or some such place in the Middle of the East in order to unwind from the pressures of show business and choosing a new O-Pair.

So when I heard through the office grape-vine that she was headed sun and sandward and would be too enarvated to write her piece, I plucked up my courage in both hands and went to see my boss (in the office in which I do actually work in, but in a typing position more) and let it all hang out.

'Giz' the job, Giz' the job,' I ejected after the style of Yosser Arrafat in *The Boys With The Black Stuff*. He smiled and said, 'Over my dead body Tiger' which he calls me because he says I'm part of an engendered species. But I just kept on and on at him till last night I finaly persuaided him that I could handle his collum and whoopee this morning he said 'I've had it Tiger. You win.' Well! I was that excited I got dressed and came to work in a taxi. The whole way.

So I expect you are bound to find my style different from Moreen's but a change is as good as arrest as my friend Elaine in Accounts is want to say and you may just find it stimmolating as might I. The thing is just between you and I, I think actressing is very different from writing and though I sometimes smile at her copy I do not think it is enough to talk about your children or your teeth or your tortus when you consider all the seriousness of which there is so much in the world of affairs.

So 'here goes nothing' as my friend Mr Anwar of Anwar Carpets of Kentish Town and Europe is want to say — Mr Anwar and I have been very thick for over a year and he keeps a place above me for when he's in town on business. Actually my friend Elaine in Accounts says I'm wasting my youth and that she's seen tastier things than him crawl out of a piece of Wensleydale, but then she is often crewd owing to unlike me not having any CSEs and her mother taking in actors. But however her heart is in the right place and it is a relief to have a bosom to lean on when you are alone in London as which who isn't?

But enough phillosofy and on to the more serious toppix and contravertial opinions which I earlier intimated.

Unemployment for a kick-off. I mean wouldn't you think that by now, Mrs Thatcher, of whom I have great respect for in other respects, would pass some law against it. I mean I have never had no trouble finding a job since the day I suddenly left secondary and I think its because I develloped a good interview technike where some of these young people with their green hair and black eyes would enarvate you just to look at them, not to mention the qualitey of the portpholios.

I would start stopping their national assurances and put them to work helping old ladies cross the street. And if that didn't work I would bring back conscripsion. Well, why not? A good spanking never hurt anyone as Mr Anwar is want to say.

Or even re-introduce the National Services again. I know there is no war on but the dissipline would do them good and they could help stop those dreadful women at Greenwood who keep cutting up the American soldiers barbed wire trying to get at them. Or those animal writes people who objects to fur coats because, as Mr Anwar is want to say, they can't afford them themselves. You could even send them to Northern Island to look for bombs or to the Falklands to round up sheep and build runways.

I mean sometimes it seems as though I could run this country single-handly and I think a woman has much more of an organizational capasity than which a man has. Even my boss says he can't believe the difference in his department since I got to grips with his software. Oh yes I've heard Mrs Thatcher is a woman too, but sometimes I think her attitude is a bit leniant. Also, if I were her secretary I would discretely guide her into Miss Selfridge or Top Shop instead of always Yaegars and Austin Reeds and maybe even suggest a blow dry with mousse rather than big rollers. Call me an old-fashioned columist but 'clothes makest man' and people take you much more serious if you are up to the minute.

My other hobbie-horse is the Royal Family because people in the medium always write that they have vast wealth and what her Majesty earns off her investitures and the amount of time Princess Di spends over her wardrobe. Quite frankly, it makes my blood boil! I just get vivid! So what? I'd just like to see them cricits try one week of Royalty's grewelling shedule and then watch them eat their words! All those ship launchings and sivic lunches and sitting in hot countries on elephants through long speeches by Ian Paysley with no-one to translate not to mention the Royal Variety Show. It must be completely enarvating. Yet they continue to perpetrate good-will all over the world over. Especially now Princess Di's got her hair back how it was. I got really depressed when she put it up as it made her look like all the others. I mean the only place in which I part company with her on is the childrens names. I know its her business not mine but Harry just reminds me of my Uncle Harry and the one with the red toupee that could never settle down and William well its alright if you don't shorten it but she should think how he'll get teased when he gets to big school.

Any road up I hope you've enjoyed my contra-vertial look at world issues. And remember, if you happen to agree with these thorny toppix why don't you drop a line to our editor and put in a good word for yours truly. Must dash now, Mr Anwar's in Marakesh and Elaine and me have got tickets for Barry Manilow. Mmmmmmm Marianne xxxxx

2

'*Dear Dairy*' by Marianne Plume
March 16th
So here I am a writer. And all because this gentleman Mr Demster with which I was dining at Stringfellows with, told me that my mind was more fuller than Selfridges Basement. And you know he was dead right because ever since I was at school in Doncaster my reports were always saying 'If there was a Noble Prize for daydreaming Marianne would cop it.' I have always known that one day my most secret innermost thoughts would be read for pastority.

Well imagine my surprise when this parcel arrives and Erin who's my daily and is called that because she's from Island which is the bit of England which belongs to all those TV stars like Robert Morley and Julie Walters comes into my Jacuzzi and brings me it in.

So it turns out not to be a book, which is good because I already have some, but it is a Fhilophax, which is a sort of big leather diary for the afour-mentioned inner-most thoughts and membership of the White Elephant and 'The Sanctuary' cards and everything. So this gentleman who is incidentally a famous writer himself and has his own collum in the paper that I always read on holiday has sent it to me, to write my memiors and has kindly offered to check it over for me, for 'label' I think he said.

First off I thought Mr Anwar would be mad, but then I remembered that what Mr Anwar most wants is for me to be inter-lectuall and since he has invested so much in my education already he could only be chuffed at me writing a best seller. Mr Anwar is the gentleman whom with I am seen in London, and he is a right important figure in the carpet world and has wherehouses all over the globe and in Bayswater. His family home is in Sordi Arabia which is in the Middle of the East, but he spends a lot of time in London and it gives him great sollice to escort me and supervise my devellopment as an inter-lectuall. Of course at the moment his family don't approve of me one bit and are forever sckeming to keep him home and praying. Like Mr Anwar says in Sordi Arabia you can't have so much as a vodka and lime but that someone will come and shout 'hands off'. And in Sordi Arabia they really mean it. So they're at him all the time to stay home with his wifes and his prayer mat. But Mr Anwar just loves London and shopping in Bond Street and I don't just mean the windows, so when he's in town you just don't know whether your coming or going. Cocktails at the Ritz, Dinner at the Dorchester then the Sporting Club till dawn and by the time he's seen one back to their flat he always seems to want to pop-in and see how one is doing with the Jeffery Archer book he send them to improve one's mind.

I mean I wouldn't tell Mr Anwar cos he'd be real disappointed but as my friend Elaine says 'She's had more enjoyment reading the side of an HP Sauce bottle than that crock of cr*p.' But Elaine is real common sometimes though and I despair of her ever acheeving her potential. Her language is dead course, and in so much as that she is a fool to herself.

March 17th

So today I got up real early round eleven and started on this diary in my negligee. Course nothing much has happened today except I took a call from one of the

My favourite part. Maggie in *Outside Edge*, rolling her own.

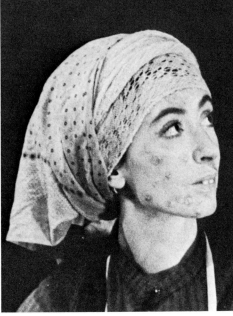

My most glamorous part. Rachel in Martin Sherman's *Messiah*, or Miss Shtetl 1675.

My most Celtic part: Kitty McShane, with Brian Murphy as Arthur Lucan, in *On Your Way, Riley*. One critic wrote it was like Barbra Streisand playing Mother Theresa.

I believe they call it a 'cameo'. As Trish, in the film *Educating Rita*.

'Are you that girl in *Agony*? — We love the woman who plays your mother!'

Back row, left to right: Peter Denyer, Simon Williams, Jeremy Bulloch.
Second row: Jan Holden, Diana Weston; front row, Peter Blake, 'Jane Lucas', Maria Charles.
The A Team, 1980!

Some founder members of the Theatre of Comedy, after 'liquid-launch'. Back row, left to right: Leslie Phillips, John Alderton, Richard Briers, Derek Nimmo and Tom Conti. Front row: Pauline Collins, Julia McKenzie, Tom Courtenay, unknown actress and Liza Goddard.

'This man has his knee on my hand!' Derek Nimmo and I as Rev. Humphrey and Miss Skillen in the Theatre of Comedy's *See How They Run*, 1983-4. ('A little more knee, Vicar?')

My husband and I . . .

gentlemen with who's aquaintance Elaine and I had struck up in Langan's Brassieres which is a restaurant a girl should really be seen in. The owner is a real scream and he will do anything for Elaine and I like sometimes he lays across our table-tops and howls like a peyote and just forces more and more champagne at us and not lets us pay our bill. No way. Elaine encourages him dreadfully but then she hasn't had the benefit of a proper finishing school such as what I did. Sometimes when I think of my poor mother doing all that escort work till the small wee hours to pay for my Lucie Clayton modeling course I could cry honestly I could just sit down and cry.

But now what was I saying in a big rush before I got digressed? Oh yes. So these gentlemen Kieth and Willy who we'd met at lunch comes over to the flat and Erin brings in some pink champagne and they show me this script which is called 'Sinopsis' which I say sounds like the operation Mr Anwar's father came over to Harley Street for with all his relatives, and well Kieth and Willy just about w*t themselves as Elaine would say — not I, since as I afourmentioned I'm afraid she is her own worst enemy. So this 'Sinopsis' is all about this sweet innocent young girl alone in London, up from Doncaster, who becomes dead interested in all this beautiful jewellery she collects from her admirers, so she finally becomes the chief owner of Hatton Gardens. So Elaine says 'Unless I'm very much mistaken someone's been bugging your maisonette for the past four years', then she tells me to consider the offer carefully since playing a part which was such a stretch from my true self would be sure to get me the BAFTA Award for character work. (Sometimes Elaine's vulgarity really gets on my bosoms!)

So I tell Willy and Kieth who are now very merry and quite giggly that I would love to read it when I've finished the Jeffery Archer, but that Mr Anwar had put an end to my promising career after I auditioned for *Oh, Calcutta!* some years back, because he turned round to me and said that what Alla had given me was sacrosanct, which sounds like the operation his mother came over to Harley Street with all her relatives for, and that he wasn't about to see his investment go on the open market, so I turned round to him and said that *Oh Calcutta!* was extremely artistic like the pictures in those museums at which he keeps wanting me to go to. But he turned round to me and put his foot down. I would have stuck up for myself but for him turning round and giving me these fabulous sweet diamond eardrops, and well I suppose it was just sentimentall but I gave up the goat. So Kieth and Willy were dead sympathetic and lay there making real groaning noises of understanding, so I told them that afterwards I'd seen in an airplane magazine a picture of the world and there really *was* a place called Calcutta!! But without the 'Oh!' Then Elaine and Kieth and Willy all seemed to be laughing at me which was exseptionaly rude since interlectuall though I am becoming, I can't be expected to know the name of every small place in Yeurope!

March 18th

So today I am feeling quite depressed and may have to go to Burns in George Street to be cheered up because I always think that a new evening dress and a re-style with mousse can give a girl a real lift especially if it is beaded. So I left Erin to get a man in to patch up the water bed and told her to get Kieth and Willy out from under it and back to their club. And I told Ricci while he was blowing me that I was going to consentrate soley on my career as a writer now and on getting more educated cos if Bertram Russell could wright *Educating Rita* then I'm sure I could do the same with *Educating Marianne* and frankly not nearly be so common. Insidentally I've seen Michael Cain in Langans and he really does look like that. And Ricci said wasn't it Anita Loose who said 'Writing is easy because you do not have to learn or practise' and I said 'Ooh, that could have been me talking' and I felt less depressed which I suppose was sychological, but I made up my mind to meet Ms Loose next time she comes up to town because I feel sure we'd have a large amount in common — Ricci said she had a fringe as well.

July 10th

I have not written any since March I know, but my felt tip has completely dried up and I

No Holds Bard

My relationship with William Shakespeare is best described as non-meaningful. By that, I mean he doesn't bother me and I don't bother him. (I'm not wild about Bacon either, but that's purely on religious grounds.) Suffice to say, that had Roy Plomley's over-populated island ever yielded up its customary offering of the Bible and the Complete Works of Shakespeare, I'd have been hard-pressed not to trade them in for a couple of Tom Sharpes, a George Eliot and a few back numbers of *Private Eye*.

It's my own fault, I know. I just don't try. Maybe I've had some bad experiences. (I think I'm going to cry.) If I took the trouble really to understand the problems of Pericles, Prince of Tyre, and really shared the Merry Wives of Windsor's merriment, then this heresy wouldn't be happening and I wouldn't be nodding off during the trumpet fanfare preceding the plays.

Look, I'm not daft. I know he's good. Everybody says so. My beloved English teacher at school said so. She was besotted. He was 'Elvis-the-King', wordwise, was William at our school. But, although I was desperate for her approval and would have eaten my bicycle for a part in the school play, I just couldn't share Miss Nicholson's love for the Avon Laddy. Why? Well, at the risk of sounding too esoteric — the plots didn't hold up, the funny bits weren't, and fancy rhyming 'on the water' with 'What's the matter'! Now I'm older and wiser, I realize that the weak plots and the low comedy don't matter (sic) — it's the brilliance of the language and the emotional insights etc. which raise it to genius level. All of which is fine, but doesn't help the poor sod playing Touchstone, who has to prance around the stage with a bell on his head, practically killing his mother for a laugh.

(I've had a similar problem over the years with opera. When

Don Giovanni and his manservant change identities (well, they just change cloaks, actually), in spite of the fact that Don Giovanni is six foot two and built like a brick maison-de-merde, and his servant three foot one and built like R2D2, everyone on stage is completely fooled. I have to bite the insides of my cheeks to stop myself shouting out: 'Excuse me! Er...it's not 'im, love...it's the little fat feller...save yourself the bother...' Three intervals later, the difference I spotted in Act 1 slowly begins to dawn on the Diva. Who then sings about it for an hour or two.)

I once appeared in a production of *The Merchant of Venice* in a provincial repertory company. It was a wet Thursday matinee, and the average age of the audience was about a hundred and seventy-five. They all chatted loudly and incessantly about the weather, their operations, and the story so far. Those on stage struggled manfully on, in wrinkled tights, lashings of mascara and heavy rouge. And that was only the men! At one point, a particularly virulent deaf-aid in the centre stalls picked up the local taxi-rank on its wavelength...*Bassanio*: 'But hear thee, Gratiano, Thou art too wild, too rude and bold of voice...' '*Roger, Roger, pick up at Green Man, account 74, Roger and Out,*' thundered a character hitherto unknown in the play, name of Roger. Exit Bassanio, clutching sides.

Later, during Portia's 'the-quality-of-mercy' speech, came the following exchange: *Portia*: 'It droppeth as the gentle rain from heaven...' *Old Lady in Pakamac in Row G*: ''Ere! Did you just put your finger in my ear?' Puzzled hiatus from cast and audience alike.

'It is twice blessed,' Portia soldiered on, 'It blesseth him that gives and him that takes.'

'What the bleedin' ell would I put my finger in your ear for?' demanded the old gentleman on the Pakamac's right. Not unreasonably, I felt.

'Well, *somebody* did,' she snapped, in a tone that demanded justice. But by now, the judiciaries on stage were rolled up into small balls, vainly trying to hide behind Shylock and emitting painful, high-pitched squeaks.

Let's face it, one generally tries to avoid what one knows one doesn't do well. Or I do. I'm more than happy to leave the great roles (or, in my case, roll-ups, see above) to those who are better equipped for it than I am. But, whenever the classics raise their noble heads, I grovel my acceptance and reveal my startling ineptitude at poncing about in panniers, twittering 'But soft, my liege, thou hast a goodly wattle', or the like.

The reason for this defensive preamble is that throughout my formative years at LAMDA studying to be the artist so aptly described as resembling a 'flamingo carrying a tea chest' and 'two yards of spaghetti overdosing on LSD' (and jolly pleased to be so), I was a National Theatre addict. Now, as you can divide Londoners into North of the River and South of the River types, so you can divide most actors into National Theatre and RSC types. I fitted firmly into the first camp. And why not? It was the golden era of Olivier's reign at the Old Vic. From the gods I saw Maggie Smith in *The Recruiting Officer*, Edith Evans in *Hay Fever*, Robert Stephens in *The Royal Hunt of the Sun*, Albert Finney and Geraldine McEwan in *A Flea In Her Ear*. This was more than acting. This was a feeling of arrival, security — coming home — which I only felt one other time in my life. And I married him.

In that season I guess I metaphorically married the Old Vic. At any rate, I gave away my heart. And it was a jealous heart. I resented the successes of the RSC at the Aldwych and Stratford as much as I revelled in the triumphs of the Vic. In 1970 I got my chance. I joined the Vic for the prestigious role of the Second Randy Lady in a musical about William Blake called *Tyger*, by Adrian Mitchell. For my audition before Michael Blakemore and John Dexter I sang Janis Joplin's 'Oh Lord, won't you buy me a Mercedes Benz' accompanying myself on thigh. I was in. There followed my happiest and most memorable three years — there I learned it all. Or so I thought. *The Front Page*, *The National Health*, *Long Day's Journey into Night*, understudying *Jumpers* and working a 13-hour day was pure 'Hi diddly de, an Actor's life for me'.

I did Shakespeare, too — I played a weird and warty witch in a production of *Macbeth*, where the actor playing Macbeth was never seen again after the first night. Which is tricky. I mean, it leaves a large-ish hole in the play and makes Lady Macbeth into a premature widow with some pretty one-sided conversations. I didn't blame him for going. It was the costume that did it. He was a stocky sort of chap and his Lady was particularly lofty. The period chosen was Jacobean. He wore wide knee-breeches, a padded tunic and a tall hat and looked like a Diddy Man. She wore an enormously wide farthingale, high shoes and an exaggerated neck-ruff. As they made their first entrance into the royal court, they bore a remarkable resemblance to a cruet. Even under my grey fright-wig and preponderance of hairy warts, I could sense his discomfort. The following night, he fled the country, leaving nothing behind him but a telegram and a pool of sweat.

In the same year the RSC asked me to audition for Celia in Buzz Goodbody's production of *As You Like It*, starring Eileen Atkins. I was flattered. Here was an actress I did not consider 'typically RSC material' — joining the company at the same time as me — a woman director who would not use bullying techniques and a part which was small enough and possibly characterful enough for me to wrestle away my Shakespeare demons in a quiet way, out in the country. Or so I thought — again.

I'd met Buzz and we got on well. Our mutual neuroses complemented each other, and Eileen had looked me over and seemed to approve. We shared suburban roots, a mutual distaste for pomposity, and an outrageous sense of humour. But the final acceptance of me could only come from John Barton. He'd never heard of me or seen my work. I got the impression that this worthy academic director lived in a circular Gothic, wood-panelled study with revolving book-lined walls, researching the inside leg measurement of Shakespeare's gardener. I was ushered into the presence. He stood up — tall, bearded and scholarly.

'I'm sorry, Miss-er- [quick glance through spectacles at dossier] Lipman — but I'm unfamiliar with your work. Could you possibly do a short extract of everything you've done?'

I was tempted to reply, as Athene Seyler is reputed to have done, 'Do you mean today?' Instead I said, 'Oh — certainly.'

Some hours later, having condensed the previous six years into a sort of 'Clap Hands, here comes Hull's answer to Sammy Davies Jnr., in drag with serious intentions', I staggered out of the building, convinced in some way that I'd just fought a truly celestial battle for survival.

I left my husband of six weeks and headed Warwickshire-wards. I moved into delightful lodgings in the Old Town, with beamed ceiling and matching landlady, and turned my attentions to Bardomania. The thing about company life away from home is that you either throw yourself into it body and soul, which means that life revolves around the theatre, the Dirty Duck pub and the greenroom noticeboard, or you lead a fairly solitary life in a tight Tory town where Shakespeare Rules, OK or not.

A conversation at the local bookshop. After close scrutiny: 'Aren't you the little girl who's giving her Celia this year?'

'Oh, yes.'

'Of course, *we* remember Suzman's Celia... quite extraordinary.' (Six syllables.) 'Well, jolly good luck to you dear.'

'Thank you,' I murmured (screaming). 'Do you have a copy of Molly Parkin's *Up and Coming*?'

I suppose I tried to fit in and couldn't. Rehearsals were a bit tense. The relationship between Rosalind and Orlando wasn't gelling. The director worried at it and chewed her hair a lot, but hadn't the strength or experience to deal with it. I was as blocked as I had been playing Dogberry at school, and only Richard Pasco's Jacques, lyrically aloof, seemed to grow daily — as a performance in rehearsal should. My feeling that a red pencil should be put through all of the low comedy in Shakespeare grew stronger. Nothing dates faster than topical satire, and I defy Les Dawson to get a laugh out of the old Mustard/Knight/Pancakes routine which Touchstone launches into as they enter the Forest of Arden.

One night, the actor playing Touchstone went so far as to fix an alarm clock into his jacket (it was a modern dress production), set to ring in each of his 'Marry, said the knight' punchlines. On the third ring he felt sure that the audience would roar with laughter. Comedic Rule of Three, see? His alarm rang three times. Nobody laughed except Rosalind and Celia, who unaccountably clutched their stomachs and wept silently.

Now for the set. The Forest of Arden — this being the RSC — was represented by a large, circular white carpet, on which all the action took place, and a ceiling full of long tubes of steel of varying lengths tied up by string, and capable of shifting to any number of positions to represent either a forest, a court or a ceiling full of steel tubes. Never has the line 'So *this* is the Forest of Arden?' had a more comic intonation. They swung in the slightest draught of air and made a strange wailing noise which I often used to think was me. One night,.Phoebe was almost decapitated by a falling rod. William S. made no provision in his lines for such an execution.

The costumes. The designs were duly laid out, and the ladies — who ranged from ultra-thin to monumental, were to wear dresses which had no waistline but fell from under the bust, Empire fashion. As I have a smallish head this is the one style guaranteed to make me look like a polythene bag full of water. I requested a waistline, to be told emphatically that none of the productions that year sported waistlines. It was not 'house-style'. My suggestion that if a style made you look like a *house*, it was time to call the removal men in, fell on half-timbered ears. Finally, Eileen and I both provided our own dresses. I actually wore my Gina Fratini wedding dress and looked like your typical Jewish bride at the court of the King of Arden.

Suffice to say that Orlando put his shoulder out during rehearsals of the wrestling scene and was never seen again. The play opened with David Suchet as Orlando and notices which were so mixed they cancelled each other out and only Richard Pasco escaped with his honour intact. For me it was a morbid experience much lightened by the jokey presence of Charlie Keating as Oliver, and of Eileen herself. On one occasion she swears I opened my mouth to bemoan the cruel fate of my beloved cousin Rosalind and instead said, 'Please release me.' I have no memory of the incident.

Throughout the season of three and a half months I never once met Trevor Nunn or Terry Hands, or re-met Mr Barton. When I left, Mr Nunn wrote me a note expressing his disappointment that I had not thrown myself into more plays and therefore more company life. I think my reply could well have cost me a deal of work. No matter.

Ten years later, almost to the day, I was recalled to the RSC. My memory played rose-coloured tricks on me and I went to meet Bill Alexander for the part of Elmire in *Tartuffe*, and Ron Daniels for a part in David Edgar's *May Days*. Mr Alexander was keen for me to play in his production. Mr Daniels patently thought I looked far too suburban to play a revolutionary. Creative casting lives!

I joined the company at the Barbican. One of the first sights I saw after groping my way around the rabbit warren which constitutes back stage, was the Blinded Gloucester banging his bloodied head against the jammed lift doors and cursing the 'f---ing machine' which refused to take him the six flights back to his dressing-room. An ominous chill ran down my spine.

Once in rehearsal it became apparent that there was no room for someone like me, somewhere like that. Everyone seemed prepared to sit around for *hours* discussing useless backroom research, invention was at its lowest ebb, and the cast and director seemed to be waiting for the star to do his extra-ordinary 'thing'. Once he began to do that, at the expense of the credibility of the rest of the characters, they could all relax. Meanwhile, my brand of naturalistic 'comedy' was a dead loss — although occasionally the leading man confessed he couldn't work with me because I was 'too funny'. This had the required effect of making me as funny as an attack of shingles, and it was clear that for the sake of the show, I should pack up the bags beneath my eyes and leave. The show, needless to say, had rave reviews, as did Sher's performance and Bill Alexander's direction. My feelings were vindicated when I saw it. Tartuffe, the imposter, the charlatan or the saint, was found on the table with Elmire, tights down and a hairy bottom practically in the audience's face. Her husband, Orgon, hidden under the table, had then to come out and say: 'I saw you *kiss* my wife.'

Naturally enough, since then I've recycled my tights and tabard and donated my bodkin to Help the Aged. However, last year the director Elijah Moshinsky asked to see me for the role of the Princess of France in *Love's Labour's Lost*. 'And don't start telling him you're terrible in Shakespeare, or why doesn't he ask Jane Lapotaire,' chided my agent/second Jewish mother (like I need *two*).

'I am and why doesn't he?' was my retort. As I'd told Jack I wasn't even going to look at the play before the meeting, I read it at 3.30 am, understood very little of it and liked less than I understood. As for the Princess — well, it was OK — but no funny walks, no regional accent, no pratfalls, nothing of interest at all to a neo-classicist such as I.

The interview went something like this: Lipman, dressed

somewhat over-casually in beige with not too much make-up for realism and glasses kept on to show 'period' feel, pokes head around door of BBC office. E. Moshinsky, a delightful fellow of antipodean derivation, greets me and asks me to sit down. Lipman, still standing, goes into quasi-Les Dawson routine. 'Were you thinking of setting the play in Barnsley?'

He: 'Why don't you sit down and I'll explain why I think you'd be wonderful in the part...'

She: 'You're setting it in Tel Aviv and you need a Jewish princess?'

He: 'I think you're right for it. Have you thought of what a great part it is?'

She: 'I think you're deranged or on a suicide mission — have you thought of Jane Lapotaire?'

He: 'The great thing about doing Shakespeare on the television is that nobody sees it.'

She (taking off glasses and sitting down): 'I'll do it.'

And here I eat my iambic pentameters, for what followed was a terrific experience. So careful was Elijah with the pastoral settings, the Watteau-like costumes, the soft, rosy lighting and the emotional content of each scene, that even *I* came out from behind my clenched fingers, watched it, and felt chirpy. He was meticulous with details. Spent three hours with me at the wig-maker's persuading me to have the hair off my face. 'Believe me,' I pleaded, 'lemme have a fringe or I'll look like Emu.'

'Believe me,' he was adamant, 'fringes were non gratis in the Court of Navarre.'

'Believe me,' I persisted, 'the King was kinky for fringes and loathed Emus.'

'No fringe, you'll look terrific.'

'A few wispy bits?'

'Not even one.' Just before we went into the studio he told me, 'You know, you have one good side and one bad.'

'For God's sake don't tell me which is which or I'm finished Princessing for keeps.'

To his credit, he didn't. Just quietly shot me from the good side and made me look as posh as all get out. 'Ravishing' in the words of one of our more discerning, myopic critics. Another chid me for my dodgy 'S' sounds. 'Do Printhethes lithp?' he wrote. I felt compelled to reply. 'You are absolutely right,' I wrote 'Printhethes do not lisp. Neither do K-K-Kings s-s-stutter.'

Actually, he had a point. In my effort to speak the Queen's English (or certainly the Princess's), I became a bit 'careful' and as the old Northern twang retreated, the tongue got shorter. Speaking of the Queen's English forces me to report that 'Royalty' only talks like that because they were Hanoverian. Yes — with a German accent. All that 'Eow, neow whey deon't we geow to mey Hyse' business is a direct result of the Hanoverians' inability to speak English vizout a broad Cherman accent. This fashion was, then, out of deference, copied by the Court, the aristocracy, the gentry and all six readers of *Tatler*.

English in Will Shakespeare's day would have surely been more of a Midland — even Brummy — sound, which explains some of his weirder rhymes; e.g. want with enchant (not, you'll note, enchahnt), tongues with belongs; room with home; prove with love — which proves my case, doesn't it, luv? Or did he just not have Pam Ayres' ear for a foin rhoim?

The most important point to remember about Shakespeare is that he was a writer working on commission and constantly to a deadline, not unlike doing *Coronation Street*. He was also an actor, with enough sensibility to realize that King Lear has to be off for long enough to have a change of rags, a pint of stout and a lie down before the final act. So, he put in enough sub-plot to cover it. Not a hack, but a practised and practical jobbing author with one eye on the box office receipts, and the other on the culture. And this was pre-Lord Gowrie. I like to think that if the Bard were alive today he'd be out at the beach in Beverly Hills, tapping out 'High Concept' Movies of the Week on his Wang Word Processor, up to his ruff in cocaine. His blockbusters would include *Much Ado About Zilch, Coriolasshole, Uptight as Andronicus* and his musical of Richard III, *I Gotta Hunch*. Meanwhile, Anne Hathaway would be doing aerobics by the pool, the Earl of Southampton would be taking a meeting with Michael Jackson in the jacuzzi, and the Dark Lady would be running a gay bank on Sunset and Vine.

It occurs to me that no one does Shakespeare after the manner of, say, Beryl Cook. 'Twould be fabulous for *A Midsummer Night's Dream*. All those smooth, fat-faced fairies with National

Health specs and huge knockers. Or an L.S. Lowry *Macbeth* in cloth caps, clogs and chip butties on the Blasted Heath. Is it too late. I wonder? Or too early?

A Potted Life

WHENEVER I FIND myself at the Walthamstow/Hounslow/
Norwood Friendship club, I start my speech with the
announcement that I don't make speeches. I follow this up by
explaining that I'll probably talk a little about my background,
and possibly my foreground, then throw the discussion open to
questions of even the most intimate nature. I then make a speech
for about an hour and a half, leaving four minutes for questions
before the arrival of the tea and sponge cakes.

Always I'm greeted at the door by several short, elderly
people who insist that I remember them to my parents, whom
they all seem to have met in Benidorm. All their names seem to
be Minnie, Manny or Moishe, and they invariably tell me I'm
too thin by half, not as good-looking as my mother, or a dead
ringer for their sister's cousin's niece with the hiatus hernia.
This is called 'running the gaunt-look'.

The organizer/chairperson of the organization imperiously
removes my friendly fans, and it's at this point I hear the magic
words 'a cup of tea'. Hearing is not seeing, however, and I must
resign myself to the cup of tea being a mirage for the next two
hours. It finally arrives with the autograph hunters, and I watch
it grow colder, browner, and finally develop a skin as I sign old
raffle tickets and buff envelopes: 'To Rochelle and Dominic with
best wishes, Maureen Lipman'. 'It's not for me, it's for my
grand-daughter, I never watch the BBC.'

If all this sounds churlish, it's not meant to. I generally have a
wonderful time at these functions, and feel a real affection for the
audience. Not all of them, but most of them.

Once I did two in a day — one at a small community centre in
East London, and one at the Glaziers' Hall in the City. The
contrast could not have been more marked. At the first, the
audience was rapt and responsive, even including the dear old
biddy in the front row who rose and sat down intermittently

181

whilst emitting a high, vibrating hum. I got quite used to timing my speech around her hums, but the rest of the audience didn't and insisted, loudly and rather unkindly, 'that she didn't ought to have been allowed in'. They were actually being embarrassed on my behalf — which was totally unnecessary, as I thought she was a riot. Anyway, they were a delightful house and I was proud to hand out the raffle prizes, and see their eyes widen with delight at winning anything, anything at all.

From here I changed into the well-worn ball-gown, gathered up Jack in his even weller-worn tuxedo, and sped to the other 'do'. Here the eyes widened with something more like disbelief, since the tickets for the fashion show/dinner were £250 a head (or £250 a 'tochas' — depending on which way you looked at it), and this house wanted their money's worth.

They sat in bored couples, dripping Armani, Arpeggio and 'arf-'eartedness; too rich to smile and too bored to clap. The fashion show brought a smattering of applause and a plethora of yawns. My speech went down like Kenny Everett's at the Tory party rally and, by the look of things at the dinner, the food went down the same way.

On an ordinary day, I'd have turned the other cheek, but today, after the warmth of the East Londoners, I decided to cheek the other turns. 'All right you lot,' I heard myself yell down the mike as raffle time reared up, 'stop picking at the smoked salmon — you've got a freezer full of it at home — and put your money where your mouths are. It's no good sitting there with short arms, long pockets and miserable bloody faces — go on, smile! See if it cracks your Ultra-Bronze!'

The raffle prizes were a £4,000 kitchen and crates of vintage wine, as opposed to a jar of bathsalts and a Toblerone — and it was the contrast, I suppose, which did for me. I seem to remember rows of stunned faces, reminiscent of the audience at *Springtime For Hitler*, and the sound of one hand clapping as I resumed my seat.

Then there are the intellectual gatherings, where they don't want jokes or self-deprecating stories, they want serious content. These are the functions where they've covered themselves by asking two or three celebrities, in the hope that not all of them will cancel. You then find yourself seated by a well-honed £950-an-hour-act, against which your stories of judging the 'Pub

Garden of the Year Competition' when your child had Belgian measles, pall into insignificance.

Of course, we professionals should be accustomed to performing with ease in front of our peers, but I'm here to tell you — we're not. Nothing chills the soul like the front-of-house manager visiting your dressing-room before a show to say: 'Do you want to know who's in tonight?' No, of course I bloody don't! Who? For the rest of the evening your erstwhile naturalistic performance becomes a parody of itself as you strive to recreate your notices for the benefit of an onlooker.

Once, after a performance of *The Front Page* at the Old Vic in 1973, in which I played Molly Molloy, the first of many 'tarts with hearts', a backstage visitor enthused, 'I just loved the things you did with your feet!'

'What things?' I demanded. Tartly.

'Oh, come on, you know what I mean — the foot business!'

I was baffled, frankly, and spent the following twelve performances bent double, playing the part of a tart with a bunion, as I gazed unceasingly down at my own feet trying to catch a glimpse of what they were doing in front of my back, and without my prior knowledge.

Acting requires absorption, but not self-absorption and, in the actor's mind, the question must always be 'Why am I doing this?', not 'How am I doing it?' That road leads to self-indulgence, and we've all seen enough of that from the West End to the local 'art.-dram. soc.' to want our ten quid back and a lift straight back to the video shop.

'How did you start to be an actress?' A voice from the hall. Thank you, dear, you've just saved me from pontificating.

It was very easy. I think I started acting even before I was on solids. I was performing from the age of four, by the simple virtue of being nailed to the sideboard by my mother, an actress manqué if ever there was one, and encouraged or coerced to do Alma Cogan impersonations. 'You dree-e-eamboat, you lovable dre-e-eamboat. The kisses you gave me ...'

'Roll your eyes, Maureen,' beamed my mother, no doubt anticipating the moment when she got to sing 'Everything's coming up roses'. 'Do the laugh in your voice!' and mock and roll I did — right around the clock. And thus was born a minor local celebrity, the sort of precocious infant I would loathe to

pieces nowadays, if I didn't know from first-hand experience
how hard it was not to 'perform'. When the act, once
encouraged, just bubbled out of you; when the people laughed
and clapped for more. No doubt I felt for the first time bigger
and brighter than my bigger and brighter elder brother.

There was never any doubt about my vocation. Nun-like,
with some prodigiously bad habits, I soon increased my
repertoire of songs and impersonations and, by incorporating
most of the neighbourhood children into a sort of backing group,
I was soon staging regular shows in the back garage. Sketches,
poems and parodies were added, and the show usually ended
emotionally with the cast singing the National Anthem, whilst
standing to attention, and saluting. A salutary experience for all
ten members of the audience.

Once at secondary school, I was clearly the lucky one.
Unremarkable in appearance, being undersized, sallow-
skinned and with a bit too much ratio of nose to face, I was
equally average in all academic subjects barring English (at
which I occasionally shone) and Maths (at which I was so
appalling I was forced to cheat in my mock 'O' levels and still
got 18%). I was lucky because I knew what I was going to be. So
when the dreaded Careers Officer — God, that must be even
more of a joke these days — came to call, I was in and out in a
flash. 'An actress?' she smirked, looking me up and down. 'Well,
it's a very hard profession, you'll need something to fall back on,
you know.' I know. I know? I'd heard nothing but 'falling
backwards' ever since I first mentioned my ambition. It was
always delivered with a faint look of pity and disparagement.
'I'll just have to fall back on the casting couch,' said the sassy
thirteen-year-old with the glasses and the brace. (I've been
awaiting that casting couch ever since! Mostly I sit on it while
they tell me their casting problems.) Still, many of my friends
ended up in banks or offices simply because their ambition
hadn't reached the simmering stage when the CO chose to call.

My big moment came whilst playing Dr Faustus in the school
play. Yes, it was an all-girls' school. At fourteen, I was a
committed, if not entirely convincing mediaeval scholar and,
save the somewhat giggly moment when I had to kiss Helen of
Troy (Susan Downing, a natural blonde) and say, 'Is this the
face that launched a thousand ships?', I was a credit to Miss

Nicholson's direction. For this performance I received my first
and best-ever review in the *Hull Daily Mail*: 'Maureen Lipman.
Remember that name, for one day you will see it alongside that
of Tom Courtenay and other well-known Hull stars.' It's the only
good review I've ever remembered, let alone kept. All the rude
ones are engraved on my gall bladder.

What I chiefly remember, though, is the feeling the morning
after the last night of the play. Plays usually had a three-night
run, and going back to being 'ordinary' again was dire. All
lessons; no rehearsals; no coming in late the next morning; no
sick feeling in the pit of the stomach at tea-time. All this coupled
with the feeling that somewhere, someone was determined to
put me back in my place for fear 'it' had all gone to my head.
Which, of course, it had!

Nowadays when a long run of a play has ended, I feel only
relief. That first evening at home, feet up and mindless telly on
by 6.30, is the showbusiness equivalent of sitting in a Radox bath
with a piece of water melon.

When the time came to apply to university, I filled in all the
appropriate forms — including the question 'Which career do
you wish to pursue?' and the relevant answer 'Actress'. In spite
of my three decent 'A' levels, none of them would even interview
me. Turning out thespians was not part of their brief.
Undaunted, I applied to a couple of drama schools. The Rose
Bruford School kept me there all day. I'd travelled down with
my mother, of course. The prospect of her seventeen-year-old
daughter getting on a train all alone filled her with a dread that
could only be assuaged by her company. Somehow, at the time,
it didn't bother me. I think I was secretly relieved — large drip
that I was.

We arrived, along with two hundred other hopefuls, to spend
a fraught six hours singing for our supper to the grand
matriarchal shape of Miss Bruford herself. At one point, I seem
to remember being asked to be a cup and saucer. Using every
trace of imagination, I placed one hand on my waist and rocked
about a bit. Later, all two hundred of us were told to be slaves
begging for our freedom — from guess who? Miss Bruford
herself! She sat on a rostrum at one end of the hall — the slaves
set off from the other. We implored, we begged, we crawled on
our bellies on the face of the earth. In short, we humiliated

ourselves, shamelessly, for the chance of a place in the academy.
At the time I was furious — in retrospect, it was a fair example of
the life to come.

At LAMDA, life was granda. A team of human beings
including the actress, Andrée Melly, heard my 'Lady Percy',
laughed at my 'Sabina' from *The Skin of Our Teeth* (complete
with imaginary flying props) and, without further ado, I was
'in'. I met Andrée recently and she told me she had never
forgotten my audition. I was thrilled as she went on to describe
to someone how I had done Titania from *A Midsummer Night's
Dream*! I'll never forget it... I hadn't the heart to tell her I was
the one who had done Lady Percy! LAMDA was two and a half
years of spade-work, some of which has remained forever, some
of which disappeared without trace the moment I scarcely heard
it. On the whole, it accomplished what all colleges of further
education *must* accomplish — in that it taught me how to live
away from my parents.

Not, I hasten to add, for fear you should detect signs of fast-
approaching maturity (which I'm still awaiting), away from
chaperones. Far from it. Through the *Jewish Chronicle*, I had
found digs with two sisters in Barons Court. Still living in the flat
of their childhood, they were now well into their middle years.
One went to market, one stayed home. It didn't take them too
long to disapprove of me. As I learned to stay out late in the Earls
Court Road, picking wax off candles and discussing the vagaries
of tongue and jaw relaxation, so the sisters learned to put the
dinner back in the oven and purse their lips. Every time I
arrived home I felt more and more like a drunk in a Donald
McGill postcard, and I quickly began scouring the *Evening
Standard* for flat-shares.

In pursuit of one such flat, I entered one of a row of telephone
kiosks in Earls Court Tube Station one Saturday morning. The
phone immediately began to ring. Being young and very green
I picked it up. 'Er— Hello— Earls Court. This is the Earls
Court—'

'Hello,' came a West Indian accent. 'Can I speak to Mr
MacNamara, please?'

'Er, I'm awfully sorry, but this is Earls Court Tube Station.'

'Oh, well, in that case, would you like to hold the end of my
penis?'

Quick as a flash (so to speak) I replied (or I like to think I replied),' No thanks, I've just put one out.' Slammed down the phone and left. As I closed the kiosk door, I saw a grinning face, and what's more, saw a lot of what the grinning face had in its hand.

I fled back to the LAMDA green-room and ordered a coffee from Joe, the Polish caretaker. 'Sugar, honey?' he said, as he would continue to say for two and a half years, in spite of my negative reply.

Nobody seemed remotely impressed with my story — just an everyday happening in SW1. Soon afterwards I moved, with fellow student, Lesley Joseph, into one half of a grim conversion off the Earls Court Road. We shared it with a student eye doctor called Rabinowitz, who had the endearing habit of taking out his eye and resting it on his cheek. When Issy said, 'I'll keep an eye out for you', he meant it. His scoring rate with the ladies was something phenomenal — particularly considering his huge girth, pallid complexion and eye-catching habits. How did he do it? One day he confided to Lesley that he only had three months to live. Soon afterwards we moved out rather than clean the oven, so we will never know whether his terminal condition was a terminal condition or simply one of the wickedest pulling acts in the business — a trompe l'oeil even.

We were an interesting mix that year at LAMDA. Annabel Leventon had been to Oxford, worked in OUDS, had a boyfriend, and a sophistication that I revered. She even had a flat of her own in which she gave Dinner Parties — divine decadence indeed. Anna Calder-Marshall had the face of an Hellenic goddess, unique talent and the instant adoration of every member of the staff. Philip Sayer from Swansea was my love and my brother from the day we met. He too had a veneer (thin) of sophistication culled from a season working at Swansea rep, and his repertoire of camp phraseology was music to my suburban ears. 'Get you, dear!' and 'Vada the bona bats, love', seemed to me the language of a very select club, and I soon learned to shriek and grimace along with the best of them. Of course, by the time I'd mastered 'the parlare', as it was called, it had become, or maybe always was, the language of wardrobe assistants and wig-makers. I told you about the 'tarts with hearts' — well, alongside them I played mothers, grandmothers, nosey neighbours and best friends who never got the man. It was difficult to find an agent on the basis of these parts and, as the end of the last term came near, the atmosphere grew tense with massed neuroses. Annabel was seeing Peter Watkins about his film *Prejudice* and Anna Calder-Marshall, Franco Zeffirelli about *Romeo and Juliet*. I'll never forget her entrance into the common-room after seeing him. Everyone wanted to know how she got on. No one could bring themselves to ask. Finally, someone did. Me. In her beautiful, husky voice, lovely face all aglow, she enthused, 'Oh, Mo, he was *so* kind, really. He took one's face in his hands and told one, one had a special quality and one felt so—' 'Anna darling, did one get the f---ing part!?' This with all the fervour of the best friend who never got the man.

The week before leaving, I had a brainwave. Armed with a bag of sixpences for the phone, and a list of every casting director who'd seen the end-of-term shows, I went down to the basement phone, rang each one of them direct, and lied, appallingly. 'Hello, I do hope you don't mind my ringing you, but I'm in a bit of a dilemma. My name is Maureen Lipman and you may have seen me playing the aged mother in Tyrone Guthrie's *The Top of the Ladder*.' (Pause for comment, none came.) 'Er, what it is, you see, is that I've been approached by a documentary film company which is making a film about a young actress leaving drama school to go to her first job. Now I've got the part but' — pause for effect — 'only if I have a job to go to — if you see what I mean.' (Shorter pause.) 'Er— so, if you could see your way to giving me one, a job, I mean, in any shape or form, well then, it would be great for me and also — er — very good publicity for your theatre . . .' Mostly what I then got was a sharp click and the dialling tone; but a couple of intrepid (or gullible) directors did see fit to interview me, and to my amazement, Giles Havergal (showing early signs of the ability to step in where angels fear to tread which has put Glasgow so firmly on the theatrical map) agreed to cast me in the part of Nancy in Ann Jellicoe's play, *The Knack*, at the Watford Palace Theatre. I was in business, and you know what they say there's no business like it — I was employed. In a play! Three men and me, and an Equity card at the end of it all. Life was rosy.

With the exception of one thing. Where was I to find a fake

documentary film crew, plus equipment in time for Monday's rehearsal? The problem was a weighty one. I mulled it over for three sleepless nights and four sleepy days. Finally, I came up with the solution. When asked, I would reply, with a blankly challenging look, '*What* documentary film crew?' Strangely enough, Giles never asked the question. Each day I braced myself for it. Each day we just rehearsed. One day the play opened, one day it closed and the question just never arose. Much later, when I was a veteran of three plays at the Palace (including a panto in which I played the Fairy of the Ring, *balanced* on a pogo stick, in blue hair and tinted specs), I finally put it to him. 'Giles, did you ever wonder what happened to my documentary film-makers?' 'No, dear,' he replied, sagely. 'It was perfectly apparent from the day we met that the whole concoction was a tissue of lies, but I decided to give you the part for chutzpah.' 'Chutzpah' is best defined as a small boy peeing through someone's letter box, then ringing the doorbell to ask how far it went.

Whilst finishing off at LAMDA I had been approached by the agent, Al Parker, who had seen me playing the classic role of a nine-months-pregnant French whore in *Mandrake*, a musical version of *Mandragola*. I turned up in his impressively panelled office wearing matching hat, dress, coat and boots in shades of toning beige. I looked like a buff envelope. He sat by the window, a Hitchcock-like figure, and, glancing up from his type-written notes (red and green 2 ply), 'Well, Miss [glance at notes] Liprian, I caught your performance last night, I think you're very talented — take off your coat and show me your figure.' I took off one layer of beige and showed him another. 'Okay, you could lose a pound or two.' (In those halcyon days I weighed $10\frac{1}{2}$ stone and was a big girl in the chest department. In fact, in Restoration plays which required corsets I was well known for being able to paint a coach and four disappearing into the horizon of my cleavage. Alas, two children and a decade of working in comedy have whittled it all down to a sort of scrag end.) 'Now,' he continued, 'let's talk nose jobs.' As you can imagine, I balked. Bridled visibly, even. To the extent that exactly fifteen minutes later I was seated in the Harley Street room of Dr Percy Jayes with a compass on my nose, bandying words like rhinoplasty (which presumably means having your horn remodelled), and post-surgical bruising. It was only after arranging an appointment and leafing through a sort of 'Which Nose?' that the thought struck me that it might be less painful to change my agent than to change my nose. I left Harley Street, and Cyrano-like I've remained ever since, for better or worse.

One good turn Al did for me was to send me to an interview for the film *Up The Junction*. This gritty, highly controversial documentary-drama had caused a sensation when it was shown on television and, although the film version would opt for tinsel rather than grit, it had to be a highly commercial proposition. The director was Peter Collinson. According to Mrs Al Parker (the actress Margaret Johnstone, who like every English actress of the 'fifties spoke the language 'as it hyed to be speyoken'), he would only interview genuine cockneys, so that was how I must present myself.

Having never met one, this posed a problem. Had she said Australian, South African, Portuguese or Polish, I could have hared straight back to the Earls Court Road and called in any café or dental surgery. But a real cockney! In London? Now that was tricky; know what I mean?

I was lucky to find one in the LAMDA common-room. Her name was Celia Quicke and she put me strite roit away with a few basic vowel sounds and a diffident, slightly aggressive manner. I've always been able to absorb people's mannerisms — it's more of a trick than a talent — and it got me through the interview with the casting director and Peter Collinson, a man very much in the Swinging Sixties mould. He was tall and lean with a craggy face, open floral shirt and the manner of a well-to-do cockney barrow-boy made good. Which indeed he was.

Somehow he bought my act, and with it, the Professor Higgins appeal of showing the film-making ropes to this gawky innocent. The part was mine. Adrienne Posta and I were to play sisters, Liz Frazer our mother, and it was a thirteen-week shoot. My cup runneth bleedin' over. I moved into Battersea, a flat beneath a dentist's surgery, and would leave at six o'clock every morning for the glamorous locations of Lavender Hill and Wandsworth Bridge. Filming, I was relieved to discover, was just like acting, only the food was better. Scrambled egg butties at 6.15 in the morning were as good a substitute for sleep as any I've found, and the more waiting around the better.

I loved the endless chat — in caravans, by tea-urns, perched on rigging equipment. I still do. More than the work, actually. And I was learning. Not a lot, but enough to get me by with some seasoned competition. There was a family feeling and I was the new baby. At weekends, Peter Collinson and his agent, Barry Krost, would show me round the King's Road, the Club del Aretusa and the Antique Hypermarket. It was very much the era of beads, bells, bell-bottoms and hashish. Reelly far out, man!

I managed to conceal that I already knew these places because of my friendship with Ricci Burns, and gooped and gawped like a regular Shirley Temple — cockney style. Because, believe it or not, after seven weeks' filming, I was still doing the act both on set and off, for fear they'd replace me if they found out. I knew about as much of the financial set-up of the film world then as I do now.

One day Peter asked me if I'd like to see the daily rushes. Now I'd never seen myself in a film since I was toddling naked in the back garden holding a snail. I was twenty-four at the time. No but truthfully, I was unprepared for the shock. There I was, warts and all, huge and celluloid, with every fault magnified. Seventeen-year-old Susan George had a tiny part in the film. When she came on, the producer, Harry Fine, said, 'That girl has something. I just love that girl.' Just like in the movies! As for me — I did the only mature thing possible. I ran out, locked myself in the toilet and sobbed hysterically.

There was a knock at the door. 'Let me in. It's Peter.' I let him in. 'What is it? What's a matter? You're terrific . . .' 'I know. It's not that,' I hiccoughed (still in character). 'It's me . . . I look . . . I look . . . so . . . sob, sob, whinge, whinge etc.' Gently, he reassured me that the film was hard in its feel and look . . . none of of us looked glamorous . . . 'You look perfect for the part . . . you *are* perfect for the part . . .' In my gratitude, I heard myself say, 'It's just that I'm . . . er . . . I'm not . . . er . . . I've got to tell you somefink, Peter . . . it's just I'm not what you fink . . . I'm not a . . . cockney. I'm— I'm from 'Ull.'

He studied me for a long moment, then said, 'That's interesting. I'm from Grimsby.'

'But I thought you were an ex-barrow-boy from the East End,' I gasped.

'How do you think I got the rights to the film for £200?' was his twinkling answer. Game, set and perfect match.

Somehow after that though, things were never quite the same. Both of us had had our covers blown and a slight wariness between us replaced the nice, comfortable Eliza/Higgins rapport of erstwhile.

The film was premièred at the Clapham Odeon, for obvious reasons, and, for equally obvious reasons, I decided on a change of image. I borrowed an amazing dress from Clive, the couturier who had dressed me as a nine-months-pregnant French whore in *Mandrake* and had remained, and still remains, a buddy. I had a false tan put on which gradually deepened into a sort of olive-drab as the evening progressed, and Ricci cut my hair into a sort of helmet. The dress was peacock-blue, floral, halter-necked and swelled into balloon trousers with built-in feet. I looked like a frozen daiquiri.

When Adrienne Posta and I walked into the spotlight, they asked me to kindly step to one side while they photographed her, and that set the keynote for the evening. Even the people who recognized me didn't recognize me. Of those who did, three screamed with fright and one, Suzy Kendal, just kept patting my arm in pity. In no way could it be said that a star was born, and I was more than relieved when Watford asked me to return in triumph to play the Fairy of the Ring in *Aladdin*. Of such stuff are dreams made....

In 1970 I joined the Stables Theatre Club (a tiny, experimental theatre built by Granada Television in the late '60s for the purpose of 'trying-out' small scale theatre productions which could later be transferred to television), there were three changing-rooms and a bar, the latter being a good deal more popular than the theatre with the staff of Granada, for Granada is a 'dry' station — Jewish television some call it — and certainly in the days of Bill Grundy, Michael Parkinson and the late beloved and wonderful Peter Eckersley, the staff was a distinctly 'liquid' one. What the theatre didn't have was a 'green-room' and in vain the actors' committee would request such an addition every time we had a meeting with the management. Finally they capitulated. A notice went up saying

'Stables Theatre Company: your new green-room is on Floor 8 of the main Granada building'. Well, it was three hundred yards from the theatre, but it was a start. We all charged across to survey our new property — past the commissionaire — flashing our identity cards, up the lift, along the corridor and through the door of Room 808. There we stood in amazement — confronted by the sight of a *green* room! Totally green. Green carpet, green curtains, green walls and chairs of a subtly clashing biliousness. Ask and it shall be given. Literally.

It reminded me of the time when I returned to Hull after my first term at drama school, fired with the thrill of improvisational theatre. (Sometimes my fellow students and I would get on the tube in different compartments and in the course of the journey, would come together and stage a 'happening'. One of us would walk up to another and slap him across the face, or unleash a torrent of abuse in a 'foreign' language. Occasionally, we would fire out a line at top voice like 'Do you know you are the father of my unborn child?' or simply 'Did you get rid of the body?' It was enough to see the faces of the passengers as we built each conflict into a full-scale confrontation.) During a visit to the New Theatre in Hull, I met the manager whilst having drinks in the enormous stalls bar. 'This place should be used more experimentally,' I chirped from the dizzy height of six weeks at a drama school. 'Have you ever thought of using it for improvisations?'

'Oh, aye,' he replied proudly, 'We are improving it bit by bit.'

It was at 'The Stables' that I met Jack. We met as the result of some kind of bet, which I can only assume he won. Oh, coy maiden — shut yer face. At first meeting he reminded me of Yves Montand, although I knew Yves Montand would never have aspired to the Marks and Spencer grey V-necked pullover with black inset dickey, which he sported on the day of our first date. He told me he was learning Hebrew (it was post Six-Day War and he, like many others, was inspired to do something for the boys), and made me laugh telling me about the elderly Yiddisher mommas in the class who regarded him with the curiosity and interest due to a personable Jewish man who seemed, startlingly enough, to be single. The following day I phoned his office and in heavy, Mittel-European Mancunian announced myself as Mrs Esther Schwarzkopf.

'I want to speak to Mr Rosenthal hisself,' I demanded of Margaret, his sanguine secretary. After a hissed exchange, Hisself came on the line.

'Hello, it's Mrs Schwarzkopf from your Hebrew class, how are you, are you busy Friday night?'

'Erm, I'm sorry — who did you...? Pardon? Er, I can't seem—'

'Mrs Schwarzkopf! From the class. I sit in front of you every Wednesday. What's the matter with you, you don't see so good?'

'Er, no, yes! It's just that — which one...er...are...er, you?'

'Mrs Schwarzkopf! Esther!' I grew excited. 'The one with grapes on my hat.'

'Er, the grapes in your, er — I'm ever so sorry, I don't seem to remem...'

'So how many women in the class have got hats with grapes on? I sit in *front* of you.'

'Yes. I'm sure if I were to see you I'd...'

'Will you listen already, I haven't got all day. I want you should come to dinner on Friday night. You got a pencil?'

'Er, Mrs er, Schwarzkopf, it's very nice of you to ask me, but I, er, I always visit my mother in Blackpool on a Fri—'

'Every Friday? You can't miss it one Friday? Listen, I've got a lovely daughter at home, very intelligent with the loveliest skin you've ever seen, like a...'

'No, I mean, I'd love to come some—'

'Listen, don't do me any favours, you don't want dinner —don't have. I'm sorry I asked.'

'No, honestly, I mean, it's extremely kind.'

'For my part I thought — a single man on his own in Manchester at the weekend...'

'Yes, but...'

'No, forget it, don't even think from it. I'll put the Helzel back in the freezer and "fartic" — it's done.'

'But, Mrs Schwar—'

'Goodbye. I'm only sorry I intruded on your time and goodbye.' SLAM.

This little jape set the seal on our future life. Even after sixteen years together I can still steal his chips by dint of a sudden glance over his shoulder and a shocked expression, indicating 'Who's

THAT?' It was several hours later in the Stables' bar when he related the episode to me, and it was only the flaring of my give-away nostrils that he caught on. 'Mrs Schwarzkopf!' he choked into his lager. 'Of course! Who else? And I've been torturing myself with guilt ever since! I was only looking up her bloody name in the phone book to send flowers, wasn't I?'

It was at the Stables Theatre that I gave of my black serving maid, Zanche, in the Jacobean tragedy *The White Devil*. For this remarkable ethnic feat I wore two coats of black and copper greasepaint — polishing each coat — a frizzed wig, time-saving black gloves, white neck ruff and more gold eyeshadow than you see at a fork supper at the Marbella Club. One night when I was merrily involved in a game of dressing-room Scrabble, I heard the unthinkable over the Tannoy: 'Miss Lipman, you're off!' (Theatrical terminology for 'Get *ON* you berk!') Like a cartoon cat I leapt down the corridor and screeched to a casual halt on stage. The cast regarded me with strange expressions. I regarded them back with the expression of one who'd never actually *seen* an actor's expression before.

My usually myopic gaze spread to the audience. It was a studio theatre and they were close, but instead of the usual comforting blur, I saw eyes, nostrils, hairs in nostrils and liquorice in dentures. It didn't take a giant intellect, which was fortunate, for I was not the possessor of one, to realize that this particular sixteenth-century black maidservant was still wearing blue-tinted, steel-rimmed, hippy-style spectacles.

I raised my hands to remove the anachronisms and couldn't help but notice that they were as white as — well, ungloved snow! My exit was as inelegant as had been my entrance, and there must be many people who, even today, remain puzzled by the unexplained symbolism of the bespectacled penguin in Act III of Webster's play. Tragic really.

After this triumph, I returned to London for a comedy series called *Don't Ask Us We're New Here*. It starred five fresh new faces (including my own), and was utterly forgettable. Jack used to visit me in London, but he was a Manchester lad, and London, to him, was a place to visit, deposit a script or an idea, and catch a train out. Somehow we commuted our relationship until with gentle pressure (like throwing myself on to the tracks at Piccadilly Central) I persuaded him to come down South. He claims it took twenty minutes to feel at home. We lived in Hampstead in a friend's vacant flat, and I used to cycle to work at the Old Vic in Waterloo. It must be about eight miles and coming home, all uphill, would render me comatose and wheezing each night. We rehearsed all day for one play and played or understudied one another at night. I was very, very happy.

We got married in '73 and I went back on stage after our two-day honeymoon. We went to a baronial castle somewhere in Norfolk, with suits of armour, four-poster beds and several stars for sumptuousness. It was as jolly as Juliet's crypt, and we fled to Bognor Regis and wet walks by the sea. It was perfect. The wedding itself was amusing. I wore a petrol-blue Gina Fratini dress, slightly period in feel, and a large cream hat. Jack wore a dark brown suit, and his only tie. My parents arrived from Hull, Mother looking lovely in a pale green coat and dress, and a pink flowered hat, and carrying five hundred fishballs in a plastic bag — for fear there wouldn't be enough food. She was right, as it happened. Jack's mother arrived from Blackpool doing the same.

All sides were relieved that we were finally legalizing our relationship. The first time I had taken Jack home was the first time I'd ever been able to take anyone home, since my earlier affairs would all have been deemed unsuitable for one reason or another. I was supposed to be living in digs in Manchester — in Fog Lane, would you believe? — though since Jack had a nearby flat, I wasn't spending a great deal of time there. At home, of course, I was placed in my own bedroom, with the teddies, and Jack got the boxroom. Naturally enough I found it hard to sleep and was pacing about when my mother, as always majoring in the rhetorical, called 'Can't you sleep?' On hearing the negative reply she suggested I came in for a chat — which I did. My father grew more and more annoyed at this intrusion into his shut-eye and finally, after dark mutterings and much thrashing about of limbs, he got up and stalked into my room, where he re-instated himself in the snooker hall of his dreams. I ultimately settled down with mother and the night passed normally away.

Except for Jack. Unaware of this game of musical beds, he awoke at 5.30, remembered where he was. Then remembered where I was, crept out on to the landing, creaked his way past my parents' room, silently negotiated the door into my room and gratefully got into the single bed with my father. It was only after he'd kissed the short hairs at the back of my father's neck that both of them realized all was not well in the state of Humberside. It took a long while for Maurice to totally trust the man who was to marry his daughter.

Of course, after four years my parents wouldn't wait. People were beginning to *talk*. There is a photo in their lounge which says it all. It shows the whole family at their silver wedding. My brother and his wife, my parents, myself, all beaming and resplendent in evening dress, and slightly away from the party to the left, my beloved, looking suspiciously like a BO advert. This was unceremoniously arranged by my mother. For fear again. This time the fear was that in the event of 'nothing coming of it' (i.e. our relationship), she could always cut him off the edge of the picture!

So, back to the wedding. Looking back, we should have been married in Hull with everyone who'd known me since cheek-pinching days, Mum and Dad in full regalia surrounded by their friends. That's what your wedding's all about, isn't it? At the time, and in my euphoria at being in the National Theatre Company, I didn't want to know that. I assumed that the people who were with me *now* would be with me *always*. Jack had rallied a colourful Manchester rabbi and we were to be wed in the West London Reform Synagogue, of which we are now members. I didn't even think to hire a limo — just a dirty old mini-cab — and I dropped in at Ricci Burns's flat on the way for a crimp and a glass of bubbly, then off we all went.

Outside the synagogue I was left alone with my Dad. Always a sentimental, emotional and highly forgetful man, he held my hand, kissed me and said, 'Mammele, I wish you every happiness in the world, you look lovely and you should only have a wonderful life together. I'll see you in there.' So saying, to my amazement, he left me outside the Shule, with the organ playing the Wedding March and no one to accompany me down the aisle. To those who know my father this will come as no surprise. He once took my mother to the pictures and, hating the film, arranged to nip into the Station Hotel for a game of snooker and pick her up after the film. After waiting twenty

minutes she went over to the hotel and found him by the pool
tables. His expression on seeing her was pure disbelief — 'What
on earth are you doing out the house at this time?'

So there I was, pulling open the big double doors — jamming
my foot in them and hissing at his departing back, 'Dad — psst!
DAD! Have you gone *mad*? Come *back* — you've got to walk me
down the BLOOMIN' AISLE!! You're my father!' Back he came,
blustering very slightly, and embarked on the moment he'd
spent his fatherhood waiting for.

I seem to remember, with horror, that the rabbi gave a list of
both our credits under the canopy. 'Er, Jack, of course, has
written *Coronation Street* and, er, *Dustbinmen* and, oh, *The Lovers* —
very, very good stuff; and his lovely bride, also, in her own right,
a member of the, er, National Theatre Company, and between
them they should have many years of success and happiness...'
I remember shifting uneasily in my fear that with such a
distinguished audience he might be tempted into a few choruses
of 'Is this the little girl I carried, is this the little girl who played?'
and perhaps a story, a hymn and a prayer.

Louie Ramsey was my 'best woman' and sang 'Happiness is
just a thing called Mo', at the reception, which broke me right
up, and it all went off like a wedding.

My dad had retired recently and announced his intention of
doing the Open University. Jack and I and my brother were
overjoyed with enthusiasm. 'That's great. What course will you
do? Sociology? Oh, Dad, I'm really proud of you, that's
fantastic! Don't you think so, Mum?' His wife, who took a more
jaundiced view of her husband's capacity for home-work, had
just entered the room. 'About Dad doing the Open University
— isn't it wonderful?' 'I've put all your long skirts on one
hanger,' she sniffed. And exited, stage left.

Shortly afterwards I joined the Royal Shakespeare Company
for reasons which escape me. I very quickly got pregnant, to my
joy and relief, and spent the next six months in a barrister's robes
in the TV series *Crown Court*, getting lumpier and lumpier, and
more and more emotional if I lost the case. Throughout the last
months of pregnancy I was driven insane by migraines and
finally stopped eating anything but vegetables until it went
away. During the worst of them I became horribly constipated
and, since drugs were out of the question, would try to make

things work by visiting the local bookshop. No, I will explain, honestly. Bookshops always have that effect on me (as I've mentioned in the chapter on habits) so my friend Edith, from the downstairs flat, would slowly walk me up the hill, every movement painful, and stand me by the section which she thought would have the greatest effect on me. Presumably Romantic Fiction. If those pink-rinsed lady authors only knew. We would stand there, swapping furtive looks, raised eyebrows, secret signs, until finally — once, I remember, it being a cookery book by Vincent and Mary Price — I'd feel the urge to schlepp my distorted body back down the hill to the loo. In every sense I was the bookshop's worst customer — never bought a thing. Never had the time.

Within six weeks of Amy's premature birth, I was back at work in some dread comedy pilot about football hooligans — filming on the M1. It is my most sordid memory. May you never know the ignominy of being stuck in a motorway toilet with a breast pump. Only those of you who've ever had cause to use one in even *normal* circumstances will know my predicament. Working was a foolish mistake. I would never have gone back so quickly after a Caesarean had I not been convinced that I'd never work again. I became sick, anaemic and totally clapped-out, and not for the first time did I regret ignoring the advice of those who knew better.

When Adam was born, I was much more relaxed about the whole thing. He had a wide, flat face, no hair, peeling skin and looked rather like Sir John Gielgud. The day after the op, I was feeling rather low and, on hearing him cry, tried to lever myself up to investigate. I got to my feet, immediately felt dizzy and sank back on the bed just as the surgeon's assistant came bustling through the door. 'Hello, Mrs Rosenthal!' she chirped, 'I've just come to look at your scar, how are you?'

'Well, I'm glad you're here because I just tried to stand up and I felt so sick and dizzy I thought I was going to faint...'

'Oh, dear,' she sympathized, 'Never you mind — I'll come back and see you when you're feeling better.' And she left.

I laughed so hard that I must have endangered the remaining stitches. Now that's what I call specialization. This time I took a good rest before going back into the theatre, to play a prim secretary in Shaw's *Candida* — starring Deborah Kerr and Denis

Quilley. We toured for three weeks (while my intrepid mother and husband took care of the children), then came into the Albery. The night I'll always remember was when Marchbanks (Patrick Ryecart) and I had a spirited exchange, leading to my making a false exit, then returning to berate him further. As I reached the door, Edwardian blouse puffed out and not-inconsiderable nose in the air, the audience exploded with a laughter far in excess of what my line-reading warranted.

Pleased but puzzled, I turned to walk downstage again — only to find that I appeared to be walking against some kind of obstruction. A glance down showed the obstruction to be my heavy black skirt which had fallen to the ground. Muttering all the while in pidgin-Shaw, I hitched it up and requested the purple-faced hysteric masquerading as my fellow-actor to kindly fasten my hook. The audience screamed its approval. He complied, and they gave us a round of applause. Bridling visibly and stiffening imperceptibly — two phrases I've always longed to write — I resumed my dialogue. Whereupon the skirt fell off again. Later that evening, the same actress was seen stalking the wardrobe mistress with intent to nail her to a wardrobe.

I love filming and I almost never do films. This could be to do with the fact that nobody ever offers me one. No — please — put away your stringed instruments — it's no cause for concern. The fact is that in the last eighteen or so years, I've actually never quite *seen* a film casting director or a film director for a job. I blame it on my bone structure!

Occasionally film people have asked for me, as Lewis Gilbert did in *Educating Rita*, so by a fluke I found myself in a box office blockbuster — albeit in a small cameo. 'There is no such thing as a small part, only small actors.' Whoever said that was nearly right but had probably never played Lychomida, nurse to Marina in *Pericles, Prince of Tyre*. Julie Walters and I improvised the last scene where Trish, Rita's friend, is in hospital after attempting suicide. Willy Russell had intended rewriting it but somehow it didn't get done. So we pieced it together in the caravan at 7.30 in the morning. As the director said 'Roll', the tears rolled with the dialogue and everyone was happy. At the end of the scene, Trish's parents were supposed to arrive and say, 'Why did you do it, love?' In contrast to their pretentious daughter, they were ordinary working-class folk. We were not, however, prepared for the two Irish extras who'd been handpicked and hand-me-downed to look like two weasel poachers on supplementary benefit with a brogue as thick as a Fair Isle sock. As I raised my tear-stained eyes from the counterpane I caught Julie's and the world became a very difficult place to live in. We shot it three times, each time with one or other of us smirking or heaving — and then they threw away the shot for ever.

It was a happy set to be working on, even for a few days, and I was grateful for the way they made me feel special in a small role. Sometime later I played a tiny cameo in a small budget film with a certain actor — hereinafter for legal reasons called Mr C!! — unknown to me, but a Colossus of Rhodes to the American public. It was a bedroom scene, though naturally enough it was the wrong bedroom. He thought he was in bed with his wife. The twist was that my character didn't want to let him out! Mr C didn't know me from Eve and didn't want to. He was directing the film in spite of the director's presence. He screwed up the only three lines I had and behaved very peremptorily, so when the cameras rolled and he tried to get out of bed, I clung to his neck and dragged him to the floor. The technicians were hugely amused by this, but Mr C complained of a bad back. So the next time I clung to his knees with my legs, and down we went again. I think he knew he was beaten, and I think I know where that scene will end up — on the floor . . . like its star.

Contrary to unpopular belief, I've only worked on Rosenthal scripts three times. Once in an episode of *The Lovers* — which was before we were married, so it doesn't count — and once in *The Evacuees*, his prize-winning autobiographical play of 1976, where I played his mother. The play marked Alan Parker's directorial debut on television. The moment most people remember was when the two evacuated Jewish boys were forced to eat pork sausages. Alan had told the two boys, Gary and Stephen, also Jewish, that the Rabbi had given permission, under the circumstances, for them to eat the pork after saying a special prayer. He then ordered some rather anaemic-looking kosher sausages. The boys looked pallid before the scene, positively ashen throughout it and Stephen almost gagged as he ate it. They were both in tears. Unethical? Yes, unethnic even, but it was the most superb piece of 'acting' in the film — for the simple reason that for the actors concerned it was a *real* personal conflict. Once more the end justified the meanness.

I also played a small part in Jack's TV play about taxi drivers *The Knowledge* — three days filming in all — and had to smart under TV critic Clive James' description of Jonathan Lynn and me as 'Jack Rosenthal's salt-beef stock company'. Very funny already.

There was one other play of Jack's. It was a stage play called *SMASH!* — the story of an English author whose small-scale hit play was expanded and ultimately exploded into a Broadway musical. It was not entirely unconnected with Jack's experience with *Barmitzvah Boy*, and all the characters were based on real life counterparts. Of the team who had turned the TV play into a stage musical, Nigel Hawthorne, Stephen Moore, John Bluthal and Peter Blake played the team. I played Jack.

Unfortunately, we lost Jonathan Lynn, our Director, to New York before the rehearsals began and it turned into an unhappy experience culminating in the producers removing their money before we came into town. It was, they claimed, too much about show business to interest the general public. The same producers seem to be doing very nicely with *Noises Off*.

Funnily enough, it's the one play that won't lie down. Every few months someone asks to read *SMASH!* They've heard such wonderful things about it, can they make a film, a play, a TV series? It never happens. But one day, I swear it will, and it will be such a smash.

On the whole, Jack writes for himself, not for anyone specific, and that includes me. He's too good to be writing 'vehicles' and I wouldn't expect it of him — so now I've started sleeping with other writers instead. No, seriously... I don't think husband and wife teams are very well received in this country, something a bit smug happens, and I'd far rather stay on parallel lines which occasionally cross, than become that afore-mentioned salt-beef stock.

My first moderately successful TV sit-com was *Agony* and in retrospect I'm proud of it. It did break some new TV barriers, and, in the words of my mother, 'put me on the map.' Now being on this map has its good points — it allows you to be in embarrassing quiz shows and bland chat shows and your mail box gets filled with requests to speak at Rotary Clubs and open lesbian workshops. The 'map' also sets you up, however, for conversations like the one I had in a sweetshop in York. The lady sweet-seller said: 'By, you remind me of that girl in that TV show — whatsit called — "Ugly", isn't it?' 'Really,' said I, loftily. 'Yes, a lot of people tell me that.' 'Well. You even sound like her,' she persisted. 'You've just the same funny voice. Are you sure you're not her?' 'I'm *quite* sure I'm not her and can I have a box of Smarties and an Aero?' 'Still, I bet you wish you had her money!' she hooted. 'I don't think she's much of an actress, anyway. Do you? 75p please.'

My brother was over from Switzerland at the time. I don't think I've heard him laugh so much since my vaccination turned septic.

Usually the public's reaction is favourable. They found the show fresh and they actually say they miss it. Invariably they add 'We loved the woman who played your mother', and then they ask if Jack wrote her part. I smile enigmatically (I hope) and tell them the names of the writers — Anna Raeburn and Len Richmond. In fact they left the show after the first series, for all sorts of reasons. I believe Anna found it difficult to relinquish Jane Lucas to someone else's hands. She found it too nerve-wracking to attend the first recording in front of a live audience, but at the second she volunteered to do the 'warm-up'. This is traditionally a few well-tried old jokes to get the audience laughing and accustom them to the studio. A typical joke would be 'I walked into a room here with WC on the door — and it turned out to be Wendy Craig's dressing room'. Not sophisticated but it fulfils its purpose. Anna talked seriously to them about 'Art imitating Life' then the cast came on and died the death. The next week we brought back the WC.

The cast, including me, did make script changes but, as Len Richmond later wrote from California, they were mainly for the better. The series formula went out in America under the 'relevant' title *The Lucie Arnaz Show*. There were no gays, no husband, no weirdos and Jane was a *doctor*. Sounds like that ol' Heart imitating Life again, doesn't it?

Our cast and production team was a joy. We did twenty-one

episodes under John Reardon's excellent direction with very few agonies. On the last recording night of each series we always took over a restaurant and had a company nosh. Dear, delightful Simon Williams would recite an original poem based on the series so far, and I would do the same in song, standing on the table. Then like proper thespians we'd all swop phone numbers, hug, kiss, shed copious tears and see neither hide nor hair of one another till the next series began.

I suppose my favourite TV role to date is Maggie in *Outside Edge*. Hardly a day goes by without someone in some grocer's store or shoe-repair shop saying, 'You know the one I really liked you in? That cricket play. With the little husband and the big fur coat!' I always grin and say, 'Oh, yes, that's everyone's favourite.' And it was.

You didn't have to play cricket to know intimately every character in that pavilion. In fact it could have been a tennis club, a golf course or an Amateur Dramatic Society hall. In the final analysis, it wasn't cricket.

When the play was sent to me there was no mention of which part I was being offered. My instinctive choice was Miriam, the harassed wife of the team captain. I phoned Sara, my agent, to convey as much to the Hampstead Theatre Club. Sara told me that Julia McKenzie was also considering the play. I was pleased. I was a great fan of hers. That same day I went to some Awards ceremony, *The Standard*, I think. It so happened that Julia McKenzie and I visited the loo at the same time. I was in there rather a long time, due to the fact that I'd worn my rings *over* my gloves, which made for a few physical difficulties. By way of conversation, and to distract myself from the problem in hand, I called out, 'Are you doing that play, Julia?' 'Oh, yes, I think so,' she replied. 'Are you?' 'Yes, I think I am, too.' 'What part are you playing?' We both laughed at having harmonized the question. Then we both said 'Miriam.' Only this time we didn't laugh.

So I opted for Maggie — and how right the casting was. Her physical characteristics were accurately described by the author, Richard Harris — big glasses, fur coat, untidy hair, gash of red lipstick — all I needed was the one 'click' which indicated that her peculiarities had fused with mine. I found it outside the school gates when one of the mothers, a wonderfully laid-back girl, leaned languorously back on her car, smoking a roll-your-own, and said in a flat North London accent: 'I've met this reeely ama-zing Aust-ra-lian Anthro-polo-gist. He's quite boring, but he's reeely ama-zing in bed.'

Click! I could have hugged her. From there it all fell into place.

Hampstead Theatre Club is a prefab of a theatre, seating only a hundred people. The summer of '78 was the hottest for years. I wore a possum fur coat throughout and dropped a stone in weight. Ian Trigger, all five foot of him, played my beloved husband, 'little Kev', and at one point had to spend five minutes inside my coat — whilst I was wearing it. Once or twice he stopped breathing in there, and, on one occasion, I swear he came out high on oxygen deprivation and Mum Rollette. I think what I loved most about Maggie was that she came on looking and sounding like a cross between Janet Street-Porter and Dame Edna Everage, but by the end of Act II she was the most 'normal' person on the turf.

In the TV version, Prunella Scales played Miriam with her customary comic brilliance. On stage, Julia's Miriam and my Maggie were a different symphony of harmony and disharmony. Playing together was bliss, and it was the beginning of a wonderful friendship.

I'm grateful to and mindful of my friends, who make all the running. I know I'm a rotten friend in the conventional sense of ringing, writing and entertaining them. I also know that *they* know that if they need me I'll drop everything to be there, to listen, to feed (so long as they don't hold their breath waiting for an invite!) and, if necessary, to fight on their behalf. As far as loading them with my problems, I fight shy of that except in the sense of turning the problems into comic routines.

Recently, I was being photographed in my kitchen, for a possible cover for this book. The photographer, Anthony Grant, and I decided a suitable image might be me in ballgown and apron, with cucumbers under my eyes and rollers in my hair, frying chips while speaking on the walkabout phone. In the absence of chips we set fire to mint wrappers in the pan. As I was smiling, frying and trying out harassed expressions, the phone, which was tucked between my chin and my shoulder, suddenly rang

and the voice of an old friend asked, 'What are you laughing at?'
'Oh God,' I cried, 'you're not going to believe what I'm doing,
I'm standing here in a bloody ballgown and rollers frying paper
with a face full of salad...' I expected her to laugh. Instead
she broke down. 'Mo, I've got to see you... I'm cracking up, I
really am... I just can't go on... I don't know what to do...'
    'Big smile,' said Anthony, clicking away. I couldn't explain
to him what was going on, so I smiled away. 'All right, love, now
just calm down, it's OK. You're feeling bad now because of —
no, listen — I promise you...' — 'Lovely — look into the
camera.' — 'You are allowed to be certifiably mad after you've
given birth — it'll go away, believe me.' Cough! 'Sorry!' The
smoke was getting out of hand. 'Now, look, can you come over
on...'
    All this, and more, with my face going from smile to surprise
to concern and the camera going click, click, click. Do you
wonder why I once confessed that life was like three episodes of
Agony? Before breakfast.

    In recent years I've joined an organization of actors, writers
and producers at the Shaftesbury Theatre to give Comedy the
theatrical status of every form of drama. It's called the Theatre
of Comedy. I joined because I love comedy, because it's what
I'm best at. Ray Cooney is the Artistic Director and two of his
own plays have run at the Theatre of Comedy — hereinafter
called TOC. I am an executive member, alongside John
Alderton, Dinsdale Landen, Liza Goddard, Paul Eddington,
Julia McKenzie, Tom Conti and Derek Nimmo. Mostly we
make lots of noises about the plays we'd like to do and then
compromise with the plays we end up doing. Everyone's free to
shout and barrack, and I suppose about 30% of our suggestions
are incorporated. I enjoy executive committee life and John
Alderton and I have a great deal of Hull aggression when we're
up against it. 'It' being our benignly-despotic Artistic Director,
Ray.
    The first play I appeared in for TOC was *See How They Run*
which, as I've already mentioned, is a farce about vicars,
escaped Germans and underwear. I was playing the frigid
English spinster, Miss Skillen, all lisle and directoire, who gets
utterly inebriated on cooking sherry. After a few days of

rehearsal, Ray Cooney said, 'Lipman, you've got comedy legs!'
I said I'd always known they'd come in handy for something.
From that moment on, those legs became my star turn. They
buckled, they bowed, they twisted into rubber knots. They did
tricks even each other didn't know about and finally they won
me a SWET Laurence Olivier Award and a Variety Club of
Great Britain Award. My first ever prizes. When I was
considering the play, Jack read it and said, 'Well, it's a very
small part. Do you think you can do anything with it?'

I spent a great deal of time during that play in a cupboard,
where I'd been unceremoniously deposited in a drunken stupor.
Rather than go back to my dressing-room, I'd stay in the
cupboard, and various members of the cast would join me for a
chat.

I especially relished my moments with Derek Nimmo because
of the fun we had comparing our days...*Derek*: 'Drove back
from Wiltshire — absolutely lovely spin — spring weather, all
the crocuses popping out. Marvellous lunch at the Hinduran
Embassy, then a business meeting in the City re the Hong Kong
tour. Then I popped into the Guildhall for a literary thing —
Kingsley Amis, terribly amusing — then just had time for a spot
of floodlit gardening at home before coming in here. Dinner
afterwards at the Garrick with Sir John and Lady M. How
about you?' *Me*: 'Similar, really. Spun down to Sainsbury's for a
bulk-buy and a row. Carrier-bag broke in car-park. Took Adam
to the doctor. Got some drops for his conjunctivitis. Wrestled on
the ground with him for two hours trying to get them in.
Emptied the cat's litter-tray on my foot. Wrote four more lines of
this piece that was due in yesterday, listened to sexual difficulties
of friend on telephone whilst frying six pounds of mince for the
freezer, stood with broken belt of Hoover in hand in utter
despair and burnt top lip with hair-remover.'

And people wonder where I get my ideas!

Over the years, as I've progressed from a self-confident
nothing to a sort of abject success, people have asked me 'How
do you combine being an actress, a writer, a mother and a wife?
How do you do it?' I give them the only honest answer —
'Badly'.

Behind every success story there's a guilt complex the size of
Mark Thatcher. I'm willing to bet that Shirley Conran

constantly borrows cups of sugar from her neighbours, that Antonia Fraser never did the two o'clock feed and that Claire Rayner's kids don't take her advice. We all just muddle through, me more than most, making chaos out of order, just like God did. In fact one of the purposes of writing this book was to pre-empt my children writing *Lipmania* — an unkind version of *Mommie Dearest*.

We must stop believing that to be 'fulfilled' we should look like Victoria Principal, cook like Prue Leith and — er — make love like Joan Collins. I mean what's so fulfilling about fulfilment anyway? I have an American acquaintance who had business cards printed, proudly saying 'Margaret Corey — Suburban Housewife'. Here's power to her elbow. And ours. And all our other pointed bits.